Southern Society and Its Transformations 1790–1860

New Currents in the History of Southern Economy and Society

This series, New Currents in the History of Southern Economy and Society, puts the history of the American South in an important new light. It demonstrates the complexity of the southern economy across time and place and its profound impact on the varieties of people who have inhabited the region. It conveys southern economic development as consistently diverse and dynamic. The series stresses the importance of comparative and transatlantic perspectives and strives to reintegrate southern history in relation to the rest of the nation and the globe. The series is purposefully organized around central themes rather than chronology to highlight new ways to conceptualize economic change and industrial growth.

The series grew out of work of the Southern Industrialization Project (SIP), a professional organization that seeks to foster a greater understanding of the history and culture of industrialization in the American South. Each year SIP meets to discuss scholarly papers organized around key themes. This series represents SIP's commitment to developing these conference themes into substantive scholarly volumes that further promote research in southern economic and social history. In addition, SIP maintains a discussion list on H-Net of more than one hundred academic and public historians with research interests that encompass many industries, eras, and geographic locations.

Southern Society and Its Transformations 1790–1860

EDITED BY

Susanna Delfino, Michele Gillespie, and Louis M. Kyriakoudes

University of Missouri Press Columbia and London

University of Missouri Press, Columbia, Missouri 65201
Printed and bound in the United States of America

5 4 3 2 1 15 14 13 12 11

Cataloging-in-Publication data available from the Library of Congress
ISBN 978-0-8262-1918-3

∞™ This paper meets the requirements of the
American National Standard for Permanence of Paper
for Printed Library Materials, Z39.48, 1984.

Designer: Kristie Lee
Typesetter: K. Lee Design & Graphics
Printer and binder: Integrated Book Technology, Inc.
Typeface: Palatino

Contents

Southern Society and Its Transformations 1790–1860

Preface

J. William Harris

The contrast between an economically "progressive" North and an economically "backward" South before the Civil War has been a staple of both popular and scholarly histories of the United States since the antebellum era itself. Northern antislavery spokesmen were sure that slavery produced economic, as well as moral, backwardness. Theodore Parker, in 1854, called the South "the foe to Northern Industry—to our mines, our manufactures, and our commerce"; New York's Senator William H. Seward asserted that slavery resulted in "an absence of enterprise and improvement" in the South and was "incompatible with all . . . the elements of the security, welfare, and greatness of nations." Many southerners were happy to agree with the economic point, while reversing its alleged moral implications. Fire eater Louis Wigfall said that southerners were "an agricultural people. . . . We want no manufactures; we desire no trading, no mechanical or manufacturing classes." A South Carolinian in 1860 told William Howard Russell, correspondent for the *London Times*, the same thing: "We are an agricultural people. . . . breeding up women and men with some other purpose than to make them vulgar, fanatical, cheating Yankees."[1]

Historians since then have made similar arguments. Progressive historians Charles and Mary Beard called the Civil War an "irrepressible conflict" over control of the national government between "planting interests" in the South who were "facing a decline in . . . economic strength" and "capitalists" in the North—the phrase "irrepressible conflict" borrowed directly from a famous speech by Seward.[2] Eugene D. Genovese, Douglas Egerton, and John Ashworth are among the more recent historians for whom the slave South was variously "precaptalist," "prebourgeois," or "premodern," the prefix always signaling a South facing backward in a progressive world. For contemporary polemicists and historians alike, a key factor—arguably, the key factor—was the presence in the North, and the corresponding absence in the South, of a vital and growing manufacturing sector.[3]

Some of the clearest statements along these lines have been published by the distinguished historian of the Civil War, James M. McPherson. In one essay, drawing on the concepts of nineteenth-century German social theorist Ferdinand Tönnies, McPherson has argued that the antebellum South had a "gemeinschaft culture," based on values of tradition and stability, while the North was "moving toward a gesellschaft culture with its impersonal, bureaucratic, meritocratic, urbanizing, commercial, industrializing, mobile, and rootless characteristics. . . . [T]he North's modernizing culture enshrined change as progress and condemned the South as backward."[4] In a widely used textbook co-authored by McPherson, he elaborates on the ways in which "American modernization" was the key factor in the coming of the Civil War:

> The antebellum United States was undergoing a process that some social scientists term "modernization": heavy investment in social overhead capital, which transforms a localized subsistence economy into a nationally integrated market economy; rapid increases in output per capita, resulting from technological innovation and the shift from labor-intensive toward capital-intensive production; the accelerated growth of the industrial sector compared with other sectors of the economy; rapid urbanization, made possible by an increase in agricultural productivity that enables farmers to feed the growing cities; an expansion of education, literacy, and mass communications; a value system that emphasizes change over tradition; an evolution from the traditional, rural, village-oriented system of personal and kinship ties, in which status is "ascriptive" (inherited), toward a fluid, cosmopolitan, impersonal, and pluralistic society, in which status is achieved by merit. In most of these respects, the United States—with the partial and significant exception of the South—was the most rapidly modernizing country in the world in the mid-nineteenth century.[5]

According to McPherson, this modernization was rooted in the Protestant ethic of Max Weber, especially strong in New England because of its Puritan heritage (and, by implication, especially weak in the South). Among the evidence cited in support of this analysis is a table showing the "Origins of Nineteenth-Century American Business Executives." Of these, 51 percent were born in New England, 34 percent in the rest of the North, and just 3 percent in the South (the rest were unknown or born abroad). Further evidence is that "analysis of property ownership based on the 1860 census revealed that, no matter where they lived, men of New England birth enjoyed greater average wealth than men born in any other part of the country."[6]

There is of course no doubt that the slave states before the Civil War were predominantly agricultural and that the North—or, more accurately the Northeast—was the region where manufacturing growth was concentrated. What can be doubted is whether this disparity is owing to some sort of profound difference in the degree of "modernization" between these regions. The difficulty with such overarching generalizations is that they tend to close off, rather than to open up, research into the realities of the antebellum South's economy and society. Symptomatic is McPherson's use of data on "business executives" and wealth. McPherson drew his table from a study of the top executives of the seventy-seven largest U.S. firms, in textiles, railroads, and steel, in the decade from 1870 to 1879.[7] In the first place, we might note that the decade of the 1870s, with the South still staggering from the destruction of its economic system (and most of its railroads) and the North in a period of explosive industrial growth, is hardly the best time to take the measure of regional differences in "modernization" between the *antebellum* regions. Second, we might point out that to define *business* in these terms, however reasonable for the purposes of the authors of the original study, automatically excludes any entrepreneurs who invested mainly in agriculture.[8] As for the reported data on wealth, McPherson's source, a well-known study of nineteenth-century wealth by historian Lee Soltow, shows that free men born in the South were, in 1860, on average the *wealthiest* in the United States. Furthermore, in the upper reaches of wealth, southerners predominated; almost three-fifths of the richest 1 percent of adult men in 1860 were southern-born.[9]

Clearly, if we were to conduct a study of the wealthiest "businessmen" in 1860, and at the same time include slave plantations as businesses, we would find that southern-born men predominated in the ranks of the most successful. The top members of this slaveholding elite—those owning at least 250 slaves—have been studied in detail in a recent work by William Kaufman Scarborough. According to Scarborough, these elite planters were "capitalists in the classical, if not the Marxian sense of the word," with many developing "extremely diversified economic portfolios," including manufacturing enterprises and corporation stock. He concludes that "in their personal lives as well as in the education of their children, they differed little from their northern counterparts in their emphasis upon such bourgeois values as industry, frugality, self-discipline, and acquisitiveness."[10] Similarly, studies of eighteenth-century rice planters and nineteenth-century sugar planters have found that these great slaveholders were often at the forefront in adopting technological innovations that greatly increased the productivity of their properties.[11]

The point here is not to deny that there were important differences between the antebellum slave and free states; it is rather that we should not assume that differences of one sort automatically meant profound differences of other kinds. Rather, as economic historian Gavin Wright has written in an earlier volume in this series, we need to "descend from the heights of macro generalizations"—about whether, for example, the South was or was not a "modern" society—"into the real historical worlds" of antebellum southern economic actors, to seek "new insights and reformulations prompted by historical experience on the ground rather than by theoretical abstractions."[12]

Among the scholars seeking to do just that in recent years have been the members of the Southern Industrialization Project. This network of historians—some trained in departments of history and others in departments of economics—have sought to promote, carry out, and publicize research on the South, especially (as the name implies) on manufacturing and related industries, and on southerners who have too often been ignored because of our understandable interest in the worlds of planters and their slaves. The present volume is the third in a series of publications sponsored by the SIP, with earlier volumes including studies of the southern economy in global context and of economic and technological innovation.[13] As with earlier volumes, case studies illustrate a broad theme, in this case "transformations" in the antebellum South.

As the editors explain in their introduction, the essays are grouped here in four sections. They can also be seen as falling into two broad categories, each dealing in one way or another with either non-slaveowning whites or with middling property owners—farmers and small planters, small merchants, professionals, and corporate entrepreneurs.

Essays by Max Grivno and Keri L. Merritt explicitly, and Michael Pfeifer implicitly, deal with what are often termed, as Merrit calls them, "poor whites." Perhaps this term, with so much ideological baggage attached, might best be retired by scholars and replaced with "the working poor." Among other things, as Grivno shows in his account of rural wage laborers in the hinterlands of Baltimore, the South's free poor did indeed work, and work hard. Not surprisingly, he portrays an existence on the margins, with income always low and usually uncertain; also not surprisingly, the worst off were blacks and women. Perhaps more surprising, black and white (male) agricultural workers received identical wages and largely identical treatment from their employers. Still, white workers manipulated race to their advantage whenever they could, attempting to enforce racial hierarchy rather than forge solidarity across racial lines. Slavery, Grivno posits, made white workers unable to see "their black neighbors and coworkers . . . as participants in the same struggle for survival."

This lack of solidarity is illustrated further by the lynchings of slaves, the subject of Michael Pfeifer's essay. White mobs put dozens of slaves to death outside the law, even if this directly harmed the economic interests of the slaveowners. In the absence of specific data on the economic status of the members of these crowds, it is unclear whether the truly poor, of the sort discussed by Grivno, were major participants. In any case, Pfeifer argues that whites involved in lynching expressed a form of "explosive popular constitutionalism" in which white men insisted on their "fundamental right" as citizens to make the law, even if that "making" did not take the form of organized elections and courts, dominated as they were by slaveholders.

Rather different conclusions about the power of poor white men are suggested by Merritt's essay on the enforcement of vagrancy laws in antebellum Georgia. Merritt shows white men (and most of her cases by far are men) could be, and were, disciplined with the use of these laws, which swept up many of them from time to time for the crime of not working. Scholars have largely ignored vagrancy laws in the antebellum South, perhaps because they appear so rarely in the easily accessible records of appellate courts. The local records examined by Merritt demonstrate that white vagrants could be and were sentenced to harsh prison terms; moreover, many white men (and a few women) lingered in local jails for months without even coming to trial. Actual trials, it seems, were not necessary to make the law effective when local powers wanted to put it to use. Freedom, for those incarcerated, was hardly identifiable with "whiteness." Since these men were not typically actually forced to work, Merritt believes the main motive of the authorities was more social than economic control—to limit petty crime, discourage public immorality such as drunkenness, and, especially, to prevent cooperation of any kind between the white poor and the black poor, free or enslaved. These three essays together suggest the complex social tensions produced in a society in which economic and racial status failed to line up as proslavery ideology demanded.

The other essays, six in all, focus on those with significant economic resources. The identity of the entrepreneurs who were establishing corporations is so far unknown; in the other five essays, the subjects belonged, economically, in the broad middle range of southern households. Jonathan D. Wells examines the ways in which lawyers, dentists, teachers, and, especially, physicians tried to create and defend their status as professionals. These practitioners worked hard to distinguish themselves in the public eye from mere amateurs. Physicians, for example, sought certified training, formed professional societies, and published specialized journals while they sought to weed out the "quacks" whose practices were based on traditional knowledge or self-taught principles. His picture of a self-conscious, energetic, ambitious, and growing group of professionals fits in poorly with the notion of a region wedded to tradition.

Jennifer Green examines the production (and reproduction) of the middle class in institutions of higher education. She focuses mainly on the network of small colleges and military schools that enrolled the sons of farmers and professionals, rather than on the prestigious public institutions, such as the University of Virginia and South Carolina College, which catered to the children of the planter elite. Many students attended institutions that offered certificates and diplomas, instead of full bachelors' degrees. These institutions were far more affordable to middling families, and, as Green shows, the graduates of these schools became, in their turn, farmers, businessmen, and professionals. Among them were several state-supported military institutes and more than seventy private military academies. Green points out that a majority of fathers of these students were themselves professionals and that graduates were more likely to become engineers than soldiers. Thus, while just one in twenty pursued military careers, two out of three entered the professions, and one in eight "worked as engineers or for the railroads." This finding is especially interesting in the light of the common perception of the South as a bastion of "martial values," as exemplified by its large number of military academies. Green's close look at these schools shows a more complex picture, with military schools among the important agencies of southern "modernization."

Both Jeff Bremer and Gary Edwards examine the economic behavior of propertied settlers on the frontier, in Missouri and Tennessee, respectively. Although Bremer's evidence focuses on merchants and Edwards on "yeoman" farmers, both find that these aspiring, middling property owners responded actively to available market opportunities. In central Missouri, Bremer sees an "enthusiastic embrace of market activity by settlers" even before the quickening made possible by the arrival of the steamboat. Settlers, he writes, "quickly seized any chance to improve their living standards" by bartering or selling farm goods to local merchants. His language is echoed in Edwards's account of middling farmers (owning land, but fewer than 150 acres) in western Tennessee who would take on "anything . . . that would pay." Unlike some students of yeoman behavior, he sees little sharp distinction between their behavior and that of large slaveowners. As in Missouri, market participation in western Tennessee was greatly accelerated by the arrival of a new mode of transportation, in this case the railroad in the 1850s. In that decade, slaveless farmers increased their cotton production by some 55 percent, and yeoman farmers who owned slaves also grew more cotton while continuing to balance this with subsistence crops. Edwards's essay in particular raises the question of how we should think about middling farmers: are they in any sense part of a middle class that also includes merchants and lawyers? The term usually implies urban professionals, businessmen, clerks, and the like, but should we consider the middling farmer who sent his son to an academy as part of the same class as the son who then became a lawyer or engineer?[14]

Elbra David's study examines credit and debt relationships in the Natchez region in the 1820s. The region had become a major center of cotton production and the home of some of the nation's richest slaveholders. David's debtors and creditors were not, however, the elite who borrowed from commission houses and banks, the giants of the plantation economy whom historians like Scarborough have been interested in. They were middling planters and businessmen, making use of a vibrant local system, in which personal IOUs, notes, and other informal instruments, often in amounts below $10, provided a flexible means of both credit and exchange. This use of local, personal networks of credit and debt can be usefully compared to the similar networks in the northeast, as recently discussed by business historian Naomi Lamoureaux.[15]

Robert Wright's examination of incorporations, like David's study, offers new data directly relevant to questions of southern entrepreneurship. Comparing Virginia and Pennsylvania, he finds that southerners, like northerners, took advantage of the emerging corporate form of capital mobilization. While, on a per capita basis, Pennsylvanians chartered more and larger corporations than did Virginians in the early nineteenth century, by the end of the antebellum era Virginia's activity "caught up to, and sometimes exceeded, that of Pennsylvania." Incorporation was also a common practice in others states, such as Georgia. Thus Wright, like several of the authors here, sees the late antebellum period as one of accelerating change in the South's economy; he urges us to dismiss "hoary claims that Southerners were by nature reluctant entrepreneurs and incompetent managers," even if they lagged somewhat behind "their somewhat more advanced Northern neighbors."

The authors tend to avoid the sort of "either/or" formulations that analyses beginning with theories of "capitalism" or "modernization" often produce. Their essays suggest that southern "transformations" were evolutionary, not revolutionary. The arrival of new forms of transportation, gradual developments in local credit markets, and the establishment of new academies and professional organizations provided new opportunities; white southerners, whether on the western frontier or in a Virginia city, responded to them. What they did not do, except in rare circumstances, is interpret these changes and opportunities as incompatible with racial slavery. If we can all agree that slavery was a moral blight on the antebellum South—and on the nation as a whole—the essays together demonstrate the uncomfortable truth that such moral blight could develop hand in hand economic and social changes that we usually label as "progress." For this reason alone, they deserve the attention of all scholars of the Old South.

NOTES

1. Quotations from James M. McPherson, "Antebellum Southern Exceptionalism: A New Look at an Old Question," in *Drawn with the Sword: Reflections on the American Civil War,* by McPherson (New York: Oxford University Press, 1997), 9, 8.

2. Charles Beard and Mary Beard, *The Rise of American Civilization. Two Volumes in One, Revised and Enlarged* (New York: Macmillan, 1933), 1:659; 2, chap. 1.

3. Genovese's views have been expressed in many books, beginning with *The Political Economy of Slavery: Studies in the Economy and Society of the Slave South* (New York: Pantheon, 1965); Egerton, "Markets without a Market Revolution: Southern Planters and Capitalism," *Journal of the Early Republic* 16 (1996): 207-21; Ashworth, *Slavery, Capitalism, and Politics in the Antebellum Republic,* 2 vols. (Cambridge, UK: Cambridge University Press, 1995-2007).

4. McPherson, "Antebellum Southern Exceptionalism," 12.

5. James M. McPherson and James K. Hogue, *Ordeal by Fire: The Civil War and Reconstruction,* 4th ed. (New York: McGraw-Hill, 2009), 13. The language here is almost identical to that found in earlier editions of this textbook, when McPherson was the single author.

6. McPherson and Hogue, *Ordeal by Fire,* 15. The table also shows the origins of inventors of "Main Technological Innovations."

7. Frances W. Gregory and Irene New, "The American Industrial Elite in the 1870's: Their Social Origins," *Men in Business: Essays in the History of Entrepreneurship,* ed. William Miller (Cambridge, MA: Harvard University Press, 1952), 193-204.

8. Gregory and New wanted data comparable to that in a previous study of executives in the early twentieth century.

9. Lee Soltow, *Men and Wealth in the United States, 1850-1870* (New Haven, CT: Yale University Press, 1975), 148-49, 101.

10. William Kaufman Scarborough, *Masters of the Big House: Elite Slaveholders of the Mid-Nineteenth-Century South* (Baton Rouge: Louisiana State University Press, 2003), 426.

11. Joyce E. Chapin, *An Anxious Pursuit: Agricultural Innovation and Modernity in the Lower South, 1730-1815* (Chapel Hill: University of North Carolina Press, 1993); Richard Follett, *The Sugar Masters: Planters and Slaves in Louisiana's Cane World, 1820-1860* (Baton Rouge: Louisiana State University Press, 2005).

12. Gavin Wright, foreword to *Technology, Innovation, and Southern Industrialization from the Antebellum Era to the Computer Age,* ed. Susanna Delfino and Michele Gillespie (Columbia: University of Missouri Press, 2008), ix.

13. Delfino and Gillespie, eds., *Technology, Innovation, and Southern Industrialization;* Susanna Delfino and Michele Gillespie, eds., *Global Perspectives on Industrial Transformation in the American South* (Columbia: University of Missouri Press, 2005). Also relevant, though not part of this series, is another volume edited by Delfino and Gillespie: *Neither Lady Nor Slave: Working Women of the Old South* (Chapel Hill: University of North Carolina Press, 2002).

14. The equation of the "middle class" with urban dwellers is clear in the title of the most comprehensive treatment, by Stuart Blumin: *The Emergence of the Middle Class: Social Experience in the American City, 1790-1900* (Cambridge, UK: Cambridge University Press, 1989).

15. Naomi Lamoreaux, "Rethinking the Transition to Capitalism in the Early American Northeast," *Journal of American History* 90 (Sept. 2003): 437-61.

Editors' Introduction

Susanna Delfino, Michele Gillespie, and Louis M. Kyriakoudes

Over the past sixty years, successive generations of historians, beginning with Kenneth Stampp and Stanley Elkins, have significantly transformed our previous understanding of the U.S. South during the slave era. Robert Fogel and Stanley Engerman's *Time on the Cross: The Economics of American Negro Slavery* in particular launched what has rightly been called a true "historiographic revolution," which sparked a long-lasting debate over the nature of slavery and the nature of the antebellum South. Was the Old South a pre-modern, pre-capitalistic society that, while marked merely by a commercially oriented mentality, stood at odds to the patterns of capitalism, as historians Eugene D. and Elizabeth-Fox Genovese contended? Or was the economic culture of antebellum white southerners imbued by a modern capitalistic ethos? Fogel and Engerman, who supported the latter view, went even so far as to suggest that slaves, in responding to positive incentives on the plantation, had internalized the same work ethic subscribed to by their owners, igniting a great controversy over the very nature of the plantation and slavery.[1]

The most significant effect of this debate was to spur a thorough reappraisal of the history of the U.S. South during the slave era in its multiple dimensions: economic, social, political, and cultural. Considering the extent of fresh research that scholars realized they needed to carry out to provide new, well-documented portrayals of the slave South, this was quite an imposing feat. Nevertheless, a sizable number of historians took on the challenge.

Many scholars, especially economic and social historians, began this work by re-examining the "traditional" image of the Old South: the plantation world and the cotton economy. Sensitive to appeals to rewrite history "from the bottom up," the social historians undertook a reconsideration of the slaves' worlds, cultures, and behaviors, delving into the psychologically devastating effects produced by violent separation from homelands, the middle passage, and the material condition of bondage in and of itself. They documented how, in order to preserve their identities, slaves had carved out a world of their own and a modicum of independence within the specific reality in which they lived, whether rural or urban. They discovered that slaves had developed a distinctive culture of their own, one that accommodated their traditional customs and ways with elements deriving from their experience in the United States. Rather than acting like puppets devoid of individual agency, they preserved a set of values among which attachment to the family, group solidarity, and thrift were paramount.[2]

The southern plantation attracted much attention too, not only so far as its organization and management were concerned, but also in the light of social and race relations. New research on the master-slave relationship projected the plantation mistress to the forefront of scholarly interests, dispelling the myth of the southern lady living a life of leisure and pleasures, well attended to by her numerous domestic servants. Besides exposing the fact that her role demanded hard work and heavy responsibilities, these studies also investigated the complex, ambiguous, and often tense relationship existing between plantation mistresses and their female slaves within a male-dominated culture, the moral code of which proclaimed the white woman untouchable while also showing indulgence toward the sexual exploitation of female slaves by their masters. This reality was met with great difficulty by planters' wives and became utterly unsettling for them when they realized the emotional involvement by their husbands. Not infrequently, plantation mistresses came to feel that their condition of powerlessness was comparable to that of the slave, and some even began to harbor antislavery attitudes.[3]

The examination of planters' business records revealed, on the one hand, that they managed their estates according to principles of rationality, carefully balancing profits and losses with a view to reinvesting their earnings in some gainful way. Improvements on the plantations, and perhaps the buying of additional slaves as deemed necessary, came first in their investment decisions. But once they had satisfied the primary needs connected with the main source of their wealth, planters turned to residual forms of investment, which they largely funnelled into the internal improvements and manufacturing sectors of the economy. On the other hand, following the insights offered by Harold Woodman in *King Cotton and Its Retainers* (1968), Gavin Wright brilliantly defined the concept of a "comparative advantage" as the paramount consideration in determining the direction and extent of the planters' investment in sectors other than agriculture.[4] A few years later, Fred Bateman and Thomas Weiss, in A *Deplorable Scar-*

city (1981), challenged Wright's argument by concluding that, despite the much higher returns offered by investment in manufacturing, large numbers of planters chose not to pursue that venue, thereby failing to produce the amount of investment that would have helped the southern industrial economy take off.[5]

Yet the conclusion that planters had not lent sufficient financial support to the development of manufacturing in their region, vis-à-vis the inadequate economic diversification of the antebellum South, only stimulated scholars to investigate more deeply the reasons for their behavior. More recently, the meaningful comparative approaches between Pennsylvania and Virginia taken by John Majewski and Sean P. Adams confirm that slavery was indeed a major limit to southern industrial development.[6] Although highly illuminating, and in some regards even conclusive, their studies did not however hit the core of the historical conundrum. Given the enthusiastic encouragement Virginians lent the development of manufacturing, as documented by both public and private contemporary sources, did the rather inadequate results obtained stem from an original aversion to industrialization as a characterizing feature of the economy, or, was it the product of a congeries of conditions and forces largely independent of human agency? In his second book, John Majewski has tackled this question directly, identifying the system of "shifting cultivation" adopted by southern planters as the main cause thwarting their endeavors at both agricultural reform and industrialization. According to this author, the chemical composition of a large part of the South's soil encouraged shifting cultivation, and the high cost of manures, compounded by the difficulties in procuring them, further undercut the attempts made by planters to till a larger share of their unimproved lands.[7]

Over the last few decades the issue of the limits posed on modernization by the region's characterization as an export-oriented, slave-based plantation economy have prompted scholars to place the South within the larger picture of the Atlantic economy and, more generally, within an international perspective. The first documentation of the U.S. South's respectable international position, as far as the main indicators of economic modernization are concerned (manufacturing, railroad mileage, per capita income) actually dated back to *Time on the Cross*. That seminal book inspired subsequent generations of historians to adopt a less dogmatic definition of *modernization* in probing its extensiveness in the antebellum era. Placing the South's political economy in the larger international context was extremely useful in documenting the reasons underlying its political course in the late antebellum period and, by extension, in providing new explanations for the origins of the Civil War. Recent works by James Huston, John Majewski, and Brian Schoen forcefully argue that white southerners envisaged the modernization of their society as an endeavor to launch a vast program of industrialization to attain multiple goals: to emancipate themselves from northern dependence, to enhance economic independence through the establishment of direct trade connections with Europe (and other parts of the world as well), and to strengthen the South's commitment to slavery.[8]

In light of these interpretations, a number of scholars have explored anew the social aspects of modernization in the slave South. The state of South Carolina, long considered the staunchest bulwark of economic and social conservatism, has received much attention in this area. Inspired by the studies carried out by Rachel Klein, Lacy Ford, and Peter Coclanis, Tom Downey and Bruce Eelman have offered recent insightful assessments of the early shaping and development of an entrepreneurial, modernizing outlook on the part of South Carolinians. Their studies help clarify why the Palmetto State came to be the hotbed of the secessionist impulse.[9]

Effectively challenging the age-old indictment for perennial immobility—and even backwardness—which long biased understandings of the Old South, these and other new studies have substituted the concept of "stasis" with that of "dynamism" as an interpretive paradigm. Acknowledging that, between the birth of the nation and the Civil War, constant change was part and parcel of the region's history, they have explored the many transformations occurring in the Old South. Their investigations strongly point to the late antebellum era, rather than the aftermath of the Civil War, as the appropriate time period in which to locate the origins of regional modernization.[10]

These critical studies on regional economic modernization have encouraged scholars to pursue comparative studies between the U.S. South's historical experience and those of other societies marked by similar systems of bonded labor and elite power structures. Notable among them are Peter Kolchin's book comparing U.S. slavery with Russian serfdom, Shearer Davis Bowman's comparison between the German Junkers of East Elbia and the southern U.S. planters, and Enrico Dal Lago's study on the agrarian elites of the Italian and the U.S. Souths, respectively. In a number of studies, Susanna Delfino has offered reflections on the similarities existing between the U.S. and the Italian Souths as staple-crop-producing and export-oriented regions, noticing that the latter region had largely partaken in the same craze for modernization that stirred the American South between the 1830s and the early 1860s, when both southern societies faced a similar confrontation with their respective northern counterparts.[11] The meaningfulness of adopting these comparative and transnational approaches as interpretational keys to grasp in all their complexity both the economic dynamics and the cultural transformations that influenced the course of southern antebellum history has clearly been enhanced by the affirmation of global studies. Framed by this perspective, a number of works have recently been produced that press scholars toward writing a comprehensive new history of the Old South.[12]

In fact, the new sensibilities developed by scholars on the issue of modernization in U.S. slave society have raised semantic concerns about the appropriateness of continuing to refer to an "Old South"—as opposed to a "new" one—to describe a region whose economy and society were in constant flux throughout the seven decades that spanned the founding of the federal Union and the coming of the Civil War. True, the abolition of slavery represented a watershed in the course of southern history. But even if its importance was paramount in affirming the great, universal principle that all human beings have the right to be free, regardless of their color, its impact on the region's economy was so devastating that the "first" New South proved a poor match with the Old one. Yet, it was precisely because of the achievements reported during the antebellum era that, although under different circumstances, the southern region could resume its march toward economic progress and modernization.[13]

This fresh departure in the study of southern history has also, unavoidably, entailed a reappraisal of traditional interpretational categories such as those defined by the intersection of time and space. As a result, territorial expansion and geographic mobility, two important features in the shaping of the South as a region, can be seen as positive factors, rather than retarding ones, in the course of its economic development. Between the founding of the nation and 1860, while the Northeast experienced a physiological aging process (comparable to the hardening and stiffening of the sinews and joints of a human body), the South, owing to the frontier dimension of so much of its territory, remained constantly young.[14] Far from embodying the pattern of constant recapitulation of successive stages of development, as outlined by historian Frederick Jackson Turner at the end of the nineteenth century, the progressive occupation of the land by southerners benefited from and partook of all the advancements already enjoyed by the more easterly regions. Yet at the same time, the frontier significantly influenced the South's historical experience. North Carolina journalist and writer Wilbur J. Cash was able to grasp its relevance in the (non)shaping of a distinctive southern identity in the pre–Civil War era and masterfully conveyed the idea with these words: "It was actually 1820," he wrote, "before the tide of immigration was in full sweep about the base of the Appalachians. . . . From 1820 to 1860 is but forty years—a little more than the span of a single generation . . . the whole period from the invention of the cotton gin to the outbreak of the Civil War is less than seventy years—the lifetime of a single man." To Cash, it was inconceivable to think of the South as being "more than a few steps removed from the frontier stage at the beginning of the Civil War." [15] Yet the persistence of a frontier dimension was not synonymous with backwardness, but rather expressed the real distinctiveness of southern life. It lay in a unique blend of diverse socioeconomic landscapes that, collectively, defined the true essence of southern history as one of continuity *within* change.[16]

The very concept of transformation, which appears in this volume's title, suggests mutability and constant adaptation to new realities and circumstances, rather than linear *progress*—a word that the editors have purposely avoided, given its ambiguous and controversial meanings when applied to antebellum America. This avoidance, which reflects the sensibilities of modern students of economic development, looks all the more appropriate if we think that conflicting ideas and understandings of "progress" lay at the core of the debate which increasingly opposed North and South from the 1830s on.[17]

During the last three decades of the antebellum era, the expansion of the market economy, the transportation revolution, urbanization, and the development of manufacturing each affected the several geographic areas of the southern region with different modalities, depending on their specific social and economic connotations. Collectively, these phenomena contributed to modernizing the South, not only economically, but also from a social point of view. Altering traditional patterns of relations among whites, and between whites and blacks, this interplay helped transform antebellum society—and the institution of slavery itself within its fold—in many significant ways.

The opening of new urban and industrial jobs and professions for southern white men, coupled with the rise of unprecedented work opportunities for women, brought about an increasing diversity in the occupational structure of the antebellum South. The emergence of women as an important component of the labor force—and, most important, as income-earners—in both urban and industrial occupations modified gender relations within the households. Simultaneously, as entrepreneurial efforts and initiatives multiplied, making the southern nonagricultural economy more and more prominent, the involvement of growing numbers of whites in the market economy prompted a redefinition of the relationship of the employee versus the employer, and the laborer versus the capitalist. As a result, from the 1840s the white laboring classes of the South became increasingly restless and impatient. They started to enact forms of covert resistance and even open protest against the work discipline to which they were subjected under the nascent industrial system, as well as against their generally abject living conditions. Their resentment was also directed toward their inherent competition with slave labor. Consider the well-known case of the strike organized by the white skilled workers of the Tredegar Iron Works of Richmond, Virginia, in 1847, soon followed by a bread riot, whose major participants were the wives of the ironworkers just laid off by mill owner Joseph R. Anderson. Indeed, scores of workers' protests and strikes, not infrequently led by the foreign immigrants who were swelling their ranks, troubled southern cities and industrial locations during the last two decades of the antebellum era.[18]

The growth of already existing urban centers, such as Savannah, Richmond, Charleston and Louisville, and the rise of many new ones, especially in the Southwest, such as Augusta, Athens, Atlanta, and Chattanooga, provided the context for the emergence of a middle class that was no longer overwhelmingly represented by yeoman farmers and small planters but complemented by the practitioners of traditional professions such as medicine, law, and teaching. From the third decade of the century, the southern middle class significantly increased in numbers and became more articulated and class-conscious, thanks to the job opportunities opened by the expansion of businesses in the fields of banking, commerce, insurance, manufacturing, and transportation. The growing demand for services largely benefited women, native and immigrant, who now found easy employment, for example as hotel maids, dressmakers, governesses, or domestic servants.[19] From the late 1840s on, a new demand for formal education arose, signalled by the decline of the small school led by women teachers and the proliferation of more ambitious institutions featuring men as principals. It also translated into the founding of new academies, colleges, and technical schools of various descriptions, adding to the variety of educational opportunities within the region.[20]

The southern countryside was not immune from change either. Starting from the 1840s, a clear process marking concentration of land ownership was evident throughout the region. Thus, while on the upper echelon of landownership holdings were becoming larger, on the lower one they were decreasing in number, causing the dispossession of many small yeomen who consequently fell back into the class of the landless. This phenomenon was largely due to the increase in land prices, which continued unabated throughout the two decades preceding the advent of the war.[21] In North Carolina and Virginia, as in Tennessee and Mississippi, farmers were affected by the coming of the market economy. Because it raised unprecedented issues of competitiveness, it prompted them to revise their economic strategies and find a new equilibrium between their traditional "subsistence first" philosophy and the new prospects for ready cash income. Southern rural families had always seen seasonal work in either the manufacturing or mining sectors as a welcome opportunity to make ends meet. From the 1840s on, however, factory employment became a necessity for many. In the mill districts of the southern Piedmont, women of all ages increasingly turned to factory work. Not infrequently, whole families, including men and children, sought employment in manufacturing, especially wherever mill villages were organized around the factories. In the new areas of the southwest, and particularly in Georgia, textile labor became more impersonal, and mills saw a massive influx of young women and children.[22] This transformation, while providing steadier and more dependable manpower for southern factories, marked a major shift in whites' understanding of labor and, indeed, in their attitude toward the plantation/slave-based economy. As a result, so-called poor whites began to nurture feelings of betrayal by the upper classes, as well as a growing acrimony toward slave laborers who, after all, seemed to enjoy better protection than they.

These developments did not fail to affect the politics of slavery. In the eyes of the slaveholding elites, the new situation revealed not only a much-disquieting waning of the deferential attitude traditionally paid to them by the lower orders but also, more dramatically, their diminished loyalty to the institution of slavery, raising unprecedented problems of social control. Much of the impatience manifested by the white lower classes stemmed not so much from the existence of any widespread antislavery sentiment among them as, rather, from what they perceived to be the actual threat that slave labor posed to the security of their jobs, even as the southern elites felt hard pressed to recover their uncompromising support of the peculiar institution. In an attempt to achieve this goal, those elites envisaged a threefold strategy. First, from the 1830s on they consented to, or were forced into, a considerable democratization of political life. Second, they endeavored to accommodate the demands for steady employment advanced by the white laboring classes by trying to enforce a segregated system of jobs. In this connection, from the early 1840s on southern textile mills increasingly resorted to white labor alone or, when employing blacks too, confined them to "external" or "menial" tasks. In manufacturing industries where blacks—and slaves—had traditionally performed even highly skilled jobs, as in iron making, they were progressively relegated to the unskilled capacities. In urban locations, blacks of both sexes—either free or slave—were confined to performing the most humble services, while the skilled occupations were becoming, by city or state ordinance, the preserve of whites. Last, toward the end of the slave era, southern elites contemplated "socializing" the whites' support to the peculiar institution by broadening access to slave ownership. This measure, which would have reconfirmed the inclusiveness of all southern whites as members of the "ruling race," was to be attained, in their view, through the reopening of the slave trade which, by stimulating an increase in the supply of bondspeople, would have led to a drop in their prices. This proposal, however, was not received favorably in the Upper South, provoking major dissension among the delegates to the commercial conventions starting in 1856.[23] Underlying this outcome was the growing differentiation between the economic and social structures of the Upper and the Lower South, respectively. During the antebellum period, whereas the states belonging to the former region had in fact enhanced their inclination to attain economic diversification through industrialization, the Lower South's stake in the cotton economy had steadily increased. The presence of fewer numbers of slaves in states such as Kentucky, Missouri, and Tennessee, as compared with the figures reported by South Carolina, Mississippi, and Louisiana, further underlined the differences. While in the Upper South economic development was not necessarily seen as intimately intertwined with the presence of a large slave population, in the Lower South feelings tended to run in the opposite direction. Because of the different milieu in which they lived and operated, many people in the border states could thus imagine scenarios in which the existing slave population adapted to an industrializing economy—eventually leading to the gradual abolition of slavery—much more easily than could people in the Deep South.

The various strategies devised by the southern elites to recover the loyalty of whites to the peculiar institution met with notable difficulties. In fact, during the 1840s and 1850s, the rise in both land and slave prices made for an increase in the number of the landless, releasing from agriculture many impoverished whites who were not only angry about their expulsion from land ownership but, more specifically, blamed the perverse workings of the slave system for their misfortunes. The southern ruling classes were thus confronted with the dilemma of how to sustain the plantation economy while promoting industrial development: two goals that were perceived as equally crucial toward the deliverance of the South from both international and domestic economic dependency. These joint concerns generated endless conflicts, the extent of which was compounded by the existence of both internal and external pressures.[24]

This volume contributes to a new understanding of the dynamism of the antebellum South by offering multiple perspectives from both established and rising scholars on the all-pervasive transformations that stirred the region between 1790 and 1860. To provide an organizing framework for analysis, the volume is divided into four parts, each devoted to a specific issue, or theme, which the editors have identified as particularly useful as an interpretive key toward a more comprehensive reappraisal of southern history. Part I discusses critical legal and extra-legal aspects of race relations as they evolved during the period under consideration. The essays included with this section document the growth of racial and class tension throughout the antebellum era, shedding additional light on the motivations lying at the basis of poor whites' increasing disaffection with the slave regime. Part II deals with the changes engendered by the advent of the market economy in the rural worlds of three Upper South areas: central Missouri, southwest Tennessee, and the Baltimore hinterland. Due to the different timing of their settlement—Baltimore the oldest, and central Missouri the most recent—farmers responded to the transformation in different ways.

Part III is devoted to the consideration of an important aspect of the transformation: the development of a modern middle class. A long-neglected subject in the study of southern society during the slave era, if not in its classical identification with the yeoman farmers, or at best through vague and scattered references to equally classical figures such as doctors and lawyers, the middle class emerges from the essays presented in this section not only as a highly diverse and dynamic segment of white society but also as an increasingly self-conscious group. Finally, Part IV of the volume concentrates on important financial aspects of the economic transformation.

The present collection of essays does not pretend to cover the whole range of social transformations that affected the American South during the first seventy years of its existence as part of an independent nation through the close of the slave era. Yet by highlighting the twisted and sometimes contradictory trajectories followed by white southerners in their pursuit of regional modernization and industrialization, it offers a meaningful panorama of the complexity of the issues involved. While no single volume of essays can provide an exhaustive account of the transformations undergone by southern society during the slave era, the editors of this volume hope this set of exciting new essays contributes toward this end in a significant way, and want the volume to constitute an important reference point for new generations of historians.

In conclusion, the editors wish to acknowledge the fine staff members of the University of Missouri Press for their highly professional and never-failing support and assistance and to express their appreciation and esteem to Clair Willcox, who is now its editor-in-chief. They also want to convey their deepest gratitude to Beverly Jarrett, the former director and editor-in-chief of the Press who recently retired, for all the enthusiasm, energy, and professional expertise she invested in launching the New Currents in the History of Southern Economy and Society series, of which the present one constitutes the third volume. Without her assistance and precious advice, none of this would have been possible, and we hope that she may now feel proud of our attainments. Finally, we once again thank Randy Patton, the Shaw Industries Chair at Kennesaw State University, for critical financial support.

This book is dedicated to historian Frank L. Owsley, whose pioneering work on the structure and tenure of land and slave ownership inspired further generations of historians—including ourselves—to engage in the investigation of the diverse social and economic landscapes characterizing the Old South.

NOTES

1. Kenneth M. Stampp, *The Peculiar Institution: Slavery in the Antebellum South* (New York: Knopf, 1956); Stanley M. Elkins, *Slavery: A Problem in American Institutional and Intellectual Life* (Chicago: University of Chicago Press, 1959); Robert W. Fogel and Stanley L. Engerman, *Time on the Cross: The Economics of American Negro Slavery* (Boston: Little, Brown, 1974). The authors' thesis substantially challenged the interpretation set forth by Eugene D. Genovese in *The Political Economy of Slavery: Studies in the Economy and Society of the Slave South* (New York: Random House, 1967) and *The World the Slaveholders Made: Two Essays in Interpretation* (New York: Pantheon Books1969) and later reiterated in *Fruits of Merchant Capital: Slavery and Bourgeois Property in the Rise and Expansion of Capitalism* (New York: Oxford University Press, 1983), written with Elizabeth Fox-Genovese. The uproar over *Time on the Cross* among historians was intense and is best summarized in Herbert G. Gutman, *Slavery and the Numbers Game: A Critique of* Time on the Cross (1975; repr., Urbana: University of Illinois Press, 2003). Recent work has supported Fogel and Engerman's position on positive work incentives. See Mark M. Smith, *Mastered by the Clock: Time, Slavery, and Freedom in the American South* (Chapel Hill: University of North Carolina Press, 1997). A more balanced rendition of the Old South's social and cultural traits is offered by *Society and Culture in the Slave South*, ed. J. William Harris (London: Routledge, 1992).

2. Revisionist literature on slavery, slave communities, and slaves as individuals is immense. See Mark M. Smith, *Debating Slavery: Economy and Society in the Antebellum American South* (Cambridge, UK: Cambridge University Press, 1998); George P. Rawick, *From Sundown to Sunup: The Making of the Black Community* (Westport, CT: Greenwood, 1972); Eugene D. Genovese, *Roll, Jordan, Roll: The World the Slaves Made* (New York: Pantheon, 1974); Herbert G. Gutman, *The Black Family in Slavery and Freedom, 1750-1925* (New York: Vintage Books, 1977); and Charles Joyner, *Down by the River Side* (Urbana: University of Illinois Press, 1977). Gutman's work openly criticized the approach taken by Eugene Genovese.

3. Ann Firor Scott, *The Southern Lady: From Pedestal to Politics, 1830-1930* (Chicago: University of Chicago Press, 1970); Catherine Clinton, *The Plantation Mistress: Woman's World in the Old South* (New York: Pantheon Books, 1982); Elizabeth Fox-Genovese, *Within the Plantation Household: Black and White Women of the Old South* (Chapel Hill: University of North Carolina Press, 1988); Deborah Gray White, *Ar'n't I a Woman? Female Slaves in the Plantation South* (New York: W.W. Norton, 1985); Michele Gillespie, "Antebellum Southern Women's History," in *A Companion to the Civil War and Reconstruction*, ed. Lacy Ford (Oxford: Blackwell, 2005), 128-51.

4. Harold Woodman, *King Cotton and His Retainers: Financing and Marketing the Cotton Crop of the South, 1800-1925* (Columbia: University of South Carolina Press, 1968); Gavin Wright, *The Political Economy of the Cotton South: Households, Markets, and Wealth in the Nineteenth Century* (New York: W.W. Norton, 1978).

5. Fred Bateman, James Foust, and Thomas Weiss, "The Participation of Planters in Manufacturing in the Antebellum South," *Agricultural History* 48, no. 2 (1974): 277-97; Fred Bateman and Thomas Weiss, *A Deplorable Scarcity: The Failure of Industrialization in the Slave Economy* (Chapel Hill: University of North Carolina Press, 1981).

6. John Majewski, *A House Dividing: Economic Development in Pennsylvania and Virginia before the Civil War* (Cambridge, UK: Cambridge University Press, 2000); Sean Patrick Adams, *Old Dominion, Industrial Commonwealth: Coal, Politics, and Economy in Antebellum America* (Baltimore, MD: Johns Hopkins University Press, 2004), and "Pits of Frustration: The Failed Transplant of British Mining Methods in Antebellum Virginia," in *Technology, Innovation, and Southern Industrialization: From the Antebellum Era to the Computer Age*, ed.

Susanna Delfino and Michele Gillespie (Columbia: University of Missouri Press, 2008), 41-67.

7. John Majewski, *Modernizing a Slave Economy: The Economic Vision of the Confederate Nation* (Chapel Hill: University of North Carolina Press, 2009).

8. James L. Huston, *Calculating the Value of the Union: Slavery, Property Rights, and the Economic Origins of the Civil War* (Chapel Hill: University of North Carolina Press, 2003); Brian Shoen, *The Fragile Fabric of Union: Cotton, Federal Politics, and the Global Origins of the Civil War* (Baltimore, MD: Johns Hopkins University Press, 2009); John Majewski, *Modernizing a Slave Economy;* Gavin Wright, *Slavery and American Economic Development* (Baton Rouge: Louisiana State University Press, 2006).

9. Rachel N. Klein, *Unification of a Slave State: The Rise of the Planter Class in the South Carolina Backcountry, 1760-1808* (Chapel Hill: University of North Carolina Press, 1973); Lacy K. Ford, *Origins of Southern Radicalism: The South Carolina Upcountry, 1800-1860* (New York: Oxford University Press, 1988); Peter A. Coclanis, *The Shadow of a Dream: Economic Life and Death in the South Carolina Low Country, 1670-1920* (New York: Oxford University Press, 1989); Tom Downey, *Planting a Capitalist South: Masters, Merchants, and Manufacturers in the Southern Interior, 1790-1860* (Baton Rouge: Louisiana State University Press, 2006); Bruce W. Eelman, *Entrepreneurs in the Southern Upcountry: Commercial Culture in Spartanburg, 1945-1880* (Athens: University of Georgia Press, 2008).

10. On the South's dynamism and openness to modernity, see Michael O'Brien's recent, comprehensive work, *Conjectures of Order: Intellectual Life and the American South, 1810-1860* (Chapel Hill: University of North Carolina Press, 2004). By the same author, see also *Placing the South* (Jackson: University of Mississippi Press, 2007). For specific examples, see Peter Coclanis, *The Shadow of a Dream,* Joyce Chaplin, *An Anxious Pursuit: Agricultural Innovation and Modernity in the Lower South, 1730-1815* (Chapel Hill: University of North Carolina Press, 1993), Tom Downey, *Planting a Capitalist South,* and Bruce Eelman, *Entrepreneurs in the Southern Upcountry.*

11. Peter Kolchin, *Unfree Labor: American Slavery and Russian Serfdom* (Cambridge, MA: Harvard University Press, 1987); Shearer Davis Bowman, *Masters and Lords: Mid-19th-Century U.S. Planters and Prussian Junkers* (New York: Oxford University Press, 1993); Enrico Dal Lago, *Agrarian Elites: American Slaveholders and Southern Italian Landowners, 1815-1861* (Baton Rouge: Louisiana State University Press, 2005); Susanna Delfino, "The Idea of Southern Economic Backwardness: A Comparative View of the United States and Italy," in *Global Perspectives on Industrial Transformation in the American South,* ed. Susanna Delfino and Michele Gillespie (Columbia: University of Missouri Press, 2005), 105-30, and, by the same author, "The Toll of Reconciliation: North and South in Post-Unification Italy and the Post–Civil War United States," in *Reconstructing Societies in the Aftermath of War: Memory Identity, Reconciliation,* ed. Flavia Brizio-Skov (Boca Raton, FL: Bordighera Press, 2004), 103-17.

12. The study of U.S. slavery in a comparative perspective owes much to the seminal work of David Brion Davis, *The Problem of Slavery in Western Culture* (Ithaca, NY: Cornell University Press, 1966). Stanley Engerman was a path-breaker in comparative and transnational studies on slavery and industrialization. See, for example, his "Notes on the Pattern of Economic Growth in the British North American Colonies in the Seventeenth, Eighteenth, and Nineteenth Centuries," in *Disparities in Economic Development since the Industrial Revolution,* ed. P. Bairoch and M. Levy-Leboyer (New York: St. Martin's Press, 1981), "Economic Growth of Colonial North America: Europe, the Lesser Antilles, and Economic Expansion, 1600-1800," in *The Lesser Antilles in the Age of European Expansion,* ed. R. L Paquette and S. L. Engerman (Gainesville: University of Florida Press, 1996), and "France, Britain and the Economic Growth of Colonial North America," in *The Early Modern Atlantic Economy,* ed. J. J. McCusker and K. Morgan (Cambridge, UK: Cambridge

University Press, 2000), and *Slavery, Emancipation, and Freedom: Comparative Perspectives* (Baton Rouge: Louisiana State University Press, 2006). Also worth mentioning is Robert W. Fogel, *Without Consent or Contract: The Rise and Fall of American Slavery* (New York: W.W. Norton, 1989). Notable among recent comparative and global studies are David L. Carlton and Peter A. Coclanis, *The South, the Nation, and the World: Perspectives on Southern Economic Development* (Charlottesville: University of Virginia Press, 2003), and James Cobb and William Stueck, *Globalization and the American South* (Athens: University of Georgia Press, 2005).

13. Eric Foner, *Reconstruction: America's Unfinished Revolution, 1863-1877* (New York: Harper & Row, 1988); Gavin Wright, *Old South, New South: Revolutions in the Southern Economy since the Civil War* (New York: Basic Books, 1986).

14. S. Max Edelson, *Plantation Enterprise in Colonial South Carolina* (Cambridge, MA: Harvard University Press, 2006); Don H. Doyle, *Faulkner's County: The Historical Roots of Yoknapatawpha* (Chapel Hill: University of North Carolina Press, 2001).

15. Wilbur J. Cash, *The Mind of the South* (New York: Vintage Books, 1941), 10-11.

16. O'Brien, *Placing the South;* James C. Cobb, *Away Down South: A History of Southern Identity* (New York: Oxford University Press, 2005), introduction.

17. Anthony F. Wallace, *Rockdale: The Growth of an American Village in the Early Industrial Revolution* (New York: Alfred A. Knopf, 1978); Susanna Delfino and Michele Gillespie, eds., *Global Perspectives on Industrial Transformation in the American South,* introduction; Delfino, "The Idea of Southern Economic Backwardness"; Susan Mary Grant, *North over South: Northern Nationalism and American Identity in the Antebellum Era* (Lawrence: Kansas University Press, 2000).

18. Suzanne Lebsock, *The Free Women of Petersburg: Status and Culture in a Southern Town, 1784-1860* (New York: W.W. Norton, 1984); Michele Gillespie, *Free Labor in an Unfree World: White Artisans in Slaveholding Georgia, 1789-1860* (Athens: University of Georgia Press, 2000); Susanna Delfino and Michele Gillespie, eds., *Neither Lady Nor Slave: Working Women of the Old South* (Chapel Hill: University of North Carolina Press, 2002); Bess B. Beatty, *Alamance: The Holt Family and Industrialization in a North Carolina County, 1837-1900* (Baton Rouge: Louisiana State University Press, 1999); Patricia A. Schechter, "Free and Slave Labor in the Old South: The Tredegar Ironworkers' Strike of 1847," *Labor History* 35 (1994): 165-86.

19. Jonathan D. Wells, *The Origins of the Southern Middle Class, 1800-1861* (Chapel Hill: University of North Carolina Press, 2004), Frank J. Byrne, *Becoming Bourgeois: Merchant Culture in the South, 1820-1865* (Lexington: University Press of Kentucky, 2006). Frank Towers, *The Urban South and the Coming of the Civil War* (Charlottesville: University of Virginia Press, 2004). On the growing participation of women in the labor market, see the essays included with parts 2 and 4 of *Neither Lady Nor Slave,* ed. Delfino and Gillespie.

20. Neither Lady Nor Slave, part 3; Jennifer R. Green, "Networks of Military Educators: Middle-Class Stability and Professionalization in the Late Antebellum South," *Journal of Southern History* 73 (2007): 39-74, and, by the same author, *Military Schools and the Emerging Middle Class in the Old South* (Cambridge, UK: Cambridge University Press, 2008).

21. James Oakes, *The Ruling Race: A History of American Slaveholders* (New York: Alfred A. Knopf, 1983); Charles C. Bolton, *Poor Whites of the Antebellum South: Tenants and Laborers in Central North Carolina and Northeast Mississippi* (Durham, NC: Duke University Press, 1994); Bill Cecil-Fronsman, *Common Whites: Class and Culture in Antebellum North Carolina* (Lexington: University Press of Kentucky, 1992).

22. See, for example, Bess B. Beatty, "I Can't Get My Bored on Them Old Lomes: Female Textile Workers in the Antebellum South," and Michele Gillespie, "To Harden a

Lady's Hand: Gender Politics, Racial Realities, and Women Millworkers in Antebellum Georgia," in *Neither Lady Nor Slave*, ed. Delfino and Gillespie.

23. Vicki Vaughn Johnson, *The Men and the Vision of the Southern Commercial Conventions, 1845-1871* (Columbia: University of Missouri Press, 1992).

24. Joseph J. Persky, *The Burden of Dependency: Colonial Themes in Southern Economic Thought* (Baltimore, MD: Johns Hopkins University Press, 1992); Brian Schoen, "Alternatives to Dependency: The Lower South's Antebellum Pursuit of Sectional Development through Global Interdependence," in *Global Perspectives*, ed. Delfino and Gillespie. Shoen provides a much broader discussion of the political economy of the Lower South and of the often contradictory motivations underlying the secession movement in his recent *The Fragile Fabric of Union*.

Part I

Legal and Extralegal Dimensions of Race Relations

Chapter 1

"A Vile, Immoral, and Profligate Course of Life"

Poor Whites and the Enforcement of Vagrancy Laws in Antebellum Georgia

Keri Leigh Merritt

In 1858, Jacob Waddel was convicted of vagrancy in Marion, a county in the heart of the western Georgia blackbelt. Waddel appealed his case to the Georgia Supreme Court on the grounds that the verdict was "contrary to evidence." Although he owned no real estate or personal property, Waddel was a thirty-three-year-old farmer with a family to support. While he had been seen plowing a potato patch and "doing some other small jobs," both the inferior and superior courts concluded that Waddel's "fancy" seemed to have been walking along the highways, "strolling about in idleness." In a unanimous opinion delivered by Chief Justice Lumpkin, the court acknowledged that the offense itself was "somewhat anomalous"; every other offense involved "doing something," but Waddel's "doing nothing" caused him to be sentenced to hard labor in the state penitentiary. Yet as the only vagrancy case to reach the appellate level in the antebellum South, the justices wanted to make Waddel an example for other southern poor whites on the eve of the Civil War. "It is time, perhaps, to give them a scare," Lumpkin wrote, "to admonish them of the old adage, that the bird that can sing, and won't sing, must *be made* to sing." And after imprisonment, Waddel sang. The 1860 census listed him as a carpenter with $100 worth of personal property.[1]

But was Jacob Waddel really arrested for being a "do-nothing"? Or was he merely a victim of circumstance, a poor white man in a slaveholder's world? Four years before the attack on Fort Sumter, Hinton Helper claimed that five million poor southern whites suffered "a second degree of slavery" precisely *because* of the peculiar institution. The *Impending Crisis of the South* asserted that no free white could compete with slave labor; it was a direct refutation of the pro-slavery argument and its purpose was to challenge the domination of the region's slaveholders. Helper, the only southerner to write about nonslaveholders as a distinct class, believed that slave ownership—not white skin—constituted southern social status. Georgia's selective implementation of vagrancy laws indicates that Helper's theories about poor whites may have been more accurate than previously assumed.[2]

While planters and slaves have been studied extensively, poor whites have been understudied and overlooked until very recently. Beginning in the 1920s, scholars like W. O. Brown, Paul Buck, and Avery Craven wrote about the southern poor, but their analyses were always compromised by racism, as well as by a desire to "redeem" the South through a subjective retelling of history. In 1949, Frank Owsley effectively shifted the focus of many historians away from poor whites and onto the South's rural middling classes. Likely because of Owsley's influence, most contemporary sources on non-elite white southerners have focused solely on yeomen farmers, classifying them as "common whites." No matter the term, though, yeomen who owned even a single slave had much more in common with planters than with poor whites, both economically and politically. It was not until after the 1990s that historians like Charles Bolton, Timothy Lockley, and Jeff Forret began to focus on the South's poorest whites, who comprised between 30 and 50 percent of the white population.[3]

Although Edmund Morgan claimed that colonial Virginia's poor and elite whites had united over racial issues by the eighteenth century, the implementation of antebellum Georgia's laws indicates that planters were uneasy about poor whites' commitment to slavery. This shift in racial solidarity between whites can be attributed to several factors, all of which stem, ironically, from the growth of the peculiar institution itself. First, slavery allowed the South's elites to overfarm for years. The subsequent soil depletion caused farmers to move frequently in search of better, more fertile land. The Old South was a highly mobile society. Second, slavery rapidly decreased the demand for white farmers, day laborers, and even mechanics, creating a large underclass of impoverished white people who spent long periods of time unemployed or underemployed. As former slave James Deane put it, "The poor white people . . . were worse off than the slaves, because they could not get any work to do, on the plantation the slaves did all the work." Third, slavery drastically kept wages of southern whites well below those of their northern counterparts. And finally, slavery produced a society in which poor whites had no stake, and thus to deal with their exclusion, many turned to alcoholism, crime, and violence.[4]

One particular crime—vagrancy—accounted for many of the criminal cases involving the South's poor whites. By definition, vagrants owned no property and thus had nothing to lose, and their "wandering about" made it easy for them to have contact with both blacks and other white rabble rousers. Conceivably the crime of vagrancy, when committed in a slave society, was more than just mere idleness. Instead, it was an ominous act that exposed the tenuousness of the upper class's position. Apprehension over the behaviors of poor whites was especially acute in areas with high percentages of blacks. Young, able-bodied whites with no ties to the southern hierarchy, who spent their days strolling about, could easily "wander" into trouble—by colluding with slaves to commit crimes, by forming intimate (and sometimes sexual) relationships with blacks, and by indulging in their propensity for drinking, fighting, gambling, and carousing.[5]

In the nineteenth-century South, vagrancy laws were used to control poor whites in the antebellum period in many of the same ways that they were used to control blacks in the postbellum period. Vagrancy is an extremely peculiar crime: while every other offense involves the perpetrator doing *something*, the vagrant could be arrested for doing *nothing*. Most historians simply assume that the South's elites began using the crime of vagrancy to control the labor of African Americans in the postbellum period. The realities of the law's implementation, though, are much more nuanced.[6]

Early modern Europeans used vagrancy to control the labor of the lower classes, especially during the transition out of feudalism. Vagrancy laws essentially reinstated many aspects of serfdom: they restricted the peasant class from moving freely throughout the country and assured the elite an abundance of cheap labor. As each American state adopted versions of British statutes, however, a subtle but definite division between northern and southern vagrancy statutes became apparent. Northern vagrancy laws depended mainly on the need for labor—rapid industrialization caused an ever-increasing demand for workers. Northern states enacted longer, more detailed vagrancy statutes; but for all of their wordiness, they identified fewer categories of vagrants than did the much more terse southern laws, and they tended to focus on maintaining a productive population. The slave-based South, on the other hand, always had a surplus of labor; it was unnecessary to force any nonslave to work. And because the South's gentry could easily command the region's laboring population, southern vagrancy statutes focused more on the prevention of criminal activity—especially interracial illegalities, from petty theft to miscegenation.[7]

Deep South lawmakers often crafted their vagrancy statutes in an extremely vague way, and these nondescript definitions of the crime allowed the local elite to justify the lengthy jailing of suspicious people—whether because of their habits, their occupations, their beliefs, or their resistance to the established social and racial order. The typical southern vagrant, therefore, was arrested not for a specific action but rather for having "a certain personal condition" or being "a person of a specified character." Vagrancy, according to Justice Hugo Black, was a crime defined in "terms of *being* rather than in terms of *acting*"; it had always been considered a crime of status, and arrests were based largely upon the elite's perception of the accused's class. In fact, class functioned as the only universal among southern vagrants. Most statutes stipulated that the offender be without means of subsistence, and many declared that property ownership negated the crime.[8]

The State of Georgia regularly prosecuted vagrants throughout the mid- and late-antebellum periods. One of the first statutes to explicitly describe the offense was enacted in 1816, condemning "any person wandering or strolling about, able to work or otherwise to support himself or herself in a reputable way, or leading an idle, immoral, or profligate course of life." Furthermore, the statute completely allowed the courts to determine the penalties for offenders. The law remained untouched until 1847, when Georgia legislators added two important clauses. First, the new statute specified that the accused "has not property to support himself or herself." Second, punishment guidelines were set between two and four years hard labor in the state penitentiary. This prison sentence was extreme in relation to the offense; manslaughter convictions generally warranted the same sentences, and prison terms for assault were usually much shorter. Clearly, vagrancy frightened Georgia's lawmakers—they made sure convicts would be locked up for several years.[9]

Paradoxically, if the offender could post bond "for his or her good behavior and future industry for one year," he or she would be released. The bond had to be under $400, but even if it averaged between $5 and $10, the law itself stipulated that vagrants could not own any property. No impoverished white could afford to pay the bond himself, and even if he could pay, he probably would not have had the actual currency. Thus, the bond had to be posted by a benefactor, which uncannily resembled the ways in which well-respected whites "vouched" for the behaviors of free blacks in local courtrooms. The bond clause obviously served to strengthen the culture of southern paternalism, but under this application, planters controlled more than blacks and women—they dominated other white men as well.[10]

To truly understand why vagrancy threatened the existing southern order, though, more needs to be known about the vagrants themselves. Superior Court Minutes for fourteen Georgia counties indicate that more than 230 poor whites were formally charged with vagrancy in the forty years prior to the Civil War. These numbers suggest that thousands of poor whites were charged with vagrancy throughout the South. The more important story, however, lies in the tales of the countless poor whites who were locked in local jails and guardhouses *without* ever being formally charged with a crime. Because of the absolute dearth of antebellum jail records, it is impossible to know how many poor whites were imprisoned for vagrancy in the South. Georgia's only jail records come from Savannah, and they verify that many vagrants spent time in and out of jail before ever being formally charged in Superior Court. Indeed, it appears that the vast majority of vagrancy arrests led only to confinement; often there was no intention of bringing these cases to court. Several short statements in the county minute books attest to the fact that people arrested for vagrancy frequently sat in jail for weeks and months awaiting indictment hearings.[11]

William Bishop, arrested for vagrancy in Bibb County in 1847, was finally released after being "confined to jail for more than a year and no person appearing to prosecute." The grand jury ordered him "discharged without payment of costs he having taken the oath of insolvency." Benjamin Farrell, a farm laborer in his thirties, served an undisclosed amount of time in Camden County's guardhouse in 1820. When Farrell finally was arraigned, the solicitor general failed to appear in court, so the jury ordered Farrell discharged. In yet another example, Chatham County's officials charged George Horlbeck, a single man in his fifties, with vagrancy twice in the late 1820s. After his first arrest, the judge described Horlbeck as "a prisoner in the county jail for some months" and ordered him "discharged for want of bond to prosecute."[12]

These stories, along with Savannah's records, suggest that vagrancy was frequently used as an excuse to imprison poor whites without the intention of ever formally charging them. While some vagrants were only held for a week to ten days, many offenders likely were held without trial for three or four months, and some were even detained for a full year. Furthermore, many of these poor whites were jailed over and over again—some just a day or two after being released. Elites could use vagrancy laws to lock away anyone who posed a threat to the southern system, even if no crime had been committed. This type of subjective incarceration clearly supports Hinton Helper's argument: depriving poor whites of personal freedom and bodily liberty *was* a second degree of slavery, and class—not race—dictated who could be enslaved.

As southerners became more geographically mobile, the idea of the intimate, face-to-face southern community was challenged, wreaking havoc on a social system long defined by personal honor. Cities, small towns, and even rural areas increasingly became overrun with "strangers." Transient poor whites had no local kinfolk, no ties to the area's churches, and no real allegiance to the institution of slavery; and white elites had no knowledge of which poor whites needed to be "controlled"—of who would help their slaves steal and drink, who would give birth to free mulatto children, who would demoralize their work force, and who might try to lead their slaves into a bloody rebellion.

The majority of Georgia's antebellum vagrancy arrests occurred in large cities, such as Macon, Savannah, Augusta, and Columbus. In urban areas, it was impossible to keep the races separated. Poor whites regularly came into contact with both slaves and free blacks in cities. White vagrants tended to be in their late teens to early thirties, and they usually had frequent contact with blacks. Whether drinking, gambling, coupling, or trading with blacks in the underground economy, poor white men easily undermined planters' complete control over African Americans. But poor white women also posed a significant threat to the established social hierarchy. As Ira Berlin has shown, the largest source of interracial sex occurred between white servant women and black men and often resulted in illegitimate babies.[13]

Planters incarcerated many female vagrants on suspicion of prostitution or sexual impropriety. Elites had good reason to control this section of the population: interracial infants took on the legal status of their mothers, meaning that poor white women had the ability to produce an entire race of free blacks—a terrifying prospect for the southern gentry. During his travels though Georgia, Frederick Law Olmsted took notice of several poor white "harlots," noting that "very slight value is placed on female virtue among this class." There must always be enough women, he reasoned, poor enough so that "their favors can be purchased by the slaves." What was much worse, though, was that the biracial offspring of these poor white women "must be constitutionally entitled to freedom." But with the offense of vagrancy, prostitutes and loose women never had to be caught in the act. Instead of having to produce proof of prostitution, fornication, adultery, or lewd behavior, elites simply jailed poor white women for roaming the streets.[14]

Perhaps it is not surprising, then, that poor white women were convicted and sentenced to hard labor at the state penitentiary in Milledgeville at a drastically higher rate than poor white men. The majority of these women, however, actually served very little of their sentences, likely because the penitentiary was unequipped to separate prisoners by sex. Like most antebellum southern jails, Milledgeville housed both blacks and whites, males and females in the same building. Nancy Walker, arrested for vagrancy in 1856, was a seventeen-year-old daughter of a poor farm laborer. As one of ten children, Walker worked as a housekeeper and a spinster. But when a county-level judge sentenced her to two years in the state prison, she was discharged after serving only six months. Her short stint in the penitentiary was easily explained by the governor's pardon. He decided to release her since she had "been imprisoned for a length of time, and in consideration of her sex and the improbability of providing for female convicts." It seems as if many female vagrants were released simply because the state was not equipped to incarcerate them.[15]

When Sarah Wynn, alias Sarah Clem, was formally charged with vagrancy in Columbus in 1860, she had already spent several years in and out of the local jail for public drunkenness. Wynn was in her late thirties and had a rather difficult past. Census records reveal that she was living with her parents and brother in 1850. The Clems were small farmers with $1,100 worth of personal property and real estate. Because of her last name, it is apparent that Wynn had been married and was either widowed, divorced, or abandoned.[16]

William Brown, the first man to testify against Wynn, was a sixty-year-old planter from New York. An extremely wealthy widower with at least twenty slaves, Brown reported that he saw Wynn "frequently drunk in the streets," that he had never known her to work, and that she often used "immoral obscene and profane language." Next, a marshal for the county admitted that he had not seen much of the defendant in the past few months. Prior to that, however, he had "hauled [Wynn] in a cart to the guardhouse" several times for being drunk and had also witnessed her use profane language. Another marshal scandalously added that Wynn frequently appeared drunk in public places "with her clothes nearly torn off of her." Finally, Davenport P. Ellis, a well-off merchant in his mid-forties, was called as the State's last witness. Ellis brought up new information about the defendant: in recent months he had seen Wynn at Colonel Osborn's house, "drunk and noisy and threatening persons." Osborn, a "man of weak intellect and very imbecile," had a legal guardian to care for him and his rather large estate. Apparently Osborn, despite being listed in census records as "insane," was extremely wealthy. In addition to land and property, he also owned thirty-two slaves. According to Ellis, after Sarah Wynn accused Osborn of "staying with other women," Osborn ordered her off the premises. Osborn said that she "annoyed him greatly . . . and that he could not get rid of her."[17]

The two witnesses for the defense, however, told a very different story. Wynn's mother, Jane Clem, took the stand first. By the time of the trial, Clem was a sixty-five-year-old widow who lived with several other jobless "paupers." She admitted that while her daughter used to be "very bad," she had "reformed within the past eight months." Wynn was now employed by Colonel Osborn: she stayed "there night and day waiting on and sewing for" him, and she earned $10 a month. Several times, according to Clem, Osborn even sent his "Rockaway and boy" to pick Wynn up. The final witness, a fiftyish woman who resided with Jane Clem, corroborated Clem's story completely. Wynn "was behaving herself very well while at Osborn's." Census records from 1860 confirm the women's testimonies. Wynn, then thirty-eight, lived with William Osborn, a sixty-five-year-old farmer with $2,500 worth of real estate and $10,000 worth of personal property. While it is not quite clear from the evidence what kind of relationship Wynn and Osborn maintained, an emotionally unstable single woman living with a wealthy, mentally deficient widower must have raised some moral concern within the community. Furthermore, Wynn's wild and erratic behavior, coupled with her alcohol problems, probably caused many planters alarm. The suggestive comment about Wynn's clothing proved that those in power feared Sarah Wynn's wanton sexuality—a sexuality that could potentially disturb the southern hierarchy. Because Wynn had acted outside of socially acceptable gender roles, she was sentenced to three years in the state penitentiary. She served all but three months of her term. Unfortunately, Sarah Wynn never seemed to improve her lot in life; in 1870 she was living in Muscogee's "poor asylum."[18]

Poor, able-bodied, young white men comprised the largest group of antebellum southern vagrants. While some of these men had wives and children, many of them at least appeared to be single, according to census records. With the transience of the poor white population, however, it is possible that many of these men simply lived apart from their families for the majority of the year. A good example of this nomadic existence of poor white men is Edward Isham, who moved every year or two to different Georgia counties, leaving behind a string of "wives," lovers, and illegitimate children. Historian Victoria Bynum wrote about the women in Isham's life, positing that they often kept him from self-destruction, but they also enabled him to live outside both state and moral law. With fathers like Edward Isham, it is not surprising that out of the poor white vagrants found in the census records as children or teenagers, many of them grew up in female-headed households. Radford White, an eighteen-year-old charged in Bibb County in 1855, resided with his jobless mother. William Holt, a twenty-year-old laborer from Macon, also grew up without a father figure. And Ezekiel Ward, charged with vagrancy in Morgan County in 1858, seemed to have been raised by a destitute mother and was financially supported by older brothers who worked as laborers.[19]

The fractured family lives of poor whites often caused these wandering men to be viewed with suspicion. As historian Lawrence Friedman wrote, although nineteenth-century America was a "society based on mobility and immigration," it "was also a society suspicious of immigrants and strangers, especially those who were detached and alone, without community or social circle or family, without fixed setting." For these reasons, the standards constituting a formal indictment for younger male vagrants varied widely. Generally, though, records show that most of these men fit a certain stereotype— a combination of idleness or laziness, drinking to excess, fighting, gambling, and sleeping with prostitutes—that often led to indictments.[20]

Jacob Waddel was convicted of vagrancy because of his perceived immorality. The court based its decision on the general, everyday actions of Waddel—not on one particular event or "act" of vagrancy. Waddel's case was not substantively different from those of other vagrants, yet somehow he had the resources to petition the county court's ruling. The brief of evidence in his case offers interesting insight into the life of a poor white vagrant. The first witness for the prosecution, Joseph Caswell, claimed that Waddel had "worked on a house" for him two years prior to the arrest and had "heard that defendant built a room last year for William Walker." Still, he swore that he did not know what Waddel did for a living; he only knew that the defendant had four or five children and that he had not seen him in the past year. During cross-examination, Waddel's lawyer asserted that Waddel worked as a carpenter and thus had "to go about frequently to get work."[21]

Next, John Kemp, a wealthy farmer in his forties, took the stand. Kemp lived about two miles from Waddel and did not know whether or not the defendant worked. Waddel had "come to him once for corn and meat," but he "did not beg it." Kemp could not recall seeing Waddel work in the past five years, although he frequently saw him drunk. He also claimed that Waddel owned no horses, cattle, or hogs and had very little furniture; everything Waddel owned "would not sell for more than ten or fifteen dollars."

James Wadsworth, the third man questioned, lived half a mile from Waddel and "saw him oftener in the road than elsewhere." He knew that Waddel had planted some potatoes that year, but he had seen no other "signs of cultivation" or "crop about the house." Wadsworth described Waddel's home as a "log cabin" and reported that Waddel had also come to him looking for meat, although he offered to pay for it. Agreeing with John Kemp, Wadsworth stated that several times he had seen Waddel drunk at Doolittle's Grocery, although not within the past two years. During cross-examination, Waddel's lawyer once again stressed that the defendant worked as a mechanic, and "mechanics work about." Wadsworth replied that he did not know whether Waddel worked or "idles his time."

Although Waddel lost his appeal, he does not show up in the penitentiary records. He may have simply served his time in the Marion County jail. Clearly, though, Waddel improved his financial situation in the years following his conviction. By 1870, he owned $150 worth of real estate and $300 worth of personal property—significantly more that the estimated $10 worth of furniture he owned in 1858. Waddell's case nicely illustrates three main points about the lives of poor whites. One, the defense of Waddel's transient ways demonstrates just how significantly poor whites were excluded from the southern labor system. Waddel's lawyer clearly expected the court to realize that, as a mechanic, Waddel frequently had to be away from home to search for work. Two, Waddel, like so many other poor whites, obviously had a severe drinking problem. Three, Waddel's inability to find work in his county, combined with his frequent drunkenness, ultimately led to a very fractured, unstable, poverty-ridden life for his wife and children.[22]

Like Waddel, William Melvin McDaniel was charged with vagrancy in the late 1850s. McDaniel, a seventeen-year-old from Muscogee County, undoubtedly led an "immoral" life. His trial made it clear that he was being condemned for his general lifestyle, not any one specific action. McDaniel, like almost all southern vagrants, came from an impoverished background. The 1850 census showed that his father, an illiterate laborer from South Carolina, owned no land and only $200 worth of personal property—and had six children to feed. Like many poor boys who felt completely disengaged by society, McDaniel began acting in a self-destructive, often lawless manner.

The first witness at McDaniel's trial, Marshal James Hughes, reported knowing the defendant for five or six years, in which time he had "seen him do nothing for a livelihood." Instead, McDaniel was "a young man of bad character" who spent time at whorehouses in "a bad part of town." He was also known to drink "whenever he can get liquor." Hughes recalled that McDaniel had been locked in the guardhouse several times during the present year—he even broke jail once. The next marshal stated that he had known McDaniel for four years and that he had seldom seen him sober (meaning that McDaniel began drinking to excess at the tender age of twelve or thirteen). The marshal confirmed that McDaniel frequented houses of ill-repute and that he had "no visible means of support." A final witness further corroborated that McDaniel, who "frolicked around whorehouses and drank liquor," had been locked in the guardhouse for the past month.[23]

Henry Johnson, a poor, illiterate merchant, was the first witness for the defense. Johnson told the jury that McDaniel had "worked sometime" on a river dam "opposite Columbus." Upon cross-examination, however, Johnson admitted to seeing McDaniel "pretty drunk . . . some two or three times about Christmas," and he also knew of at least two fights in which the defendant had participated. Witnesses Garland B. Terry and John Allen had both previously employed McDaniel. A master carpenter in his fifties, Terry hired McDaniel to work on a bridge for five days, and then to work on a racetrack in LaGrange for five or six weeks. Although Terry admitted that the defendant had a "reputation of being a rowdy," he had never seen him drunk. Allen, also a carpenter in his fifties, had a slightly different experience. He hired McDaniel to cut wood, but after a few days the defendant quit. Allen "could not prevail upon him to continue work"—instead, McDaniel "strolled about town drinking."[24]

The petit jury obviously took all of the testimonies about McDaniel's wayward "character" seriously. They condemned McDaniel to two years in the state penitentiary, where he served the majority of his sentence working as a carpenter. It seems that prison may have helped change some of McDaniel's untamed ways: the 1870 census listed McDaniel as a twenty-seven-year-old farm laborer with a wife and young son.

Perhaps the most interesting thing about McDaniel's case, however, was the latter part of Henry Johnson's testimony. Johnson told the court that McDaniel had once professed "that he had as soon be in the penitentiary or any where else, and didn't care a damn." McDaniel's depression-fueled apathy about his future deserves closer analysis. In *Roll, Jordan, Roll*, Eugene Genovese reinterpreted what was considered fatalism among slaves, demonstrating that much slave resistance (from feigning illness to tool breaking to running away) actually resulted from submerged anger and resentment. Shirking, drinking, whoring, stealing, and fighting were all ways that southern vagrants could buck the system—a system in which they had no stake. These types of resistance, while ultimately self-destructive, were all ways of not submitting to the present. Nell Irvin Painter's recent work on "soul murder" also may help explain the position of many poor whites. Reared in cycles of poverty, alcoholism, violence, and oppression, poor, nonslaveholding whites felt the tentacles of slavery much more acutely than did any other group of white southerners.[25]

The harsh realities of the lives of poor whites—like William McDaniel and Jacob Waddell—make it easy to understand *why* they might have felt cut off from the southern "system." Slavery stripped poor whites of their jobs, drove down their wages, and crushed their sense of self-worth, their honor, and even their most sacred trait: their "whiteness." Historian Stephanie McCurry held that yeomen farmers derived their sense of white masculinity from the "inviolability of the household, the command of dependents, and the public prerogatives of manhood." Yet poor whites could not even function as masters of their own homes: even Hinton Helper questioned their ability to control "social dependents."[26]

With so little to lose, poor whites' sense of defeatism obviously gave southern elites cause to worry. Planters' most serious fears about poor white vagrants concerned the possibility of revolt, whether class-based or bi-racial. Most scholars, of course, agree that the southern elite had little to worry about—in reality, the likelihood of rebellion was very low. Nevertheless, upper-class whites were concerned; both their letters and their actions attest to this fact. Aside from the well-known rebellions and "unhatched plots," many recent historians have discovered evidence of smaller, generally inchoate, planned revolts. While more research is needed on the topic, several late-antebellum conspiracies between slaves and poor whites to overthrow the prevailing hierarchy occurred in various parts of the Deep South. Charles Bolton uncovered one plan for insurrection in North Carolina. An 1845 letter, written by a slave, tells of at least two poor whites who were supposed to help with the revolt. William Taylor, a landless white farmer, and Eli Penry, a poor dram-shop keeper, were to serve as "captins." After freeing both blacks and poor whites from the county jail, the men planned to "tye all the whites" and shoot "evry man that want go with them." Eli Penry even offered all "his powder and shot for haf the mony." Penry's job made him an obvious leader; he could "make all the men drunk an . . . make em doo enny thing."[27]

Georgia too had several failed revolts. In 1857, a Chatham County jury acquitted William McGuire of "attempting to excite an insurrection and revolt of the slaves." In Camden County, Emily Burke wrote about an attempted rebellion involving white lumbermen and local slaves. And in Hancock County, Georgia, poor white John Pool heard about John Brown's Harper's Ferry raid and mindlessly told an overseer that he would "black himself" and join "the strong side" when war broke out. He was tried for "uttering abolitionist sentiments," but after being labeled a "poor, simple native," Pool was finally discharged with a stern lecture.[28]

Still, aside from the slight possibility of insurrection, planters also worried about any kind of conviviality between African Americans and poor whites. And from rebellion to miscegenation to the joint commission of crimes, alcohol was central to much of the mayhem created by the South's poor. Averaging forty cents a gallon, a pint of liquor only cost a nickel in antebellum Georgia. As a relatively inexpensive commodity, even the poorest whites and slaves could afford to purchase alcohol. More commonly, though, the South's two underclasses used liquor itself as currency. Planters knew that runaways could usually spend a night or two with a poor white in exchange for alcohol. Indeed, spirituous liquor seemed to be the driving force behind many of the region's crimes, especially larceny. One African American woman recalled the relationship between slaves and poor whites on the eve of the Civil War: her masters "didn't never allow us niggers to mix with what they called the po' white trash; they always said they would learn us how to steal and drink; it was the truth, too."[29]

Historian Avery Craven summarized the importance of alcohol in black–poor white interactions: "Sometimes the Negro slipped away to labor at night in the fields of a less energetic white in return for his liquor; sometimes a system of theft was perfected by which plantation equipment and supplies passed in payments; sometimes the black economized his own rations that he might secretly exchange his surplus for the means of a spree." Traveler Daniel Hundley also noticed the effect that alcohol had on black–poor white interactions. He proposed that abolitionists focus their attention on the South's white groggery-shop keepers: "they can tell you who are the most reckless, daring, villainous, and discontented of negro men." He wondered why abolitionists did not "initiate" these poor whites into their "secret plots for fostering negro insurrections, for poisoning, maiming, and murdering the white families of the South." Furthermore, because both cities and rural areas housed brothels and "disorderly houses," liquor was often assumed to play a part in black men's "improper association" with white women, especially prostitutes. Alcohol, a known social lubricant, clearly enabled—and even encouraged—personal ties between the races.[30]

Ann Willis was charged with vagrancy in Columbus, Georgia, after furnishing a slave with a half pint of liquor "without the knowledge and consent of the owner, overseer, or employer." Most white men would have been charged with "supplying liquor to a slave." Yet Willis was arrested for the more serious offense of vagrancy simply because the sharing of intoxicating spirits between a black man and a white woman could preface "indecent" and "lewd" actions between the two; liquor once again functioned as a social conduit between the races.[31]

While it seems logical that planters would be more concerned about sexual relationships between white women and black men, several vagrancy cases involving poor white men and black women seem to indicate otherwise. Since all children born to slave women increased the wealth and workforce of the South's elite, planters probably did not worry much about affairs between white males and enslaved females. But perhaps it was poor white men's commingling with free black women that bothered planters: the offspring of these relationships would also add to the free black population.

Census records seem to corroborate this theory. For example, Washington Allen, arrested for vagrancy in Morgan County in 1844, was in his twenties and employed in manufacturing. He lived with an older white woman, who was most likely his mother (she was between sixty and seventy years old). However, Allen also resided with two "free colored" females —one between ten and twenty-four years, and one under ten years. It is very probable that these free blacks were Allen's lover and daughter. Allen was convicted the year after his arrest, although it is unclear what his sentence entailed. John Mitchell, arrested for vagrancy in 1842 in Chatham County, was a sixty-two-year-old seaman from Virginia. Mitchell lived in Savannah with two free black men, three free black women, and three female slaves. It seems very plausible that he was involved in a sexual relationship with an African American woman. Sentenced to two years in Milledgeville, Mitchell died a year and a half into his sentence. And Lewis H. Gregory, charged in 1820 in Richmond County, was in his sixties and employed in manufactures. He lived with one white female between ten and sixteen years old, and two free black females. One black woman was between twenty-six and forty-five years old, and one was over forty-five. In all likelihood, these three women were Gregory's lover and daughters—perhaps one daughter was white enough to "pass," or maybe both he and his partner had children from previous relationships. Gregory's bond was set at an exorbitant $500 and could be voided on "the condition that the said defendant was industrious and orderly for the space of one year." The convictions of these three men probably served as warnings to other poor white men who fraternized with black women. According to another (rather infamous) Georgian, Edward Isham, getting "too intimate with a free girl" seemed to have been a relatively common occurrence among the poor white men of the state; perhaps the southern elite decided to use vagrancy law to help combat this type of interracial relationship.[32]

Perhaps more important, though, the South's elite wanted to keep the races separate because they believed that poor whites "demoralized" slaves by laboring so infrequently while still managing to live in apparent comfort. As one planter explained, "the intercourse of *these people* with the negroes was not favorable to good discipline." Poor whites, he thought, could not command slaves' respect and thus would weaken the prevailing racial hierarchy. This idea of "demoralization" is important: if slaves realized how little poor whites had to work to lead lives that differed only slightly from their own material realities, surely they would become more discontented. Furthermore, if blacks recognized the absolute differences—both economically and socially—between poor whites and all other whites, they could start to question the ideological privileges associated with race. Poor whites not only undermined slavery through crime, miscegenation, and personal relationships with African Americans; they also served as a constant reminder that race in itself did not constitute any type of "scientific" superiority.[33]

At the same time that poor whites—who were often unemployed or underemployed—demoralized the work ethic of slaves, slavery both financially and psychologically devalued labor to poor southern whites. Aside from Hinton Helper, though, only a handful of whites ever admitted the injurious influence that the peculiar institution had on the South's poor whites. Traveler James Redpath reported that he "met and conversed with many of the poorer class of whites in my journey. All of them were conscious of the injurious influence that slavery was exerting on their social condition. If damning the negroes would have abolished slavery, it would have disappeared a long time ago, before the indignant breath of the poor white trash. But—it won't." Fanny Kemble, the English-bred wife of planter Pierce Butler, echoed the same opinions, writing that the "filthy, lazy, ignorant, brutal, proud, penniless savages," otherwise known as the "pine-landers" of Georgia, comprised the most "degraded race of human beings claiming an Anglo-Saxon heritage." These "wretched creatures," she reasoned, refused to "labour for their own subsistence," because "labour belongs to blacks and slaves alone here."[34]

Perhaps the emasculation of working alongside slaves added to the poor's sense of defiance, whether consciously or subconsciously. Indeed, many poor whites balked at the prospect of taking orders from a "master." Olmsted commented that the South's poor white laborers were often drunk and always undependable; they simply refused to "work steadily at any employment." In one instance a laborer had received some of his wages in advance—to buy some church clothes, he said—and absconded the next day, "right in the middle of harvest." Olmsted also reported that if a planter requested certain types of work from poor whites, like fetching water or wood or taking care of the cattle, the poor white "would get mad and tell you he wasn't a nigger." Their "distinct and . . . rather despicable class," he concluded, "are worse off in almost all respects than slaves." Slavery, according to Olmsted, was essential "in encouraging vagabond and improvident habits of life among the poor."[35]

Poor whites truly occupied a tenuous place in antebellum southern society. Politically, even if poor whites could afford to pay the poll tax, their votes would not have affected the planter-controlled oligarchy. To compete with slave labor, poor whites had to work for pay considerably lower than that of the "wage slaves" in the North, often in jobs deemed too dangerous for blacks. Slavery also caused many poor whites to move every few years in search of work, which created fractured family lives—poor white men could not even feel a sense of paternalism within their own households. Socially, planters could geographically isolate the destitute, cultivate their slaves' disdain for poor whites, and generally treat them with condescension and contempt. Legally, the southern elite could arrest poor whites for essentially "doing nothing," lawfully intimidating and incarcerating the lower class whenever they needed to reinforce the poor's submission to their authority.

Thus, as nonslaveholders in a world based on slavery, as white laborers in a culture that equated blackness with work, as paupers in a region of patriarchs, and as southerners who had no semblance of honor, poor whites had nothing—and thus nothing to lose. So instead of toiling ungodly hours just to scrape by, perhaps many poor whites disconnected from society, preferring to give in to the few earthly delights that brought them some sense of pleasure and escapism. This escapist philosophy, however, only served to solidify the elite's fears about poor whites' tendencies to commit crimes, conspire with slaves, and even help propagate the region's free black population. In short, Hinton Helper was right: poor whites in the antebellum South were not slaves, but neither were they wholly free.

After the Civil War, however, the lives of the South's poor whites changed dramatically—both legally and socially. Although southern states had been forced to give off an appearance of compliance with the federal Civil Rights Act of 1866 by repealing laws that solely targeted African Americans, the vast majority of people arrested for vagrancy in the postwar Deep South were black, generally outnumbering whites by about four to one. While many poor whites would still have qualified as vagrants *de jure*, scholars such as Alex Lichtenstein and Lawrence Friedman have demonstrated that post-emancipation vagrancy laws were specifically intended to keep freedmen in a type of quasi-slavery. Friedman wrote that postwar vagrancy arrests "played a sinister role in the system of race oppression." The southern legislatures may not have been able to equate blackness with vagrancy in letter, but law enforcement officials across the former Confederacy clearly understood the statutes' intended targets.[36]

Georgia's new vagrancy law criminalized people "who have not some visible and known means of a fair, honest and reputable livelihood," meaning former slaves who left the employ of their plantations. It also included people "without a fixed abode"—qualifying all newly freed blacks. The "vagrant" category extended to anyone involved in trading or buying stolen property, presumably property carried off of plantations by freedmen. Furthermore, the state's 1865 statute deemed it lawful for "any person to arrest said vagrants," giving even the poorest whites legal power over blacks. After arrest, vagrants could be fined, imprisoned, or sentenced to work on "public works or roads." Alternately, they could "be bound out to some person" for a year, for a bond not exceeding $300. This short-term master would agree to provide food, clothing, and medical attention, making the black vagrant's virtual slavery complete.[37]

Emancipation, therefore, heralded the end of the imprisonment of thousands of poor southern whites who had defied the social hierarchy. This swift change in the color of the southern vagrant—overwhelmingly white during slavery, overwhelmingly black after emancipation—gives credibility to the fact that the maintenance of slavery greatly exacerbated class tensions between whites. Southern elites used a variety of different legal and psychological means to keep poor whites and blacks separate, and vagrancy arrests seemed to help the elite reach their end goals: no bi-racial coalition ever formed, no class-based rebellion ever happened. But slavery economically crippled many white southerners, and it also caused nonslaveholders to completely disengage from society. Almost a hundred years after slavery's end, Dr. Martin Luther King Jr. explained this alienation—an alienation that has plagued the impoverished underclasses of every civilization: "There is nothing more dangerous than to build a society, with a large segment of people in that society, who feel that they have no stake in it; who feel that they have nothing to lose. People who have a stake in their society, protect that society, but when they don't have it, they unconsciously want to destroy it."[38]

Following the passage of the Fourteenth and Fifteenth Amendments, the South's elite embarked on a long campaign to make even the poorest whites feel superior to blacks. African Americans were voting, sitting on juries, and holding office. Poor whites were no longer the southern elite's targets; instead, the rich needed poor whites as racial allies. As poor whites gained more legal and social freedoms, though, blacks realized that they had emerged from one kind of slavery only to suffer the "second degree of slavery" that poor whites had long endured. Blacks became the elites' new legal targets for victimless "crimes," such as vagrancy. Ironically, upper-class whites used many of the same hegemonic practices on African Americans in the postbellum period that they had used to keep poor whites in line during the antebellum period. Elites simply adapted these hegemonic structures to the Jim Crow era, but they made sure that the consequences for blacks were much more extreme and vicious than they had been for poor whites. For African Americans, the New South became an extremely chaotic, violent, racist society. Waters McIntosh, enslaved as a child in Arkansas, clarified who, precisely, emancipation helped. As a boy, McIntosh sang a song called "Rather Be a Nigger Than a Poor White Man." After gaining legal "freedom," however, he changed his tune. "It was the poor white man who was freed by the war," concluded McIntosh, "not the Negroes."[39]

NOTES

1. *Jacob Waddel v. The State of Georgia,* 27 Ga. 262 (1859 Ga. Lexis 50); U.S. Bureau of the Census, Population Schedules, Sixth Census, Decatur County, Georgia, 5-6; Seventh Census of the United States, 1850, Marion County, Georgia, 92; *Waddel v. Georgia,* italics in original; Eighth Census of the United States, 1860, Chattahoochee County, Georgia, 59. Chattahoochee County was formed from parts of Marion County in 1854.

2. Hinton Rowan Helper, *The Impending Crisis of the South,* ed. George M. Fredrickson (1857; repr., Cambridge, MA: Harvard University Press, 1968). For a new, comprehensive examination of Helper's theories, see David Wayne Brown, *Southern Outcast: Hinton Rowan Helper and the Impending Crisis of the South* (Baton Rouge: Louisiana State University Press, 2006).

3. W. O. Brown, "Role of Poor Whites in Race Contracts of the South," *Social Forces* 19, no.2 (Dec. 1940): 258-68; Paul H. Buck, "The Poor Whites of the Ante-Bellum South," *American Historical Review* 31, no. 1 (Oct. 1925): 41-54; Avery O. Craven, "Poor Whites and Negroes in the Antebellum South," *Journal of Negro History* 15, no.1 (Jan. 1930): 14-25; Frank L. Owsley, *Plain Folk of the Old South* (1949; repr., Baton Rouge: Louisiana State University Press, 1977); Charles C. Bolton, *Poor Whites in the Antebellum South: Tenants and Laborers in Central North Carolina and Northeast Mississippi* (Durham, NC: Duke University Press, 1994); Timothy James Lockley, *Lines in the Sand: Race and Class in Lowcountry Georgia, 1750-1860* (Athens: University of Georgia Press, 2001); Jeff Forret, *Race Relations at the Margins: Slaves and Poor Whites in the Antebellum Southern Countryside* (Baton Rouge: Louisiana State University Press, 2006). Other influential histories on antebellum non-elite white southerners include: Bill Cecil-Fronsman, *Common*

Whites: Class and Culture in Antebellum North Carolina (Lexington: University Press of Kentucky, 1992); Clement Eaton, "Class Differences in the Old South," *Virginia Quarterly Review* 33 (1957): 357-70; Lacy K. Ford, *Origins of Southern Radicalism: The South Carolina Upcountry, 1800-1860* (New York: Oxford University Press, 1988); Michele Gillespie, *Free Labor in an Unfree World: White Artisans in Slaveholding Georgia, 1789–1860* (Athens: University of Georgia Press, 2000); Steven Hahn, *The Roots of Southern Populism: Yeomen Farmers and the Transformation of the Georgia Upcountry, 1850-1890* (New York: Oxford University Press, 1983); J. William Harris, *Plain Folk and Gentry in a Slave Society: White Liberty and Black Slavery in Augusta's Hinterland* (Baton Rouge: Louisiana State University Press, 1985); Samuel C. Hyde Jr. "*Plain Folk* Reconsidered: Historiographical Ambiguity in Search of Definition," *Journal of Southern History* 71, no. 4 (Nov. 2005): 803-30; Grady McWhiney, *Cracker Culture: Celtic Ways in the Old South* (Tuscaloosa: University of Alabama Press, 1988); Stephanie McCurry, *Masters of Small Worlds: Yeoman Households, Gender Relations, and the Political Culture of the Antebellum South Carolina Low Country* (New York: Oxford University Press, 1995); and Bell Irvin Wiley, *The Plain People of the Confederacy* (Baton Rouge: Louisiana State University Press, 1943; repr., Columbia: University of South Carolina Press, 2000).

4. Edmund S. Morgan, *American Slavery, American Freedom: The Ordeal of Colonial Virginia* (New York: W.W. Norton, 1975), 310. All WPA and Fisk interviews appear in George P. Rawick, ed., *The American Slave: A Composite Autobiography*, vols. 1-19 (Westport, CT: Greenwood, 1972). Following the lead of Stephanie Shaw in "Using the WPA Slave Narratives to Study the Impact of the Great Depression," *Journal of Southern History* 69 (Aug. 2003): 623-58, subsequent references to specific interviews will be cited thus: James V. Deane, WPA, *American Slave*, 8 (MD), 9.

5. Many recent works on poor whites concern the interactions they had with slaves and free blacks, from the internal (or underground) economy to social and sexual bonds. Much of this newer history stemmed from the call for research in Eugene D. Genovese, "'Rather Be a Nigger Than a Poor White Man': Slave Perceptions of Southern Yeomen and Poor Whites," in *Toward a New View of America: Essays in Honor of Arthur C. Cole*, ed. Hans L. Trefousse (New York: B. Franklin, 1977), 79-96. Also see Ira Berlin and Philip D. Morgan, eds., *The Slaves' Economy: Independent Production* (Portland: Frank Cass, 1991); Alex Lichtenstein, "'That Disposition To Theft, With Which They Have Been Branded': Moral Economy, Slave Management, and the Law," *Journal of Social History* 21 (Spring 1998): 413-40. One recently published primary source, Charles C. Bolton and Scott P. Culclasure, eds., *The Confessions of Edward Isham: A Poor White Life of the Old South* (Athens: University of Georgia Press, 1998), also offers several good articles on race relations between poor whites and blacks.

6. Scholars who have studied postbellum southern vagrancy include Eric Foner, *Reconstruction: America's Unfinished Revolution, 1863-1877* (New York: Harper Collins, 1988), 55, 62, 200-201, 206, 208-9, 363, 372, 519, 593; Lawrence M. Friedman, *Crime and Punishment in American History* (New York: Basic Books, 1993), 94, 100, 102-4, 201, 385-86; Alex Lichtenstein, *Twice the Work of Free Labor: The Political Economy of Convict Labor in the New South* (New York: Verso, 1996); David M. Oshinsky, *Worse than Slavery: Parchman Farm and the Ordeal of Jim Crow Justice* (New York: Free Press, 1996).

7. Keri Leigh Merritt, "'A vile, immoral, and profligate course of life': Poor Whites and the Enforcement of Vagrancy Law in Antebellum Georgia" (master's thesis, University of Georgia, 2007); A. L. Beier, *Masterless Men: The Vagrancy Problem in England, 1560-1640* (London: Methuen, 1986), xxii.

8. Quoted in Forrest W. Lacey, "Vagrancy and Other Crimes of Personal Condition," *Harvard Law Review* 66, no. 7 (May 1953): 1203, 1204 (italics in original). Other crimes of personal condition included "being a common drunkard, common prostitute, com-

mon thief, tramp, or disorderly person." For other works on vagrancy and its legal history, see William J. Chambliss, "A Sociological Analysis of the Law of Vagrancy," *Social Problems* 12, no. 1 (Summer 1964): 67-77; Arthur H. Sherry, "Vagrants, Rogues and Vagabonds—Old Concepts in Need of Revision," *California Law Review* 48, no. 4 (Oct. 1960): 557-73; and Robin Yeamans, "Constitutional Attacks on Vagrancy Laws," *Stanford Law Review* 20, no. 4 (April 1968): 782-93.

9. Georgia's nineteenth-century statutes and legal codes concerning vagrancy can be found in Howell Cobb, *A Compilation of the Penal Code of the State of Georgia: with Forms and Bills of Indictment Necessary in Prosecutions under It, and the Rules of Practice* (Macon, GA: Joseph M. Boardman, 1850), 38-39; *Acts of the General Assembly of the State of Georgia*, 1816, pp. 181-86; 1835, pp. 332-34; 1847, pp. 199-200; 1855-56, p. 344; 1857, p. 314; 1859, pp. 69-70; 1860, pp. 44-45; 1865-66, p. 234; 1868, p. 122. These Acts can all be found online at http://docsouth.unc.edu/imls/gagenas/georgia.html.

10. Cobb, *Penal Code,* 38.

11. Merritt, "'Vile, immoral, and profligate,'" chap. 2; Lacey, "Vagrancy," 1214, 1224.

12. William Bishop: Bibb County, Superior Court Minutes, Georgia Department of Archives and History (GDAH), drawer 183, box 12, 1846-52, microfilm; Benjamin Farrell: Camden County Superior Court Minutes, GDAH, drawer 28, box 64, 1820-42, microfilm; Sixth Census, Decatur County, Georgia, 5-6; George Horlbeck: Chatham County Superior Court Minutes, GDAH, drawer 68, box 37, vols. 12-13, 1826-36, microfilm; Fifth Census, Charleston County, South Carolina, 182.

13. Ira Berlin, *Many Thousands Gone: The First Two Centuries of Slavery in North America* (Cambridge, MA: Harvard University Press, 1998), 44-45.

14. Frederick Law Olmsted, *A Journey in the Seaboard Slave States: With Remarks on Their Economy* (New York: Dix and Edwards, 1856), 507-9. Online at http://odur.let.rug.nl/~usa/D/1851-1875/olmsted/jourxx.htm.

15. Nancy Walker: Central Registration of Convicts, microfilm, Governor Convict and Fugitive Records—Pardons, GDAH, record group 1-4-16, vol. 1-1241; Seventh Census, Floyd County, Georgia, 249; Eighth Census, Floyd County, Georgia, 261; Ninth Census, Floyd County, Georgia, 24.

16. Muscogee County Superior Court Minutes, GDAH, drawer 80, box 66, vol. K, 1859-63, microfilm. Sarah Wynn: Seventh Census, Muscogee County, Georgia, 358; Eighth Census, Muscogee County, Georgia, 356.

17. William B. Brown and Davenport P. Ellis: Eighth Census, Muscogee County, Georgia, 303, 309; Eighth Census, Slave Schedule, Muscogee County, Georgia.

18. Jane Clem and Mrs. Maugham: Eighth Census, Muscogee County, Georgia, 315. Both women were listed as paupers with no occupation. William Osborn: Eighth Census, Muscogee County, Georgia, 356, and ibid., Slave Schedule. Sarah Wynn: State of Georgia Board of Corrections; Ninth Census, Muscogee County, Georgia, 708.

19. Bolton and Culclasure, eds., *Edward Isham,* 1-18; see also chap. 6. Radford White: Bibb County Superior Court Minutes, GDAH, Drawer 183, Box 13, 1852-56, microfilm. William Holt: Bibb County Superior Court Minutes; Seventh Census, Bibb County, Georgia, 308. Ezekiel Ward: Morgan County Superior Court Minutes; Seventh Census, Morgan County, Georgia, 271.

20. Friedman, *Crime and Punishment,* 102, 103.

21. *Jacob Waddel v. The State of Georgia,* 27 Ga. 262. Georgia Reports, GDAH, *Jacob Waddel v. The State,* brief of evidence, filing 9/16/1858, judgment 2/4/1859, Case A-2666, drawer 313, box 13, microfilm.

22. John Kemp: Eighth Census, Marion County, Georgia, 84. James Wadsworth: ibid., 321. Jacob Waddel: ibid., Chattahoochee County, 7. Waddel, listed as a forty-five-year-old farmer, lived with his wife and three of his children, who worked as farm laborers.

23. William M. McDaniel: Muscogee County Superior Court Minutes; Seventh Census, Gwinnett County, Georgia, 220. McDaniel was eight years old. He does not appear in the 1860 census.

24. Henry Johnson: Eighth Census, Muscogee County, Georgia, 64. Johnson had $100 of personal property and no real estate. Garland B. Terry: ibid., Quitman County, Georgia, 483. John Allen: ibid., Muscogee County, Georgia, 6.

25. William McDaniel: Muscogee County Superior Court Minutes; Ninth Census, Harris County, Georgia, 212; Georgia Board of Corrections. Eugene D. Genovese, *Roll, Jordan, Roll: The World the Slaves Made* (1972; repr., New York: Vintage, 1976); Nell Irvin Painter, "Soul Murder and Slavery: Toward a Fully Loaded Cost Accounting," in *Southern History across the Color Line* (Chapel Hill: University of North Carolina Press, 2002).

26. McCurry, *Masters of Small Worlds,* 304; David Brown, "Hinton Rowan Helper: The Logical Outcome of the Non-Slaveholders' Philosophy," *Historical Journal* 46, no. 1 (2003): 49, 42.

27. Bolton, *Poor Whites,* 109.

28. Lockley, *Lines in the Sand,* 128; Harris, *Plain Folk and Gentry,* 64-65.

29. Genovese, *Roll, Jordan, Roll,* 641-42; "Now Supported by Children She Raised," Fisk, *American Slave,* 18:215.

30. Craven, "Poor Whites and Negroes in the Antebellum South," 18-20; Daniel R. Hundley, *Social Relations in Our Southern States* (New York: Henry B. Price, 1860), 231; Bolton, *Poor Whites,* 50.

31. Ann Willis: Muscogee County Superior Court Records, GDAH, drawer 80, box 65, vol. J, 1858-9, microfilm. Willis does not appear in the census records.

32. Washington Allen: Morgan County Superior Court Minutes; Sixth Census, Gwinnett County, Georgia, 145-46. John Mitchell: State of Georgia Board of Corrections; Sixth Census, Baldwin County, Georgia, 58-59. Lewis H. Gregory: Richmond County Superior Court Minutes; Forth Census, Richmond County, Georgia, 19; Fifth Census, Bibb County, Georgia, 58-59. Bolton and Culclasure, eds., *Edward Isham,* 9.

33. Olmsted, *Journey,* 674.

34. James Redpath, *The Roving Editor, or Talks with Slaves in the Southern States,* ed. John R. McKivigan (University Park, PA: Pennsylvania State University Press, 1996), 88; Fanny Kemble, *Journal of a Residence on a Georgia Plantation in 1838-1839* (New York: Harper, 1863), online at http://www.questia.com/PM.qst?a=o&d=9668355.

35. Olmsted, *Journey,* 73, 83, 84, 452.

36. I arrived at the four-to-one (black to white) ratio by examining the following sources: Chatham County, Georgia, Prison Records, 1891-99, GDAH, drawer 75, box 28, microfilm; Savannah (Chatham County), Georgia, Jail Records, 1866-73, GDAH, drawer 116, box 38, microfilm; State of Georgia Board of Corrections, Inmate Administration Division: Central Registration of Convicts, 1866-85, GDAH, drawer 230, box 37, vol. 2, microfilm; and the Superior Court Minutes for Morgan, 1866-1900, and Rabun, 1866-1900. Foner, *Reconstruction,* 55, 63, 200-201; Friedman, *Crime and Punishment,* 95, 104.

37. *Acts,* 1865-66, p. 234.

38. Martin Luther King Jr., interview in *Eyes on the Prize: America's Civil Rights Years, 1954-1964,* produced by Henry Hampton (PBS/Blackside, 1987), episode #8, "Two Societies (1965-1968)."

39. Waters McIntosh, WPA, *American Slave,* 2 (AR), pt. 5, p. 20.

Chapter 2

The Lynching of Slaves

Race, Law, and the White Community in the Antebellum South

Michael J. Pfeifer

In July 1859, whites in Navarro County in east central Texas hanged a slave accused of murdering and robbing a white man, Mr. English, who was traveling through the area en route to his home in Fort Worth. The white community reportedly offered to compensate the slave's master with the same sum that he would have received from the state if his slave had been legally executed. The 1859 mob hanging in Navarro County reveals how white communities in the antebellum South sometimes deflected slaveholders' claim of their right to human property by resorting to collective killing of slaves.[1]

Scholars in recent years have told us much about lynching in the postbellum South.[2] Yet we still understand little about collective racial violence in the South before the emancipation of the slaves. Influential monographs on slavery and antebellum southern violence study the matter only slightly and take contradictory views of the issue.

In *Roll, Jordan, Roll,* Eugene Genovese argued that the lynching of slaves was relatively rare. Estimating that a mere 10 percent of the three hundred or so persons lynched in the South between 1840 and 1860 were black, Genovese asserted that slaveholders preferred legal executions to mob executions, because slaveholders were compensated by states if their slaves were legally executed. Genovese conceded that planter-class and lower-class whites sometimes turned to collective violence amid the racial panic of insurrection scares.[3] In contrast to Genovese, Kenneth Stampp argued, in *The Peculiar Institution*, that mob killings of slaves occurred frequently, typically by burning or hanging.[4] However, neither of these historians conducted a thorough analysis of mob violence against slaves in local sources. Local studies of slavery in fact suggest that collective killings of slaves were fairly common. Thomas G. Dyer found that between 1847 and 1859, at least eleven slaves were murdered by mobs of whites in Missouri, most in the area along the Missouri River known as Little Dixie, where that border state's slaveholding concentrated; mobs burned three of the slaves to death.[5] Scholars of slavery in Arkansas, Alabama, Texas, Georgia, and Missouri have asserted that the lynching of slaves occurred fairly frequently, although these events often went unreported in newspapers.[6] One scholar has argued recently that when it comes to slaves, the term *lynching* may not be especially meaningful, since slaves were so often subject to homicidal violence that may or may not have taken collective or extralegal form.[7] Other scholars have recently unearthed evidence that southern whites collectively murdered slaves when their interests diverged from those of slaveholders, who sought in vain to protect their property from the punitive demands of the larger white community after allegations of murder or rape.[8]

Examining accounts of mob executions in newspaper sources and in state, local, and regional histories (which often quoted newspaper sources verbatim), this essay analyzes the social and legal dynamics of the lynching of slaves. In doing so, it complicates understandings of antebellum slavery, the law, black-white relations, social and cultural differentiation among whites, and the lineage of racial violence in the South. While slaves' status as property left them vulnerable to the punitive whims of individual slaveholders, slaves' position as the investment of masters provided some protection from the legal consequences of serious crimes and the racial antipathies of nonslaveholding whites. Southern mob executions of African Americans, informed by a praxis of the formal and informal capital punishment (sometimes by burning alive) of slaves stemming from the colonial era, were increasingly labeled "lynching" after the mid-1830s and excoriated by the northern abolitionist press as an aspect of an atavistic system of racial slavery. The antebellum lynching of African Americans flowed from the imperfections of the slave system and disparate southern whites' commitment to an explosive popular constitutionalism, the notion of the fundamental right of citizens to make and supervise law.[9]

The lynching of slaves, which may have occurred more frequently than some scholars have acknowledged, transpired when the master's claim to the protection of his investment in human property was effectively nullified, either through a slave's murder of a master or his family or by the white community's insistence that the collective execution of a slave outside of law served a good greater than the preservation of the value of the master's investment. Lynching punctuated a vigorous conversation among whites with divergent relations to slavery over the role of the criminal law in securing control of African Americans. Nearly half of documented southern white mobs burned alive their African American victims, asserting that immolation offered a more terrifying message to black miscreants than the most common legal punishment in the antebellum South, hanging. In an era marked by the territorial expansion of slavery, the staunch defense of the Peculiar Institution from internal and external threats, and the erosion of the status of "free negroes" as an intermediate legal and social caste, mobs of whites also collectively murdered free blacks. Evidence suggests that the lynching of African Americans may have been most common on the expanding western periphery of slavery, in Missouri and Texas, where the slave population was rapidly growing, slaveholders possessed comparatively less social and political power, and nearby cultural challenges to bond-holding made slaveholding whites especially defensive about the perpetuation of the Peculiar Institution.[10] The lynching of blacks, while seemingly contradictory in a society that placed a high premium on the value of a master's slave property, emerged organically from traditions of crime and punishment in slavery, the response of white southerners to legal reforms, and, most important, the inability of slaveholders to ever achieve the full mastery of African Americans and southern society that they sought. Hardly anomalous in the antebellum South, the practice of the lynching of blacks would be seized upon and reinvented by white southerners after emancipation, absent the consideration of the master's property interest that had previously shaped and constrained the actions of southern mobs.

Through an examination of primary and secondary sources, I have compiled an inventory that includes fifty-five mob executions of blacks in the South in the years 1835-1862. This is necessarily an incomplete database, shaped by my selective research in southern and northern newspapers, the choices that southern editors made regarding the coverage of events in their localities, northern editors' decisions concerning coverage of slavery and events in the South, and the emphases of state historians of slavery. Nonetheless, the partial tally suggests that lynching violence against blacks in the South may have been more pervasive than historians such as Genovese have asserted, and that the phenomenon of the mob execution of African Americans in the South substantially pre-dated the Civil War and Reconstruction. The sources document at least forty-three mob killings of slaves and at least three mob murders of free blacks (the slave or free status of black mob victims was not specified in some cases). Viewed conservatively, the evidence indicates that a practice of the mob execution of blacks had emerged in the South by the 1830s, if not well before,[11] and that the practice had become a familiar one in the South by the 1850s (more than two-thirds of documented lynchings of blacks occurred between 1850 and 1862).[12] However, the evidence falls short of indicating that the collective execution of slaves occurred on anything like the scale of lynching violence that would ensue in the decades after emancipation.[13] The inventory does not include the hundreds of slaves summarily executed during insurrection panics in the antebellum era. While retaliatory white violence in the wake of real and purported slave rebellions bore substantial similarities to the mob executions of individual slaves accused of particular criminal offenses such as murder and rape, anti-insurrection violence resulted from the perception of large scale crises in racial control and thus tended to be considerably more indiscriminate and far-reaching.[14]

The issue of the property value of a slave, and the potential uncompensated loss to the master of that sum if a slave were to be lynched, loomed large in the calculation of whether a slave would be mobbed or left to the punishment provided by the legal system. The issue was significant enough in Texas that in 1857 state legislators considered a bill that would have provided compensation to the owners of slaves "executed by the people without the authority of law."[15] Texas, following the practice in other southern states, compensated the slaveholder in the event that a slave was legally executed. An 1852 Texas statute stipulated that the jury of conviction assessed the value of the slave condemned to death, with the amount not to exceed $1,000, with half the assessment to be paid to the executed slave's master. However, the proposal to also compensate masters for the loss of their chattel property to lynchers was rejected by the state senate as a possible encouragement to mobs. A senate committee instead advocated that masters who lost their human property to lynchers might turn to the courts for redress.[16] This was exactly the remedy several slaveowners sought in 1857 when they sued the city of Louisville, Kentucky, for the value of two slaves, George and Bill, who had been taken from the city jail by a mob and hanged, and for the value of a third slave, Jack, who had cut his throat to avoid death at the hands of the mob. The three slaves had been accused of murdering the Joyce family.[17] Despite the importance of the issue of compensation, it did not necessarily deter the lynchers of slaves and those who defended their actions by asserting that dramatic, communal punishment outside the law would bolster the social control of slaves.

The lynching of slaves occurred within a legal context that privileged slaveholder authority and property-holding.[18] Antebellum southern states possessed slave codes inherited from colonial statutes that offered legal sanction to masters and overseers who killed slaves in the process of correcting them and that offered compensation to the owners of slaves who were legally executed.[19] In Louisiana, Virginia, and South Carolina, separate systems of slave courts administered a harsh and swift mode of criminal justice for slaves accused of crimes. In Louisiana, special slave tribunals denied slaves basic due process procedural safeguards and ensured that slaveholders would be adequately compensated for any loss of their property through a legal execution. Tribunals, staffed by slaveholders, often sentenced slaves convicted of killing other slaves to floggings and to wearing iron collars or shackles for periods of years. Such punishments meant slaves could continue to labor for a master as they served their sentence.[20] Capital crimes for which slaves could be sentenced to death in the late antebellum era in Louisiana, with a method of execution to be chosen by the special slave tribunal, included a broad array of offenses that emphasized the lethal punishment of virtually any act of overt African American slave resistance or criminality. These included "wilful murder," assault with a dangerous weapon with the intention to kill, poisoning, strangling, drowning, the rape of a white girl or woman, plotting insurrection, arson, "striking the master, mistress, their children, or white overseer," burglary, and theft.[21] A judge or magistrate sitting on the special tribunal was required to appraise the value of the convicted slave and pay half the value to the slave's owner and the other half to the victim of the slave's crime in the event of a death sentence.[22]

In most other slave states, however, the tendency in the antebellum era was toward bringing slaves into the same courts and under the same formal legal procedures as whites.[23] Courts could be solicitous of slaves' rights, particularly if influential masters sought to protect slaves or employed skilled legal counsel. A growing tendency toward the protection of slaves' legal rights aligned with an antebellum defense of slavery that asserted the slave system's essential benevolence and its consistency with American laws, legal culture, and an increasing emphasis on procedural fairness in American criminal law.[24] In lieu of execution, in a practice that originated in the early nineteenth century as an attempt to avoid the spectacle of public hangings, slaves convicted of capital crimes were often instead sold to contractors and transported out of the country; around nine hundred slaves were transported from Virginia from 1801 through 1858.[25] In practice, then, the law served the interests of slaveholders and ensured that the administration of criminal law would not unduly threaten their control or disposition of their property-holding, but the planter's prerogative was sometimes in tension with the views of the larger white community and an expanding emphasis on legal fairness for slaves.

Regardless of antebellum legal trends, most slaves who resisted white authority never made it into court. Masters and overseers typically exacted physical and sometimes lethal punishment without the formal process or deliberation of a court or tribunal, although the consideration of the master's property investment offered a check against indiscriminate lethal violence. Moreover, the testimony of blacks against whites was not admissible in court, which in some cases effectively protected whites from legal repercussions for their assaults and homicides of blacks. Recalling legal systems as experienced by slaves in Louisiana to a white interviewer decades after emancipation, Octavia George highlighted the mercurial nature of white authority: "There were no jails; the white man was the slaves' jail. If whipping didn't settle the crime the Negro committed—the next thing would be to hang him or to burn him at the stake."[26] Similarly, in 1836, an escaped slave, Moses Roper, questioned the very concept of the neutrality of the law as he described a legal execution by burning in South Carolina. Roper posited that with regard to "the protection which the law is supposed to extend to the slave's life," in his view "that whatever the law may be, no such protection is in reality enjoyed by the slave."[27]

Beyond slaveholders and overseers, southern law and practice institutionalized an important role for the white community in policing slave behavior, thereby linking whites of diverse socioeconomic statuses in a common defense of the slave system and white supremacy. The slave patrol originated in the early eighteenth century in South Carolina and Virginia in response to fears of slave rebellion, and it became a means of controlling the movement of slaves and preventing their unauthorized assembly. Slaveholding and nonslaveholding whites joined forces in the patrol, which was authorized to go on to private property to inspect slave cabins and to demand to see the passes of slaves who traveled on the roads. Often making nocturnal rounds in bands of four or five, sometimes costumed in dark clothing or in hoods that suggested ghosts, patrollers flogged slaves who lacked permission for travel, bound them, and turned them over to the sheriff or their master. The master's interest in preserving his property may have mitigated the degree of violence the patrollers could inflict.[28] Many years after emancipation, former slaves recalled the violence of the "patterollers" and how masters sometimes clashed with the patrol and sought to protect slaves from its punitive activities. The patrol offered the larger white community a significant function in the supervision and punishment of slave behavior and the control of racial boundaries, albeit one that frequently conflicted with the authority over slaves that masters claimed for themselves.[29]

The southern legal system thus sought to mediate between the competing goals of the control of black deviancy, the sanctity of slaveholders' property-holding, and the observation of the formal legal procedures that existed for the prosecution of slaves accused of committing particular crimes. Allegations that slaves had committed crimes such as murder and rape could disrupt the delicate balance between crime and racial control, the preservation of the value of the master's property, and the observation of legal process. Thirty-nine of the fifty-five documented antebellum mob executions of African Americans (71 percent) involved allegations of murder. Significantly, fifteen out of forty-three slaves who were lynched (35 percent) were collectively executed for murdering, or attempting to murder, their master, mistress, or other members of the master's family. Slaveholders perceived the killing of a master or his family as a grave threat to the preservation of slaveholding authority, a literal destruction of the master's patriarchal authority over his slaves and family. Killing the master or his family negated, at least in an emotional sense (although not necessarily in a practical sense, in terms of the legal claims of the master's surviving legatees), the property interest that normally would have led slaveholders to attempt to intercede in the legal system for the mitigation of the severity of punishment and the preservation of the life of the slave offender. Murder of the master or his relatives typically flowed from slaves' anger at the far-reaching and often cruel effects of authority exercised by members of the master class, sometimes in the context of the personal toll upon slaves of the westward expansion of slavery.[30] These dynamics were at play in April 1859, when Alfred, a slave in Tyler County in southeast Texas, axed to death his master, Mr. Roper, and burned his corpse. Alfred believed the master's death would mean the family's return to Alabama, from where they had recently immigrated at the behest of Mr. Roper against the wishes of the rest of his family. A "large number of the citizens of the counties of Liberty, Polk, and Tyler" immolated Alfred near the site where he had murdered Mr. Roper. An "eye witness" newspaper correspondent explained that "Judge Lynch opened and adjourned the Court."[31] The trauma of forced migration westward provided a similar context for the collective killing of a slave in 1836. William allegedly axed to death the members of a party migrating to Texas, including his master, another white man, and five slaves. Tennessee law officers apprehended William in his previous home near Memphis and conveyed him to the locale of the crime, Hot Springs County, Arkansas, where whites seized the slave from the sheriff and burned him to death.[32]

Another case of the murder of a master occurred in Montgomery County in central Alabama in 1854. A planter, Dr. McDonald, punished a slave for disobedience. The slave allegedly responded by lying in wait for McDonald in a stable and clubbing the slaveholder to death when he came to get his horse. After the slave surrendered to authorities, hundreds of whites came into town demanding rapid punishment, with most of the crowd advocating burning. After the mob seized the slave, they [tied] him to a stake, piled on pine knots, and applied turpentine and a torch. After burning the slave to death, the crowd reportedly raised a collection of $850, the equivalent of the value of the deceased slave, and gave it to the dead master's family, thus honoring the principle of compensation for taking the life of slave property.[33] While the *Huntsville Democrat* quibbled with the mob's choice of method, it defended the collective killing as an orderly act done in the public interest of racial and crime control: "We think it would have been better simply to have hung the scoundrel with the promptness with which he was burned. But in matters involving the control of that class of population, we hold that the law of self-protection, which abrogates all other law, must necessarily find its exponent in the action of the majority of those immediately interested."[34] A mob execution similarly ensued in Lincoln County in Missouri's slaveholding Little Dixie region in January 1859, after a slave stabbed to death his master, Simeon Thornhill. At the "annual Negro sales" at the county seat of Troy, James Calaway, the deceased slaveholder's brother-in-law, mounted a box and exhorted the crowd to "take the black murderer out of jail and burn him at the stake in the presence of all the negroes that were there, to set an example before them, and show them what will be the result of all such conduct if there should ever be such again."[35] The mob of whites, estimated at eight hundred to one thousand, used crowbars, axes, and sledgehammers to extricate the prisoner from the jail, then tied him to a stake that they had planted in the jail yard. The lynchers borrowed the didactic formula of the gallows speech from the antebellum rite of legal execution. Before the mob set alight the wood it piled around its victim, it compelled him to address the two hundred to three hundred blacks gathered to watch the execution in a final statement asserting that he had had a good master, had been treated better than he deserved, and had been given too many liberties, and that they must take warning and heed the lesson of his execution.[36]

Unprotected by prevailing white understandings of gender and deviancy, slave women were also executed by mobs for harming members of the master class. In his travelogue of his journey through East Texas in early 1854, Frederick Law Olmsted chronicled a case near Fannin in which a mob hanged a slave woman who had murdered her mistress and her two children with an axe.[37] In May 1850 in Clay County, Missouri, a mob similarly hanged a slave woman after she struck her mistress with an axe, while another Missouri mob, in Callaway County in 1860, hanged a young slave female accused of murdering a young white woman in her master's family towards whom she had "known ill feeling."[38] While a slave's murder of a slaveholder and his family could easily lead to calls for punishment outside of legal channels, so could other slave offenses. Mobs also executed African Americans accused of organized criminality and the murder of whites off of the plantation. For instance, in 1841 a crowd of Mississippi whites in a river town south of Natchez burned to death a "runaway slave" accused of participation in a criminal gang's spree of murder and robbery. The pyre was lit by a white woman the gang had kidnapped and raped.[39]

Allegations of rape could also catalyze southern mobs that pursued African Americans. Eleven percent of documented mob executions of blacks in the antebellum South resulted solely from an allegation of rape, whereas 27 percent of documented black victims were accused of rape in addition to other serious crimes such as murder. Recent scholarship has complicated our understanding of the white community's response to sexual relationships between black men and white women in the early to mid-nineteenth-century South, finding that harsh repercussions for interracial sex depended upon factors of class and circumstance. White communities sometimes cleaved along class lines, as planters manipulated the legal system to protect slaves accused or convicted of raping lower-class white women. Such tensions may have been a factor in an 1861 Georgia case in which a master sued the lynchers of his slave, George, who was to stand trial for raping a white woman but was instead seized and burned to death by neighborhood whites who could not abide "the law's delay."[40] In another instance of lynching for rape, a mob seized a slave from jail and hanged him after he was arrested for attempting to rape a white woman in Hopkins County in northeast Texas in 1859.[41] Mobs similarly murdered slaves accused of rape in North Carolina,[42] and in Missouri in 1850 and 1859.[43] The relatively small number of slaves executed by mobs solely on an accusation of rape may have reflected the fluidity of antebellum southern white responses to interracial sex, as well as the ability of slaveholders to wield their social authority and legal influence to shield slaves from communal violence.

The antebellum southern mob's choice of a method of execution occurred within the context of traditions of racialized punishment and alterations in the administration of the death penalty. More than 43 percent of documented lynchings of blacks involved execution by burning (twenty-four victims), whereas mobs murdered 47 percent of documented black victims through hanging (twenty-six victims). Execution by burning had been a staple of capital punishment in Colonial America, inherited from English jurisprudence (where it had been used as a punishment for heresy and witchcraft in the late medieval era), but reserved by the seventeenth and eighteenth centuries for those convicted of petit treason, the reversal of the patriarchal order of the household through the revolt of wife against husband or slave against master. In the American colonies, the highly dramatic punishment of burning at the stake was reserved for slaves convicted of participating in insurrection plots or of murdering their masters or, less frequently, for wives convicted of murdering their husbands. However, colonial authorities seldom inflicted death by burning, often preferring to hang slaves who had murdered masters and wives who had killed husbands.[44] Execution by burning was eliminated in northern states with the extensive statutory reforms that sought to rationalize the capital code in the era of the American Revolution. Influenced by Enlightenment notions that emphasized sympathy with the humanity of the offender, the reformability of the criminal, and the deterrent effect of mild but predictable (as opposed to the traditional system of severe but random) punishments, legislators discarded traditional punishments such as the gibbet (hanging in irons), dismemberment, and burning.[45] Despite the reform of the capital code in much of the United States, execution by burning persisted in the antebellum South. In states such as South Carolina, special tribunals tried slaves and selected the method of their punishment, occasionally choosing to burn convicted slaves alive.[46] Even as legal tribunals in some slave states still imposed burning at the stake, hanging became the predominant method of legal capital punishment in the antebellum South. Some southern white mobs and their apologists asserted by contrast that the sanguinary tradition of burning African Americans at the stake provided an especially powerful assertion of racial supremacy.

Antebellum southern mobs, and those who pondered their actions, debated the propriety of burning versus hanging in a conversation in which white citizens sought to define the jurisprudence of racial mastery in a white republic. A Mobile, Alabama, editor defended a mob's immolation of two African Americans convicted of murdering two white children in May 1835, by asserting that the only legal punishment available, hanging, was not adequate to the "barbarity" of the crime: "As the Court pronounced the only sentence known to the law—the smothered flame broke forth. . . . Their lives were justly forfeited to the laws of the country, but the peculiar circumstances demanded that the ordinary punishment should be departed from—they were seized, taken to the place where they had perpetrated the act, and burned to death."[47] In some cases the matter of whether to burn or hang an African American offender was determined in republican fashion, through a public meeting and then a vote. In July 1851, a slave was arrested for the murder of Mr. and Mrs. Baker near Austin, Texas. Whites in the vicinity held a meeting in which a minority advocated burning at the stake, but the majority "were not so barbarous" and voted down the idea. The meeting appointed a committee which, denied access to the defendant by the sheriff, broke into the jail, seized the slave, tried and found him guilty, sentenced him to death, and hanged him.[48] Similarly, a mob of whites hanged two slaves "according to a statute of Judge Lynch" in southern Mississippi in 1843. A Gallatin editor argued that the mob would have been justified had it fulfilled its original intention to burn the slaves alive in retribution for their rape, assault, and robbery of a white woman and her child, which constituted grave offenses against "the domestic circles of life": "if the perpetrators of this excessively revolting crime had been burnt alive, as was first decreed, their fate would have been too good for such diabolical and inhuman wretches."[49]

A public debate among whites over the efficacy of burning versus hanging an African American offender erupted in a courtroom in Columbia, Missouri, in August 1853. A slave on trial for the attempted rape of a white woman confessed his guilt. Spectators watching the trial determined to immediately burn or hang the accused, but the prosecutor, Odon Guitar, admonished the crowd that if they insisted on executing the prisoner outside of legal process they should "go about it coolly and . . . decently and in order, not as demons." The crowd then formed a committee, chaired by a prominent slaveholder, Eli E. Bass. Bass took a voice vote of the crowd, the majority of which voted for hanging over burning. The vigilantes seized the prisoner and hanged him.[50] Yet the republican mob, faithful to racialized traditions of the execution rite, reserved burning at the stake exclusively for black miscreants. A posse of whites in Chicot County, Arkansas, in 1857 captured a biracial gang of rapists and murderers. The posse burned the blacks alive but shot the white ringleader.[51] Even as southern lynchers debated among themselves the propriety of burning African American victims, some antebellum northern commentators saw the propensity of southern mobs to burn their victims alive as an atavistic vestige and a profound marker of sectional difference. The *New York Times* rejected a Tennessee editor's spirited defense of a mob that had burned its black victim alive, asserting that "civilized communities, as a general thing, have long since discarded the notion that they were to inflict punishment for the sake of torture,—or that the deserts of the culprit were to be the measure of the personal torment they should bestow upon him."[52]

Just as antebellum southern mobs sometimes argued that the conventional capital punishment, hanging, did not transmit a sufficiently harrowing message to African American offenders, mobbers and their apologists similarly asserted that an avowedly neutral legal process could not respond with the speed and harshness necessary to deter black deviancy. As slaveholders in many cases controlled the courts, and masters sought to employ legal counsel to protect their chattel property (and indeed were required to do so in some states), such cases reflected tensions between slaveholders and nonslaveholders over the proper response to slave crime as well as a more general reaction against an expanding tendency toward legal fairness for blacks (and whites) in southern courts. Mobs responded with anger at instances of observation of legal procedure that delayed the punishment of black offenders. In Sumter County in western Alabama in 1855, a slave allegedly murdered a white girl. When the circuit court granted a change of venue to another county, a mob extricated the slave from the jail and burned him to death before a crowd of two thousand.[53] The next year in Barbour County in southeastern Alabama, the state supreme court voided the death sentence of a slave, Bob, by granting him a new trial. Over the reported objections of some residents, a mob took the slave from the jail and hanged him anyway.[54] In September 1855, after a judge granted a continuance, a mob in East Tennessee hanged a "runaway negro" accused of murdering a white woman.[55] Beyond frustration at the slowness and unpredictability of legal process, southern mobbers sometimes insisted that a court's sentence was too lenient. A mob in Montgomery in southeast Texas in 1857 reportedly hanged a slave accused of the attempted murder of his mistress because they "were impatient of the law's delay, and indisposed to let him off with less than capital punishment."[56] A portion of the white community in Columbus, Georgia, in August 1851, held a mass meeting to protest the governor's pardon of a slave, Jarrett, who had been convicted of raping a white girl and sentenced to death. The mass meeting transformed into a mob that stormed the jail, pulled out Jarrett, and hanged him.[57] Frustration over the lacunae of a racially disparate criminal justice system could also lead mobs to claim white victims. A mob hanged a slave woman and a white man, McClintock, in Clay County in western Missouri in 1850 because her inability to testify as a witness against him (slaves could not give testimony against whites in Missouri courts) meant that he would have escaped legal repercussion for his purported role in her axe attack on her mistress.[58]

A mob similarly cited the purported leniency of the criminal justice system in October 1854 on Maryland's Eastern Shore. In Denton, a free black, Dave Thomas, was tried for the murder of William H. Butler. The court convicted Thomas of manslaughter and sentenced him to sixteen years and seven months in the penitentiary. Neighbors and friends of the murdered man, angered at what they perceived as a light sentence, took Thomas out of the jail and hanged him to fulfill "the sentence of Judge Lynch to its deadliest extent."[59] The lynching of Dave Thomas underlined the precarious status of free blacks in the antebellum South. Lacking whatever protection a slaveholder's interest in his property may have afforded slaves, at times viewed as a threat to the survival of the slave system, and increasingly stripped of the legal rights that had distinguished them from slaves, free blacks also fell victim to the wrath of antebellum southern white mobs.[60] In 1858, a Louisiana mob murdered a free black who had allegedly raped a white child.[61] Northern African Americans traveling in the slave states were also at risk. In April 1836 a St. Louis mob burned to death Francis L. McIntosh, a "mulatto" boatman from Pittsburgh who had killed a deputy sheriff.[62]

Mob executions of African Americans resulting from frustration over the deliberative and unpredictable nature of legal process highlighted the lack of unanimity among southern whites.[63] Amid circumstances of racial crisis, and in light of legal institutions that privileged slaveholders' interests, whites with varying relationships to slavery did not necessarily agree on what the proper response was to allegations of slave criminality. This may have been especially true in western portions of the upper, border-state South, where slaves and slaveholders were less numerous, large portions of the white population were less invested in the peculiar institution, and laws and legal institutions less perfectly meshed with the prerogatives of slavery and racial control.[64] For instance, in central Missouri in July 1859, whites hanged and burned four slaves whom they accused of murdering, assaulting, and raping whites. After the conviction of one of the slaves, John, for murder in the first degree, the judge enraged the crowd in the courtroom by telling John's attorneys that he would listen to motions to put aside the verdict for a new trial before sentencing him. Shortly afterward, the crowd, angered by the formalities of legal procedure, transformed into a mob that pulled John from the jail where he had been placed as the court temporarily recessed and chained him to a tree and burned him to death.[65] The central Missouri lynchers were enraged by the possibility that slaveholders might intercede to thwart criminal justice. One of the slaves, named Holman, had been arrested for assault. His owner had sent him from jail to a locale outside of the county with the hope of selling him; authorities captured the slave and jailed him again. A mob seized Holman and hanged him shortly after they had collectively immolated John.[66] White defenders of the lynchers of the four slaves argued that the legal punishment for slaves convicted of rape in Missouri, castration, was not severe enough, and that slaveholders had evaded their responsibility in controlling the behavior of their slaves.[67] Although the participants in and apologists for the mob executions in Missouri's Little Dixie in 1859 apparently supported slavery and evinced "prosouthern political views,"[68] their brutal actions nonetheless highlighted the limitations of formal law in sustaining a comprehensive white supremacy. Gestures of legal fairness and the efforts of slaveholders to protect their property investment could confound the will of a white community that demanded racial vengeance.

In sum, the antebellum lynching of African Americans forecast the wide-scale disavowal of formal law by many southern whites after emancipation.[69] If formal southern legal systems existed to bolster slavery and left substantial space for the expansive personal authority of slaveholders, the collective killing of slaves and free blacks served to highlight divisions among whites in a vigorous republican polity organized around slaveholding and white supremacy and to underline the contradictions of legal systems that attempted to control persons held as property, to protect the slaveholder's investment in them, and to extend them legal fairness. When emancipation and Radical Reconstruction dissolved slavery and its legal systems, conservative southern whites would seize and expand upon the precedent of the region's history of racial lynching as a template for how to impose white control independent of formal law.

NOTES

I am grateful to Christopher Waldrep and William Carrigan for their comments on a draft of this essay.

1. *Galveston (TX) Weekly News*, August 6, 1859.

2. See, for example, George C. Wright, *Racial Violence in Kentucky, 1865-1940* (Baton Rouge: Louisiana State University Press, 1990); W. Fitzhugh Brundage, *Lynching in the New South: Georgia and Virginia, 1880-1930* (Urbana: University of Illinois Press, 1993); Stewart E. Tolnay and E. M. Beck, *A Festival of Violence: An Analysis of Southern Lynchings, 1882-1930* (Urbana: University of Illinois Press, 1995); Michael J. Pfeifer, *Rough Justice: Lynching and American Society, 1874-1947* (Urbana: University of Illinois Press, 2004); William D. Carrigan, *The Making of a Lynching Culture: Violence and Vigilantism in Central Texas, 1836-1916* (Urbana: University of Illinois Press, 2004).

3. Eugene D. Genovese, *Roll, Jordan, Roll: The World the Slaves Made* (New York: Pantheon, 1974), 32-33. For additional interpretations stressing the infrequency of the lynching of slaves, see Clement Eaton, "Mob Violence in the Old South," *Mississippi Valley Historical Review* 29 (Dec. 1942): 351-70; Gilles Vandal, *Rethinking Southern Violence: Homicides in Post–Civil War Louisiana, 1866-1884* (Columbus: Ohio State University Press, 2000), 94, 244-45n20; Vandal found 5 instances of lynching that claimed 8 black victims in Louisiana in the 1850s. In parallel with Genovese's estimates, David Grimsted enumerated approximately 49 African-American victims of "anticriminal mobs" in the antebellum South. Grimsted, *American Mobbing, 1828-1861: Toward Civil War* (New York: Oxford University Press, 1998), 101, 103.

4. Kenneth M. Stampp, *The Peculiar Institution: Slavery in the Ante-bellum South* (New York: Knopf, 1956), 190-91. Additional interpretations arguing that the lynching of slaves was fairly common can be found in Ulrich B. Phillips, *American Negro Slavery* (1918; repr., Gloucester, MA: Peter Smith, 1959), 511-12; Bertram Wyatt-Brown, *Southern Honor: Ethics and Behavior in the Old South* (New York: Oxford University Press, 1982), 388-89; and Philip Schwarz, *Twice Condemned: Slaves and the Criminal Laws of Virginia, 1705-1865* (Baton Rouge: Louisiana State University Press, 1988), 291-92.

5. See Thomas G. Dyer, "A Most Unexampled Exhibition of Madness and Brutality: Judge Lynch in Saline County, Missouri," in *Under Sentence of Death: Lynching in the South*, ed. W. Fitzhugh Brundage (Chapel Hill: University of North Carolina Press, 1997), 98-99.

6. Orville W. Taylor, *Negro Slavery in Arkansas* (Durham, NC: Duke University Press, 1958), 235-36; James Benson Sellers, *Slavery in Alabama* (1940; repr., Tuscaloosa: University of Alabama Press, 1994), 262-64; Randolph B. Campbell, *An Empire for Slavery: The Peculiar Institution in Texas, 1821-1865* (Baton Rouge: Louisiana State University Press, 1989), 105; Ralph Betts Flanders, *Plantation Slavery in Georgia* (Chapel Hill: University of North Carolina Press, 1933), 268-69; R. Douglas Hurt, *Agriculture and Slavery in Missouri's Little Dixie* (Columbia: University of Missouri Press, 1992), 248-50.

7. Christopher Waldrep, ed., *Lynching in America: A History in Documents* (New York: New York University Press, 2006), 61. For an important discussion that emphasizes growing northern criticism of southern collective violence after the mid-1830s, violence that was increasingly labeled "lynching" and that included mob executions of slaves, see Waldrep, *The Many Faces of Judge Lynch: Extralegal Violence and Punishment in America* (New York: Palgrave Macmillan, 2002), 27-47, esp. 41-45.

8. See Dyer, "A Most Unexampled Exhibition," 81-108; Martha Hodes, *White Women, Black Men: Illicit Sex in the Nineteenth-Century South* (New Haven, CT: Yale University Press, 1997), 58-59, 60, 235-36n56; Diane Miller Sommerville, *Race and Rape in the Nineteenth-Century South* (Chapel Hill: University of North Carolina Press, 2004), 29-30, 52-53.

9. For vital analyses of the history of popular constitutionalism in the United States, see Larry Kramer, *The People Themselves: Popular Constitutionalism and Judicial Review* (New York: Oxford University Press, 2004); Christian G. Fritz, *American Sovereigns: The People and America's Constitutional Tradition before the Civil War* (Cambridge, UK: Cambridge University Press, 2008). For a cogent interpretation that analyzes the history of the federal response to lynching in the context of popular constitutionalism, see Christopher Waldrep, "National Policing, Lynching, and Constitutionalism," *Journal of Southern History*, 74, no. 3 (Aug. 2008): 589-626.

10. Missouri and Texas tallied, respectively, 12 and 9 documented African American victims of mobs. The proximity of Kansas, the locus of a fierce national debate over the territorial expansion of slavery and the site of intense conflict between pro-slavery and abolitionist settlers, may have heightened white fears about the effects of abolitionism upon an "insufficiently obsequious slave population" in Missouri. Dyer, "A Most Unexampled Exhibition," 82-83. The nearness of Mexico, a haven for escaping slaves, and the presence of large numbers of culturally distinct Tejanos, whom Anglo American slaveholders suspected might aid slave insurrection, lent a distinctive character to slaveholding culture in Texas. Carrigan, *The Making of a Lynching Culture*, 72-74; Campbell, *An Empire for Slavery*, 218-19; Enda Junkins, "Slave Plots, Insurrections, and Acts of Violence in the State of Texas, 1828-1865" (master's thesis, Baylor University, 1969), 9, 17-24. Comparatively low rates of legal execution on slavery's western periphery may also have played a role in the relative prevalence of the lynching of slaves there. Although his evidence is incomplete, Watt Espy documents merely 11 executions of blacks in Missouri and 10 of African Americans in Texas from 1835 to 1862, compared to 185 executions of African Americans in Alabama and 174 executions of blacks in Virginia. For Espy's historical execution database, see http://www.deathpenaltyinfo.org/executions-us-1608-2002-espy-file (accessed Feb. 15, 2011).

11. Evidence suggests that the collective killings of slaves began before the nineteenth century. For instance, in Accomac County, Virginia, in 1791, a group of "disguised men, numbering from six to fifteen," hanged Ralph Singo and James Richards, for reasons not specified in the historical record. W[illia]m P. Palmer and Sherwin McRae, *Calendar of Virginia State Papers* (Richmond, VA, 1885), 328. This incident is cited in Phillips, *American Negro Slavery*, 311. Race is not specified in the source, and Phillips' discussion of the episode is ambiguous on the question of the race of the offenders. Less ambiguously, Waldrep, ed., *Lynching in America*, 62, includes documentation of a 1797 Georgia case in which a posse decided to burn to death a slave accused of murder.

12. Thirty-nine of the documented lynchings of slaves and free blacks occurred between 1850 and 1862. While northern abolitionist newspapers relished reporting such events during this period of sectional crisis, southern newspapers reported them as well, albeit with concern over how Northerners might interpret such incidents.

13. For the transformation of lynching violence against African Americans in the wake of emancipation, see Michael J. Pfeifer, *The Roots of Rough Justice: Origins of American Lynching* (Urbana: University of Illinois Press, 2010), chap. 5, "The Civil War and Reconstruction and the Remaking of American Lynching."

14. Insurrection panics precipitated extensive episodes of lethal violence against African Americans, sometimes legally constituted, sometimes extralegal. David Grimsted tabulated that 35 incidents of collective violence by southern whites against real and purported slave "insurrections" claimed 448 lives in the antebellum era, with most of the victims slaves. Grimsted, *American Mobbing*, 135-36. For the dozens of slaves killed by militia or executed in highly public punishments following judicial proceedings in the suppression of a large-scale slave rebellion in the Louisiana sugar parishes of St. John the Baptist and St. Charles in 1811, see Adam Rothman, *Slave Country: American*

Expansion and the Origins of the Deep South (Cambridge, MA: Harvard University Press, 2005), 106-17. For the summary executions of blacks and whites amid an insurrection panic in Texas in 1860, see Donald E. Reynolds, *Texas Terror: the Slave Insurrection Panic of 1860 and the Secession of the Lower South* (Baton Rouge: Louisiana State University Press, 2007). For the hangings and lethal floggings with which whites sought to suppress an alleged slave conspiracy in Mississippi in 1861, see Winthrop D. Jordan, *Tumult and Silence at Second Creek: An Inquiry into a Civil War Slave Conspiracy*, rev. ed. (Baton Rouge: Louisiana State University Press, 1996). The classic interpretation of African American slave resistance and the white response is Herbert Aptheker, *American Negro Revolts* (New York: International Publishers, 1963).

15. Campbell, *An Empire for Slavery*, 101.

16. Ibid.

17. *Boston Liberator*, October 16, 1857; James Elbert Cutler, *Lynch-Law and Investigation into the History of Lynching in the United States* (New York: Longman, Green, 1905), 125.

18. For analyses of the treatment of slaves in the formal criminal justice system and in extralegal "plantation justice," see Michael Stephen Hindus, *Crime, Justice, and Authority in Massachusetts and South Carolina, 1767-1878* (Chapel Hill: University of North Carolina Press, 1980), 130-61; Edward L. Ayers, *Vengeance and Justice, Crime and Punishment in the 19th-Century American South* (New York: Oxford University Press, 1984), 132-37.

19. Howell M. Henry, "The Police Control of the Slave in South Carolina," (PhD diss., Vanderbilt University 1914; New York: Negro Universities Press, 1968), 4-6. Walter Hening, *The Statutes at Large: Being a Collection of all the Laws of Virginia, from the First Session of the Legislature in the Year 1619* (New York: R & W & G. Bartow, 1823), vol. 1.

20. Judith Kelleher Schafer, "Slaves and Crime: New Orleans, 1846-1862," in *Local Matters: Race, Crime, and Justice in the Nineteenth-Century South*, ed. Christopher Waldrep and Donald G. Nieman (Athens: University of Georgia Press, 2001), esp. 56, 74, 84-85n5.

21. Ibid., 62.

22. Ibid., 58.

23. Ibid., 56, 84-85n5.

24. For a case study with these dynamics, see Timothy Huebner, "The Roots of Fairness: *State v. Caesar* and Slave Justice in Antebellum North Carolina," in *Local Matters*, ed. Waldrep and Nieman, 29-52. For evidence of concern for slaves' legal rights, proper legal procedure, and a variety of legal outcomes in cases involving slaves in Texas, see Campbell, *An Empire for Slavery*, 106-8. For the legal culture of southern slavery, see Daniel J. Flanigan, *The Criminal Law of Slavery and Freedom, 1800-1868* (New York: Garland, 1987); Mark V. Tushnet, *The American Law of Slavery, 1810-1860* (Princeton, NJ: Princeton University Press, 1981); Thomas D. Morris, *Southern Slavery and the Law, 1619-1860* (Chapel Hill: University of North Carolina Press, 1996); Ariela J. Gross, *Double Character: Slavery and Mastery in the Antebellum Southern Courtroom* (Princeton, NJ: Princeton University Press, 2000).

25. Schwarz, *Twice Condemned*, 27-29; Stuart Banner, "Traces of Slavery: Race and the Death Penalty in Historical Perspective," in *From Lynch Mobs to the Killing State: Race and the Death Penalty in America*, ed. Charles Ogletree Jr. and Austin Sarat (New York: New York University Press, 2006), 100.

26. WPA Slave Narratives, Oklahoma Narratives, vol. 13, Octavia George, 113.

27. Moses Roper to Thomas Price, London, June 27, 1836, from *Slavery in America* 2 (Aug. 1836): 45-46, in *Slave Testimony: Two Centuries of Letters, Speeches, Interviews, and Autobiographies*, ed. John W. Blassingame (Baton Rouge: Louisiana State University Press, 1977), 24-25.

28. For analyses of the slave patrol, see Sally E. Hadden, "Colonial and Revolution-

ary Era Slave Patrols of Virginia," in *Lethal Imagination: Violence and Brutality in American History*, ed. Michael Bellesiles (New York: New York University Press, 1999), 69-85, and Hadden, *Slave Patrols: Law and Violence in Virginia and the Carolinas* (Cambridge, MA: Harvard University Press, 2001).

29. For the commentary of former slaves on the slave patrol, see, for instance, WPA Slave Narratives, Ohio Narratives, vol. 12, Perry Sid Jemison, 52; WPA Slave Narratives, Georgia Narratives, vol. 4, pt. 2, Easter Huff, 24. For analysis of the clash between masters and the slave patrol and how this was informed by a tension between slaveholders and nonslaveholders regarding the regulation of African American behavior, see Henry, "The Police Control of the Slave in South Carolina," 39-41.

30. For the profound social effects of the expansion of slavery in the early to mid-nineteenth century, an event that Ira Berlin calls "the Second Middle Passage," see Berlin, *Generations of Captivity: A History of African-American Slaves* (Cambridge, MA: Harvard University Press, 2003), 161-243.

31. *Galveston (TX) Weekly News*, May 17, 1859.

32. Taylor, *Negro Slavery in Arkansas*, 235-36.

33. Sellers, *Slavery in Alabama*, 262-64.

34. *Huntsville (AL.) Democrat*, September 7, 1854, quoted in Sellers, *Slavery in Alabama*, 263.

35. *Maysville (KY) Eagle*, January 8, 1859. *New York Times*, January 28, 1859, erroneously reports that this incident occurred in Kentucky.

36. *Maysville (KY) Eagle*, January 8, 1859. For the ritual of the condemned person's "dying declaration" in eighteenth- and early nineteenth-century England and America, see Stuart Banner, *The Death Penalty: An American History* (Cambridge, MA: Harvard University Press, 2002), 48-52.

37. Frederick Law Olmsted, *The Cotton Kingdom; A Traveler's Observations on Cotton and Slavery in the American Slave States* (New York: Alfred A. Knopf, 1953; repr., New York: Da Capo Press, 1996), 303.

38. Hurt, *Agriculture and Slavery in Missouri's Little Dixie*, 248; Harrison Anthony Trexler, *Slavery in Missouri, 1804-1865* (Baltimore, MD: John Hopkins University Press, 1914), 254n61; *St. Louis (MO) Bulletin*, November 8, 1860, quoted in *Santa Fe (NM) Gazette*, December 15, 1860.

39. *(Natchez) Mississippi Free Trader*, March 8, 1854, reprinted in Waldrep, ed., *Lynching in America*, 76-77.

40. Hodes, *White Women, Black Men*, 39-122; Sommerville, *Race and Rape in the Nineteenth-Century South*, 19-101. Hodes, 59-60, cites the 1861 Georgia case.

41. Campbell, *An Empire for Slavery*, 105.

42. Sommerville, *Race and Rape in the Nineteenth-Century South*, 29-30.

43. Dyer, "A Most Unexampled Exhibition," 87; Hurt, *Agriculture and Slavery in Missouri's Little Dixie*, 249-50.

44. Banner, *The Death Penalty*, 70-72.

45. Ibid., 72-76, 88-111, 151.

46. I am grateful to Peter Charles Hoffer for information on this point. "Execution by Burning in the 19th century U.S.?" thread, H-Law, July 18, 2008. I am also indebted to Michael Radelet for information on this matter. E-mail correspondence with the author, July 15, 16, 2008. For a description of a legal execution by burning in South Carolina in the 1830s, see Roper to Price, London, June 27, 1836, in *Slave Testimony*, ed. Blassingame, 24-25. Special freeholder courts tried slaves and free blacks in South Carolina from the colonial era through the antebellum period; blacks gained the right to appeal the decisions of the "negro courts" in 1833. Henry, "The Police Control of the Slave in South Carolina," 58-65.

47. *Boston Liberator*, July 4, 1835, quoted in Cutler, *Lynch-Law*, 108. For discussions of southern whites and ritualistic aspects of lynching in the late nineteenth and twentieth centuries, see Pfeifer, *Rough Justice*, 48-49, and Amy Louise Wood, *Lynching and Spectacle: Witnessing Racial Violence in America, 1890-1940* (Chapel Hill: University of North Carolina Press, 2009), 19-44.

48. Junkins, "Slave Plots, Insurrections, and Acts of Violence," 40. The quotation is from Junkins's source, the *San Antonio (TX) Ledger*, July 31, 1851.

49. *Gallatin (MS) Signal*, quoted in *Courier de La Louisiane (Louisiana Courier)*, March 1, 1843.

50. Hurt, *Agriculture and Slavery in Missouri's Little Dixie*, 249. Hurt quotes *Weekly Tribune* (Liberty, MO), September 2, 1853.

51. Wyatt-Brown, *Southern Honor*, 389; *Boston Liberator*, October 16, December 4, 1857.

52. *New York Times*, September, 17, 1857. For another northern editor's condemnation of a "negro-burning" in Tennessee as the inevitable product of "the inhuman relations of slave and owner," see *New York Tribune*, July 11, 1854.

53. Sellers, *Slavery in Alabama*, 263.

54. Ibid., 263-64.

55. *Boston Liberator*, October 19, 1855, reprinted in Waldrep, ed., *Lynching in America*, 74-75.

56. *Galveston (TX) Weekly News*, June 2, 1857.

57. Flanders, *Plantation Slavery in Georgia*, 268-69.

58, Trexler, *Slavery in Missouri, 1804-1865*, 254n61; Hurt, *Agriculture and Slavery in Missouri's Little Dixie*, 248.

59. *Baltimore (MD) Republican and Argus*, October 10, 1854.

60. For the declining social and legal status of free blacks in the antebellum South, see Berlin, *Generations of Captivity*, 182-84, 224-25; Campbell, *An Empire for Slavery*, 112-14; John Hope Franklin, *The Free Negro in North Carolina, 1790-1860* (Chapel Hill: University of North Carolina Press, 1943), 67-81.

61. H. E. Sterkx, *The Free Negro in Ante-Bellum Louisiana* (Rutherford, NJ: Fairleigh Dickinson University Press, 1972), 189-90.

62. *(St. Louis) Missouri Republican*, April 30, 1836, reprinted in Janet S. Hermann, "The McIntosh Affair," *Bulletin of the Missouri Historical Society* 26 (Jan. 1970): 123-43; John F. Darby, *Personal Recollections* (St. Louis: G.I. Jones and Co., 1880), 237-41.

63. For an interpretation that argues that the unevenness and flexibility of local criminal justice in the antebellum South stemmed from the need for courts to mediate class differences among whites, see Bertram Wyatt-Brown, "Community, Class, and Snopesian Crime: Local Justice in the Old South," in *Class, Conflict, and Consensus: Antebellum Southern Community Studies*, ed. Orville Vernon Burton and Robert C. McMath Jr. (Westport, CT: Greenwood Press, 1982), 173-206.

64. Genovese argues that Kentucky's slave code was comparatively mild but that Kentucky apparently saw more "personal violence and lynching" than many other southern states, "although much more often directed against allegedly negrophile whites than against blacks." *Roll, Jordan, Roll*, 32.

65. Dyer, "A Most Unexampled Exhibition," 89-91.

66. Ibid., 86, 92.

67. Ibid., 93.

68. Ibid., 93-94.

69. The most accurate count available, that of Stewart E. Tolnay and E. M. Beck, is that nearly 2,500 African Americans were murdered by lynch mobs from 1882 through 1930 in the ten southern states of Mississippi, Georgia, Louisiana, Alabama, South Carolina, Florida, Tennessee, Arkansas, Kentucky, and North Carolina. Tolnay and Beck,

A Festival of Violence, ix. South-wide statistics for Reconstruction violence are not available, but Gilles Vandal has enumerated 124 black and 46 white victims of lynching in Louisiana from 1866 through 1876, a much higher rate of lynching than occurred in the succeeding years of the early Redemption era, when 47 blacks and 22 whites died at the hands of mobs from 1877 through 1884. More broadly, Vandal has identified 402 cases of collective murder in Louisiana between 1865 and 1876, with whites committing most of the acts of collective violence (85 percent); in two-thirds of cases of Reconstruction-era collective killings, whites murdered blacks (68.7 percent). Vandal, *Rethinking Southern Violence*, 67-93.

Appendix: Slave Lynchings, 1835–1862

Locale and/or County	Date	Name	Status	Alleged Offense
Near Mobile	May 1835	"Negro"	Unknown	Murdered children
Near Mobile	May 1835	"Negro"	Unknown	Murdered children
Mount Meigs, Montgomery County	August? 1854	"Negro of Dr. McDonald"	Slave	Murder of master
Sumter County	May 1855	"negro man"	Unknown	Murder and rape
Clayton, Barbour County	August 6, 1856	"Bob"	Slave	Unknown
Near Tuskgee, Macon County	October 9, 1860	"boy belonging to Maj. Cocke"	Slave	Unknown
Phillips County	1849	Unknown	Slave	Murder of master
Phillips County	1849	Unknown	Slave	Murder of master
Hot Spring County	1836	William	Slave	Murder of master, another white man, and five slaves
Chicot County	1857	Unknown	Unknown	Murder and rape

Method of Execution	Source
Burning	James Elbert Cutler, *Lynch-Law and Investigation into the History of Lynching in the United States* (New York: Longman, Green, 1905), 108. Source: *Liberator,* July 4, 1835.
Burning	James Elbert Cutler, *Lynch-Law and Investigation into the History of Lynching in the United States* (New York: Longman, Green, 1905), 108. Source: *Liberator,* July 4, 1835.
Burning	James Benson Sellers, *Slavery in Alabama* (1940; repr., Tuscaloosa: University of Alabama Press, 1994), 262-64.
Burning	*New York Times*, June 2, 1855; James Benson Sellers, *Slavery in Alabama* (1940; repr., Tuscaloosa: University of Alabama Press, 1994), 263.
Hanging	James Benson Sellers, *Slavery in Alabama* (1940; repr., Tuscaloosa: University of Alabama Press, 1994), 263-64.
Burning	James Benson Sellers, *Slavery in Alabama* (1940; repr., Tuscaloosa: University of Alabama Press, 1994), 264.
Burning	Orville W. Taylor, *Negro Slavery in Arkansas* (Durham, NC: Duke University Press, 1958), 235.
Burning	Orville W. Taylor, *Negro Slavery in Arkansas* (Durham, NC: Duke University Press, 1958), 235.
Burning	Orville W. Taylor, *Negro Slavery in Arkansas* (Durham, NC: Duke University Press, 1958), 235-36.
Burning	Bertram Wyatt-Brown, *Southern Honor: Ethics and Behavior in the Old South* (New York: Oxford University Press, 1982), 389, 564n38. Source: *Fuller Diary*, October 16, November 15, 1857; *Boston Liberator*, October 16, December 4, 1857.

Chicot County	1857	Unknown	Unknown	Murder and rape
Columbus	1851	Jarrett	Slave	Rape
"Georgia's plantation belt"	1861	George	Slave	Rape
Unknown	1842	"two runaways"	Slave	Murder, rape, and kidnap-ping
Unknown	1842	Two runaways	Slave	Murder, rape, and kidnap-ping
Unknown	October? 1858	Free negro	Free	Rape and murder of white child
Louisville	1857?	George	Slave	Murder
Louisville	1857?	Bill	Slave	Murder
Near Peak's Mill Franklin County	Early Janu-ary 1862	Slave of "Miss Pearce"	Slave	Rape and murderous assault
Denton, Caroline County	October 1854	Dave Thomas	Free	Murder
Near Union Point	1841?	"runaway slave"	Slave	Murder, rape, and robbery

	Burning	Bertram Wyatt-Brown, *Southern Honor: Ethics and Behavior in the Old South* (New York: Oxford University Press, 1982), 389, 564n38. Source: *Fuller, Diary*, October 16, November 15, 1857; *Boston Liberator*, October 16, December 4, 1857.
	Hanging	Ralph Betts Flanders, *Plantation Slavery in Georgia* (Chapel Hill: University of North Carolina Press, 1933), 268-69.
	Burning	Martha Hodes, *White Women, Black Men: Illicit Sex in the Nineteenth-Century South* (New Haven, CT: Yale University Press, 1997), 58. Source: *(Columbus, GA) Daily Sun*, February 22, March 2, 29, 1861.
	Burning	Bertram Wyatt-Brown, *Southern Honor: Ethics and Behavior in the Old South* (New York: Oxford University Press, 1982), 388-89, 564n38. Source: Davis, *Barrow Diary*, June 17, 1842, p. 262.
	Burning	Bertram Wyatt-Brown, *Southern Honor: Ethics and Behavior in the Old South* (New York: Oxford University Press, 1982), 388-89, 564n38. Source: Davis, *Barrow Diary*, June 17, 1842, p. 262.
	Unknown	H. E. Sterkx, *The Free Negro in Ante-Bellum Louisiana* (Rutherford, NJ: Fairleigh Dickinson University Press, 1972), 189-90. Source: *New Orleans Bee*, October 9, 1858.
	Hanging	James Elbert Cutler, *Lynch-Law and Investigation into the History of Lynching in the United States* (New York: Longman, Green, 1905), 125. Source: *Liberator*, October 16, 1857.
	Hanging	James Elbert Cutler, *Lynch-Law and Investigation into the History of Lynching in the United States* (New York: Longman, Green, 1905), 125. Source: *Liberator*, October 16, 1857.
	Hanging	*New York Times*, January 14, 1862.
	Hanging	*Baltimore Republican and Argus*, October 10, 1854, p. 2.
	Burning	Christopher Waldrep, ed., *Lynching in America: A History in Documents* (New York: New York University Press, 2006), 76-77, source: *Mississippi Free Trader*, March 8, 1854.

Near Union Point	1841?	"runaway slave"	Slave	Murder, rape, and robbery	
Near Gallatin, Copiah County	February? 1843	"negro men . . . of Mr. Burdy"	Slave	Rape, murderous assault, and robbery	
Near Gallatin, Copiah County	February? 1843	"negro men . . . of Mr. Burdy"	Slave	Rape, murderous assault, and robbery	
St. Louis	April 28, 1836	Francis L. McIntosh	"free mulatto" boathand	Murder of deputy sheriff, stabbed deputy constable	
Near Peverly, Jefferson County	1842?	"negro"	Unknown	Murder and robbery	
Franklin County	April 1847	Eli	Slave	Murder and attempted rape of white woman, attempt to kill her son	
Clay County	May 1850	"slave woman"	Slave	Assaulted mistress with an ax	
Boone County	August 1853	"a slave"	Slave	Attempted rape	
Carroll County	October 1855	Slave of Judge Thomas Clingman	Slave	Murder of master	
Troy, Lincoln County	January 1, 1859	"negro" of "Mr. Simeon Thornhill"	Slave	Murder of master	

Burning	Christopher Waldrep, ed., *Lynching in America: A History in Documents* (New York: New York University Press, 2006), 76-77. Source: *Mississippi Free Trader*, March 8, 1854. .
Hanging	*Courier de La Louisiane (Louisiana Courier)*, March 1, 1843.
Hanging	*Courier de La Louisiane (Louisiana Courier)*, March 1, 1843.
Burning	Janet S. Hermann, "The McIntosh Affair," *Bulletin of the Missouri Historical Society* 26 (Jan. 1970): 123-43; John F. Darby, *Personal Recollections* (St. Louis: G.I. Jones and Co., 1880), 237-41.
Hanging	*Goodspeed's History of Franklin, Jefferson, Washington, Crawford, and Gasconade Counties, Missouri* (Chicago: Goodspeed Publishing, 1888), 405; http://www.rootsweb.ancestry.com/~nebuffal/jeffcomo/courts.htm.
Unknown	Harrison Anthony Trexler, *Slavery in Missouri 1804-1865* (Baltimore, MD: Johns Hopkins University Press, 1914), 254n61. Source: *Goodspeed's History of Franklin, Jefferson, Washington, Crawford, and Gasconade Counties* (Chicago: Goodspeed Publishing, 1888), 283.
Hanging	R. Douglas Hurt, *Agriculture and Slavery in Missouri's Little Dixie* (Columbia: University of Missouri Press, 1992), 248. Source: *(Columbia) Missouri Statesman*, May 24, 1850; Harrison Anthony Trexler, *Slavery in Missouri 1804-1865* (Baltimore, MD: Johns Hopkins University Press, 1914), 254n61. Source: *History of Clay and Platte Counties* (St. Louis, 1885), 158-59.
Hanging	R. Douglas Hurt, *Agriculture and Slavery in Missouri's Little Dixie* (Columbia: University of Missouri Press, 1992), 249. Source: *Weekly Tribune* (Liberty, MO), September 2, 1853.
Hanging	*New York Times*, October 16, 1855.
Burning	*Maysville (KY) Eagle*, January 8, 1859, p. 2.

Arrow Rock, Saline County	July 18, 1859	"slave belonging to Dr. William Price"	Slave	Assaulted white girl
Marshall, Saline County	July 20?, 1859	John	Slave	Murder
Marshall, Saline County	July 20?, 1859	Jim	Slave	Attempted rape
Marshall, Saline County	July 20?, 1859	Holman	Slave	Had allegedly stabbed white man
Callaway County	Early November 1860	Unknown	Female Ssave	Murder of young white woman
Unknown	Unknown	"slave"	Slave	Rape of slaveholder's daughter
Unknown	1840	"runaway slaves"	Slave	Cattle theft, murder of member of posse

	Hanging	Thomas G. Dyer, "A Most Unexampled Exhibition of Madness and Brutality: Judge Lynch in Saline County, Missouri," in *Under Sentence of Death: Lynching in the South,* ed. W. Fitzhugh Brundage (Chapel Hill: University of North Carolina Press, 1997), 87.
	Burning	R. Douglas Hurt, *Agriculture and Slavery in Missouri's Little Dixie* (Columbia: University of Missouri Press, 1992), p. 250. Source: *Glasgow (MO) Weekly Times,* July 21, 1859. Thomas G. Dyer, "A Most Unexampled Exhibition of Madness and Brutality: Judge Lynch in Saline County, Missouri," in *Under Sentence of Death: Lynching in the South,* ed. W. Fitzhugh Brundage (Chapel Hill: University of North Carolina Press, 1997), 87.
	Hanging	R. Douglas Hurt, *Agriculture and Slavery in Missouri's Little Dixie* (Columbia: University of Missouri Press, 1992), 250. Source: *Glasgow (MO) Weekly Times,* July 21, 1859. Thomas G. Dyer, "A Most Unexampled Exhibition of Madness and Brutality: Judge Lynch in Saline County, Missouri," in *Under Sentence of Death: Lynching in the South,* ed. W. Fitzhugh Brundage (Chapel Hill: University of North Carolina Press, 1997), 87.
	Hanging	R. Douglas Hurt, *Agriculture and Slavery in Missouri's Little Dixie* (Columbia: University of Missouri Press, 1992), 250. Source: *Glasgow (MO) Weekly Times,* July 21, 1859. Thomas G. Dyer, "A Most Unexampled Exhibition of Madness and Brutality: Judge Lynch in Saline County, Missouri," in *Under Sentence of Death: Lynching in the South,* ed. W. Fitzhugh Brundage (Chapel Hill: University of North Carolina Press, 1997), 87.
	Hanging	*St. Louis Bulletin,* November 8, 1860, quoted in *Santa Fe (NM) Gazette,* December 15, 1860, p. 2.
	Burning	Diane Miller Sommerville, *Race and Rape in the Nineteenth-Century South* (Chapel Hill: University of North Carolina Press, 2004), 29-30. Source: 270n55 cites Guion Griffis Johnson, *Antebellum North Carolina,* p. 508.
	Shooting	David Grimsted, *American Mobbing, 1828-1861: Toward Civil War* (New York: Oxford University Press, 1998), 111-12, 311n72. Sources: *Wilmington Chronicle* in *Fayetteville Observer,* January 13, 1840; *Raleigh Register* in *Liberator,* January 22, 1841.

Unknown	1840	"runaway slaves"	Slave	Cattle theft, murder of member of posse	
Interior of state	1861	"favorite household servants"	Slave	"Revolt"/ murder of master's family	
Interior of state	1861	"favorite household servants"	Slave	"Revolt"/ murder of master's family	
Unknown	1854	Unknown	Unknown	Murder and rape of white woman	
Near La Grange	1855	"negro boy . . . belonging to Mr. Wm. Turner"	Slave	Murder of overseer	
Near Sparta	September 1855	"runaway negro"	Slave	Murder of woman	
Unknown	1857?	"negro"	Unknown	"sundry foul, revolting, and hellish crimes"	
Near Fannin	Early 1850s?	"negro woman"	Slave	Murder of mistress and mistress's two children	
Near Austin	July 1851	"Negro"	Slave	Murder	
Ft. Bend County	May? 1853	"young man"	Slave	Murder of master	

	Shooting	David Grimsted, *American Mobbing, 1828-1861: Toward Civil War* (New York: Oxford University Press, 1998), 111-12, 311n72. Sources: *Wilmington Chronicle* in *Fayetteville Observer*, January 13, 1840; *Raleigh Register* in *Liberator*, January 22, 1841.
	Burning	*New York Times*, December 1, 1861.
	Burning	*New York Times*, December 1, 1861.
	Burning	Martha Hodes, *White Women, Black Men: Illicit Sex in the Nineteenth-Century South* (New Haven, CT: Yale University Press, 1997), 58. Source: *New York Daily Tribune*, July 4, 11, 1854.
	Hanging	Christopher Waldrep, ed., *Lynching in America: A History in Documents* (New York: New York University Press, 2006), 74. Source: *Boston Liberator*, October 19, 1855.
	Hanging	Christopher Waldrep, ed., *Lynching in America: A History in Documents* (New York: New York University Press, 2006), 74. Source: *Boston Liberator*, October 19, 1855.
	Burning	*New York Times*, September 17, 1857.
	Hanging	Frederick Law Olmstead, *The Cotton Kingdom; A Traveler's Observations on Cotton and Slavery in the American Slave States* (New York: Alfred A. Knopf, 1953; repr., New York: Da Capo Press, 1996), 303.
	Hanging	Enda Junkins, "Slave Plots, Insurrections, and Acts of Violence in the State of Texas, 1828-1865" (master's thesis, Baylor University, 1969), 40. Source: *San Antonio (TX) Ledger*, July 31, 1851.
	Hanging	Enda Junkins, "Slave Plots, Insurrections, and Acts of Violence in the State of Texas, 1828-1865" (master's thesis, Baylor University, 1969), 44. Source: *State Gazette* (Austin, TX), May 28, 1853.

Ft. Bend County	May? 1853	"Negro Preacher"	Slave	Had influenced young man to murder master
Smith County	August? 1853	"Negro"	Slave	Rape and murder
Montgomery, Montgomery County	May? 1857	"negro"	Slave	Attempted murder of mistress
Near Smithfield, Polk County	April 30, 1859	"Alfred, was the property of a Mr. Roper"	Slave	Murder and robbery of master
Dresden, Navarro County	Mid-July, 1859	"A negro man, belonging to a Mr. Blanton, of Ellis county"	Slave	Murder and robbery
Hopkins County	July? 1859	Unknown	Slave	Attempted rape of white woman
Harrison	Early September 1861	Green	Slave	Rape and Murder of twelve-year-old white girl

	Hanging	Enda Junkins, "Slave Plots, Insurrections, and Acts of Violence in the State of Texas, 1828-1865" (master's thesis, Baylor University, 1969), 44. Source: *State Gazette* (Austin, TX), May 28, 1853.
	Hanging	Enda Junkins, "Slave Plots, Insurrections, and Acts of Violence in the State of Texas, 1828-1865" (master's thesis, Baylor University, 1969), 45. Source: *Standard* (Clarksville, TX), August 13, 1853.
	Hanging	*Galveston (TX) Weekly News*, June 2, 1857, p. 1.
	Burning	*Galveston (TX) Weekly News*, May 17, 1859, p. 1.
	Hanging	*Galveston (TX) Weekly News*, August 6, 1859.
	Hanging	Randolph B. Campbell, *An Empire for Slavery: The Peculiar Institution in Texas, 1821-1865* (Baton Rouge: Louisiana State University Press, 1989), 105.
	Burning	*Marshall (TX) Republican*, September 7, 1861, quoted in *New Orleans (LA) Picayune*, September 12, 1861.

Part II

The Advent of the Market Economy and the Agricultural World

Chapter 3

Frontier Capitalism

Market Migration to Rural Central Missouri, 1815–1860

Jeff Bremer

Gottfried Duden, a German writer who lived in central Missouri in the 1820s, encouraged the immigration of his fellow countrymen into antebellum Missouri in his *Report on a Journey to the Western States of North America*, published in 1829. After three years of living on a farm located on the Missouri River west of St. Louis he wrote of the great opportunities available for European immigrants. He glorified pioneer life and emphasized the plentiful natural resources and the availability of cheap land in Missouri. It was "extremely alluring to settle down in regions where one has such complete freedom of choice," he explained. Americans benefited from the fertility of the land and the plentiful game and fish; livestock even foraged in the forests and fed themselves. The climate was almost perfect for agriculture and he claimed that corn grew more than twelve feet high. Taxes were also low, he boasted. River connections were "splendid" and the Missouri River was "navigable without interruption for over 2,500 miles." Communication via steamboat was "exceedingly easy" and the region's rivers tied Missouri settlers to the rest of the nation. In short, Missouri was ideally suited for commerce and farming.[1]

Duden's narrative provides a fine introduction to the enthusiastic embrace of market activity by settlers in the region of central Missouri, broadly defined here as the forty-two counties within fifty miles of the Missouri River. He noted that "wherever population had grown to a certain level, there also a market will soon develop for the products of the soil, and no one would be more pleased than the farmer who can leave it to the merchant and to speculators to send goods long distances." No immigrant or settler could "get along without the intermediary service of a merchant," he added. Anyone who had something to sell turned to storekeepers, who then sold the goods on commission or bought them from their customers. Farmers brought in wax, tallow, furs, skins, and minerals and received brandies, flour, and other goods in return. According to Duden, Missouri farmers tried to produce as many of their necessities as possible themselves—this was the "ambition of every farmer"—so no money had to be spent on basic foodstuffs. He wrote that American farmers "spend their cash with a much easier mind for luxury articles, for things of one's fancy." Such luxury items, as well as manufactured goods, could only be obtained from one source—merchants. The desire for mercantile goods—and their long-standing commercial orientation—drove farmers to try and earn as much store credit or cash as possible. He also noted the interest in commercial activity of local farmers, writing that "some farmers, for instance, use the hours of bad weather for making shoes, for building barrels, and for making other implements. All of this is then transmitted to a storekeeper for sale."[2]

Americans who migrated west after the Revolutionary War carried with them a general acceptance of the market economy and the opportunities that commercial participation provided. There was little resistance to the market in rural central Missouri, as immigrants to this region usually came in pursuit of personal economic advantage, and they normally seized any chance to improve their living standards through selling or bartering farm goods for items they could not or chose not to make themselves. But such activity was not immediately possible, and newcomers had to focus their early efforts on carving a farm from the wilderness. In this initial phase of pioneer agriculture, families depended on hunting and gathering, corn, pork, and garden vegetables to feed themselves. They also relied on neighborhood exchange networks to meet labor, food, and other needs. Settlers quickly looked to barter or sell a portion of their production for access to goods they could not produce themselves, such as sugar, coffee, or gunpowder, to earn money to buy more land. Here they began the transformation to what historian Richard Bushman has called "composite" farming, where families produced goods for household use, market sale, and neighborhood exchange. Downriver transport, small towns, peddlers, and occasional general stores eased the shift toward market production, but the difficulties of importing goods against the Missouri River's currents limited economic activity. Geography interfered with the chance for more market involvement, but steam power opened central Missouri to increased market penetration. In the 1830s merchants began to export and import goods in large amounts with the assistance of steamboats, which could easily move upriver. The region became increasingly tied to the larger economy, and residents could express their pent-up desires for mass-produced staple foods and goods. Households produced more goods (such as corn, hemp, and pork) for credit at local stores and purchased more luxury goods, as well as many items they had initially made at home, such as soap and candles. The region never became as commercialized as the Northeast—most families remained involved in composite farming throughout the late antebellum period—and most white residents did not face the challenges to household independence, such as wage labor, serious land scarcity, and the curtailment of neighborhood credit, that existed in more economically developed states such as Massachusetts.[3]

American immigrants had been transforming central Missouri since the late eighteenth century, importing an individualistic, market-oriented worldview that replaced the communal attitudes of earlier Native American and European residents. Missouri was a borderland between European and native peoples, where British, Spanish, French, Osage, and Americans competed for influence. The initial European settlers exploited a fertile landscape, seeking wealth from agriculture and trade until Americans overwhelmed them in the early 1800s. When the first French settlers had arrived at the start of the eighteenth century, they brought with them a medieval agricultural system that emphasized cooperative farming. French farmers exercised little personal initiative and shared common farmlands with others. The Native American tribes of the region, such as the Osage, practiced agriculture and hunting that mirrored the communal structure of French farmers. A limited population and overwhelmingly subsistence farming produced only a small surplus for export and discouraged commercial production. Thus, the region was virtually undeveloped at the start of the nineteenth century. But beginning in the 1790s, immigrants from the United States—from both the North and the South—brought commercial values that were at odds with European and Indian agricultural ideologies. American farmers rejected the communal farming practices of the earlier inhabitants of the region and established independent and separate farms, free from outside regulations or limits. They pursued their own economic goals, and their ambition to make money led to rapid economic development, as sawmills, mines, salt production, livestock herding, artisan activity, and thousands of new farms began to transform the countryside. By 1820, more than fifty thousand Americans lived in Missouri. These immigrants changed the economic structure of the region and laid a foundation for the evolution of a commercial world where one had not existed before.[4]

Most immigrants came from the South, but their commercial motivations differed little from those of northerners. Antebellum Missouri contained a small number of plantations, and most farmers produced a large variety of goods for household and market consumption. Significant amounts were produced for commercial sale, including corn, tobacco, wheat, and hemp. Only about 10 percent of Missourians owned slaves by 1860—one of the smallest percentages in the South—and most families had fewer than 10 slaves. A large majority of the slave-owning families sold sizeable amounts of tobacco and hemp, which earned farmers cash to purchase goods from merchants, buy land or slaves, or educate their children. Immigrants from the upper South, such as Kentucky, shared this commercial outlook, and the question for them was not whether to participate in commerce, but how to take part. Southerners, like their brethren from colder climates, looked to improve their lives through market activity.[5]

Farmers in the Mississippi River Valley preferred to live near rivers, because waterways provided access to markets and the land was more fertile. Settlement usually followed a narrow economic geography decided by these two main factors. Those who lived near transportation routes with the most productive land enjoyed the greatest opportunities to participate in commerce. Others, without the ability to buy more expensive land with market access or who chose to live in areas away from more developed regions, were less able to take part in the expanding economy. Methodist minister Jacob Lanius found a clear division between the primitive frontier life of the remote southern sections of the state and the more developed regions near the Missouri River. He called the life of a frontier settler "not enviable." Lanius wrote in his diary about his travels during the 1830s, noting that one old man lacked furniture or utensils and ground his coffee beans in a mortar. Near Springfield, in the southwest corner of the state, he recorded that "the country at present is in a very bad state of cultivation and improvement. People mostly live in log huts, with small farms and plenty of stock, such as horses, cattle and children." He was relieved when he headed north toward the Missouri River, where residents "seemed to live comfortably. Have good farms and good log houses. How changed the aspect since I crossed the Osage River. I feel like I entered the old world again that is the north part of the state."[6]

American farmers in the West began to search for ways to sell surplus produce and purchase non-necessary items soon after immigration and settlement. In the Ohio River Valley, farmers began to market surplus crops by the third year after establishing a farm. In Missouri, families moved equally quickly to produce extra crops for sale or barter. Those who lived near rivers found it easier to find a market for their produce. Initial commerce often involved selling farm products to new immigrants who arrived with some cash to buy their food, seeds, or tools to start their own farm. Historian R. Douglas Hurt argued in *Agriculture and Slavery in Missouri's Little Dixie* that farmers in central Missouri moved "as quickly as possible" from subsistence to commercial agriculture, selling tobacco, hemp, livestock, bacon, pork, flax, linen, and cowhides in local towns to earn much-needed cash or merchant credit. Historian Craig T. Friend agreed, writing that most Kentucky farmers "aspired to more than subsistence simplicity" and desired to take part in local and regional markets, which provided "profit and comfort."[7]

As soon as immigrants had surged over the Appalachian Mountains in the late eighteenth century, they had pursued commercial opportunity, often using rivers as a way to reach markets. The Harvard-educated Presbyterian minister Timothy Flint wrote that the Ohio and Mississippi rivers contained scores of boats full of Americans selling farm produce from Kentucky to Illinois to Missouri. "The products and ingenuity and agriculture of the whole upper country of the west" were for sale. Boats had arrived from regions thousands of miles apart, he noted with some exaggeration; sometimes a collection of these vessels covered "some acres." He wrote that boats loaded with planks from southwest New York mixed with "Yankee notions from Ohio" and that pork, flour, whiskey, hemp, bagging, and tobacco could be found in Kentucky boats. Cattle and horses were for sale from Illinois, and furs and lead were exported from Missouri. Some boats, he recalled, were loaded with bulk ears of corn or turkeys "that gobble most furiously," while others had barrels of apples and potatoes or cider or dried fruits. "Every kind of spirit manufactured in these regions" was sold onboard as well.[8]

The American drive to make money was shown by the great variety of goods and services for sale on these waterborne crafts. Some boats operated as floating mercantile shops; others were the equivalent of a floating dram shop, or pub. While traveling on the Mississippi River he found that more than one hundred boats had landed in New Madrid, a small river town in southeast Missouri. He watched a "tinner's establishment" float by, where various metal articles were manufactured and sold. Another vessel, a blacksmith's shop, manufactured axes, scythes, and other iron tools and even shod horses. There also was a dry goods shop on a boat. Indeed, he declared, every spring brought forth "new contrivances of this sort, the result of the farmer's meditations over his winter's fire." Missourian Thomas Beckwith also noted the commercial orientation of western residents. He recalled that farmers in western Kentucky had loaded boats with corn, hogs, cattle, lumber, or "whatever they had for sale." Other flatboats sold "every thing you could buy in a store," including wagons, plows, ropes, bells, silk, sugar, coffee, and molasses. These floating merchants tied up their boats near a town or village and remained for a few days until the residents were supplied with the goods they wanted. Then, the small ship would head downriver to another neighborhood.[9]

Merchants moved west with their customers, crossing over the Appalachian Mountains and settling across the Old Northwest and the South in the late eighteenth century and early nineteenth century. As Americans surged westward and pioneers became farmers and focused on selling some surplus goods, itinerant peddlers and roving merchants helped meet their demand for material goods. The importance of floating stores has been detailed above, but itinerant peddlers and mobile merchants served an important purpose in antebellum America. These businessmen were often the only source of merchandise for frontier settlers until populations became large enough to justify permanent stores.[10]

"Yankee traders" served the less populated western areas, such as Illinois or Missouri, in the first decades of the nineteenth century, and moved by boat or by wagon, taking merchandise that they sold to residents from their transient stores. These peddlers sold basic goods such as corn, textiles, whiskey, flour, and chickens, as well as brooms, cider, coffee pots, clocks, almanacs, plows, hats, rope, and even furniture to a dispersed population with few towns. Like river traders, they stayed in a neighborhood until they disposed of their goods or moved on to better markets. They visited inns or county courthouses on court days in search of customers. A number of peddlers would then provide a wider variety of goods to local residents who came into town. One such peddler, Jared Warner, who later established his own store in Wisconsin, traveled more than one thousand miles in the summer of 1834 in Ohio, Indiana, and Illinois. The famed naturalist John James Audubon was a partner in a store in Kentucky until financial problems pushed him west. Audubon and his partner loaded their merchandise onto a boat and set off down the Ohio River, eventually selling their goods and making a profit in Ste. Genevieve, Missouri, a town with a pent-up demand for merchandise and low supplies. Some permanent merchants began their careers as peddlers but accumulated enough capital through hard work and thrift to open up their own businesses. Westward migration and the increase in population provided new opportunities for merchants and traders, who flocked west in the wake of post–War of 1812 settlement.[11]

Americans came to central Missouri seeking fertile land that would allow them to achieve economic independence, a higher standard of living, and a better quality of life. Although frontier settlers were limited to the pioneer stage of agriculture for the first few years of settlement, most quickly produced surplus goods for market sale when possible. Some families chose to remain relatively isolated, finding security in creating a mostly subsistence life from the fertile countryside. However, few farmers preferred the spartan and primitive life of the rude pioneer, where dirt floors, drafty cabins, backbreaking work, and a monotonous diet dominated their lives. This initial phase of agriculture was a difficult period of transition for new immigrants. Farmers in central Missouri, according to historian R. Douglas Hurt, did not see subsistence farming as particularly noble. Fortunately for settlers in the region, a ready-made highway already existed that allowed them to take advantage of commercial opportunities. Without inexpensive and easy access to markets downriver, farmers in Missouri would have remained on the fringes of the American economy. Farm families welcomed the chance to buy glass windows, iron stoves, utensils, tools, and clothing that allowed them to enjoy a higher standard of living, and most chose market involvement whenever possible.[12]

The Missouri River played a key role in the state named after it and operated as a "major highway for the state." The river opened the region to settlement and to commercial development, as well as to the export of farm goods and the immigration of settlers. Missouri's rivers flowed through eight million acres of fertile land, about twenty percent of the entire state. The vast inland interior of the United States was particularly dependent upon river transportation, and few Midwestern farmers lived more than twenty miles from a river. This was fortunate, for roads in the antebellum United States were terrible. Most roads barely deserved the name, as mud holes, stumps, and stones made transport hazardous; when wet, they became rutted and swampy. Frontier communities simply lacked the resources or the labor to build a decent transportation infrastructure, and roads were built to serve local needs. Even late in the antebellum period, travel by road was challenging. Lisbon Basye, who traveled to the lead mines of southwest Missouri in the spring of 1852, usually only made about ten miles a day by road. Only good weather, occasional "solid roads," or good luck allowed him to travel faster than this.[13]

Until the advent of the steamboat, commerce flowed almost entirely in one direction—south. The cost for upstream freight was five times the downstream cost, and it took four or five times as long to make the upstream trip. Therefore, because of such difficulties, most of the trans-Appalachian west had limited access to the imported merchandise and manufactured goods that areas with easy transportation links did. The vast majority of all river commerce flowed downstream before 1820, and traffic upstream was very limited, with only a few keelboats and about twenty barges making the trip each year. But this one-way market system began to come to an end in 1817, when the first steamboats began to make their way up and down the river highways of the West.[14]

Between 1815 and 1860, the United States experienced a transportation revolution that made the transition to a market economy possible. Central Missouri benefited most from water transport, as few railroads penetrated the state until the 1850s. Steamboats replaced primitive roads and one-way river shipping, providing inexpensive long-distance transport. The transportation revolution changed the trans-Appalachian west from an isolated frontier region into a thriving commercial area that exchanged agricultural produce for eastern manufactured goods. Improved transportation integrated western states into the growing northeastern market economy and fostered the growth of a national economy. It tied disparate regions together and allowed the easy exchange of products, helping the United States develop a vast, self-sustaining domestic economy. An example of this integration occurred in southern Wisconsin in 1838 when lumber harvested in New York State was used to build a new home. The wood was cut in Pittsburgh sawmills and then transported by steamboat to the Wisconsin Territory, astonishing settlers.[15]

The rapid and inexpensive transportation provided by steamboats in the West dramatically reduced travel time. The first steamboat docked in St. Louis on August 2, 1817, and by 1819 there were thirty-one in the West, mainly running between Louisville and New Orleans. Steamboat operations began on the Missouri River in 1819 when the *Independence* reached the towns of Franklin and Chariton, 250 miles above St. Louis, and brought flour, whiskey, sugar, and iron. There was no regular steamboat service on the Missouri River until 1829, but ships made it upriver occasionally. In 1821, it took ten days to travel by land from St. Louis to Franklin; steamboats cut this time by 80 to 90 percent a decade later. By the mid-1830s, steam power had linked the towns and rural regions in central Missouri to the larger American economy; port towns such as Jefferson City, Franklin, and Boonville became thriving commerce centers for their agricultural hinterlands. According to historian Louis Hunter, the fast and cheap transportation provided by steamboats, which carried eastern merchandise and manufactured goods north and returned south with the agricultural products of western states, brought about the "economic emancipation" of the whole region. Steam navigation began to tie the nation together after the War of 1812 and caused a revolution in the standard of living in western states.[16]

The inexpensive transport provided by steamboats helped transform the Mississippi River Valley from a primitive frontier society into a bustling commercial region. Upriver freight costs were greatly reduced, and the cost to move goods fell by up to 90 percent between the War of 1812 and the 1830s. The cost of manufactured items, as well as that of sugar, coffee, glass, and other products, fell drastically. Prices for sugar, coffee, salt, and other goods fell from 50 to 75 percent in the West. Lower costs and increased supplies of such items gave Missouri residents access to material goods that improved their standard of living. Steamboat transportation also reduced serious price differences between St. Louis and other cities. Large quantities of merchandise at competitive prices were chiefly available in St. Louis and upriver in Missouri, according to historian James Neal Primm, because of the reduced transport cost. In 1842, twenty-six steamboats worked on the Missouri, accelerating the import and export of goods and western migrants. This number swelled to fifty-eight by 1849, when the California Gold Rush brought tens of thousands of migrants to the transcontinental trailheads in western Missouri and Iowa.[17]

As the regional economy expanded, St. Louis became a major collection point for agricultural produce. The city accepted pork, bacon, tobacco, whiskey, hemp, flax, beef, and corn from Missouri, as well as farm goods and iron from Illinois and the upper Mississippi River Valley, for down-river shipment. Steamboats gave Missouri farmers an advantage over their Ohio Valley rivals because the Missouri River and its tributaries were navigable even at lower water stages. Furthermore, the Missouri was also less likely than the Ohio River to freeze, and Missouri farmers were hundreds of miles closer to New Orleans than those along the Ohio. St. Louis became part of a waterborne transportation network that reached from the east coast and New Orleans to Pittsburgh and Cincinnati. The booming agricultural business pushed the fur trade into secondary status as the export of farm goods and the import of retail and manufactured products brought the expanding national market to central Missouri.[18]

Numerous towns grew along the banks of the Missouri River. It operated as a ready-made highway, and as with today's interstate highways, settlements grew up along its route. Towns from St. Louis to St. Joseph—five hundred miles upstream—were located on the Missouri River because of the easy transportation it provided. St. Louis remained the state's largest city throughout the nineteenth century and served as a link between the smaller towns to the west and New Orleans. Upriver towns exported their surplus products to southern and eastern markets though St. Louis and imported merchandise that was needed in the rapidly expanding central and western portions of the state. The towns, and the services they provided, helped develop their surrounding areas. They were economic and social centers for the settlers and migrants, serving as outfitting or supply stations for the rural areas around them. Beginning in the 1830s, steamboat service replaced the primitive road system and spurred migration, settlement, and commerce.[19]

A town initially arose because it was a river port or a center of trade, had a county seat, contained public institutions like a land office, bank, or college, or because it was at the intersection of transportation routes. Towns then grew because of these advantages, which allowed them to outstrip smaller villages in the surrounding countryside. One example of such growth is Franklin, the westernmost town in central Missouri in the 1810s and 1820s. Its location gave it a monopoly on the trade of the quickly populating area. It was the initial seat of Howard County, had a post office, a public land office, a newspaper, and a circuit court, and served as the starting point for the Santa Fe trade in the 1820s. Franklin was therefore able to reap the advantages from this rendezvous of this unique set of favorable circumstances. Its merchants offered a wide variety of services to area farmers and sold items including fine cotton cloth, construction materials, groceries, and household furnishings. Because currency was scarce, farmers bartered salt pork, beef, tallow, beeswax, and tobacco for store goods. Such towns worked—with the aid of profit-seeking local merchants and commercially minded farmers—to send agricultural production downriver to St. Louis and New Orleans via mercantile middlemen or by farmers themselves who floated their farm goods to market. The *Missouri Intelligencer* wrote that Franklin presented to the observer "a busy, bustling, and commercial scene, in buying, selling, and packing goods, practicing mules, &c, &c, all preparatory to the starting of the second spring Caravan to Santa Fe."[20]

Commercial growth such as Franklin's contributed to the economic development of the region. Other towns grew along the river as well, serving the same functions for their small hinterlands as Franklin did for its area. Columbia was established in 1821 and quickly became a trading center for Boone County. Jefferson City became the state capital because of its central location and proximity to the river; it prospered as a commercial center for its area and gained a telegraph line and a stage route by the 1830s. The town of Independence was founded in 1826 and became a major center for western trade and emigration. Like other towns, it had a variety of businesses that served disparate groups, from overland migrants to fur trappers. Independence became the jumping-off point for the Santa Fe trade in the 1830s, once steamboats were able to carry merchants and their outfits upriver and farther west.[21]

The Santa Fe trade and overland emigration contributed significantly to the growth of towns such as Independence. In his classic account of the southwestern trade, *The Commerce of the Prairies*, Josiah Gregg wrote that Independence was "a place of much bustle and active business." Rocky Mountain traders, trappers, emigrants, and merchants bought supplies or outfitted themselves in the town. Gregg wrote that he purchased flour, bacon, coffee, sugar, beans, and crackers in the town before he headed for Santa Fe in 1830. Merchants usually also bought other provisions as well as mules, oxen, and wagons before departing. Later, in the 1840s, Independence became a starting point for the Oregon and California trails. Historian Francis Parkman detailed his 1846 trip to the Northwest in his book *The Oregon Trail*. He wrote that the hotels were crowded and that the gunsmiths and saddlers were "constantly at work providing equipment" for departing migrants. Almost every day, he noted, "steamboats were leaving the levee and passing up the Missouri, crowded with passengers on their way to the frontier." The upper decks of vessels were filled with large wagons for the Santa Fe trade, while their holds were crammed with merchandise for sale. More than one thousand emigrants camped out near Independence. "A multitude of shops had sprung up to furnish the emigrants and Santa Fe traders with necessaries for their journey; and there was an incessant hammering and banging from a dozen blacksmith's sheds, where heavy wagons were being repaired and horses and oxen shod."[22]

The string of towns that dotted the counties along the Missouri River served as commercial centers for the inhabitants of central Missouri. Rural farmers brought their produce in for sale or barter and received needed—or desired—merchandise in return. Agricultural goods were sold to those that wanted them, facilitated by local merchants, while goods that were not in local demand were sold downriver to St. Louis or New Orleans. Emigration to Missouri—as well as migration westward through the state—helped create a home market that encouraged the production of surplus crops for sale. In 1849, an agricultural journal reported that overland emigrants bound for California had purchased most of the extra mules and oxen in the state of Missouri.[23]

The great engine of growth in the North and the West was the creation of a self-sustaining domestic market, which was largely based on population growth and migration that spurred economic development. Immigration into any region, such as central Missouri, transformed it, led to the creation of towns, and laid the foundation for economic activity. The migration of thousands of people not only expanded the national market but also created a local market that extended into new territory and brought new farmland and resources into use. Composite agriculture was built on trade routes and market access, and increased population helped overcome the problem of undeveloped markets weakened by a lack of customers or producers. A dispersed population separated by long distances increased the costs of moving goods and doing business. Limited settlement prohibited the construction of the infrastructure that encouraged commercial activity. Immigration and increasing populations allowed for the creation of a social and economic system that promoted commercial agriculture. Roads, bridges, ferries, and boat landings helped farmers export their products, while mills, inns, stores, warehouses, and artisans encouraged trade, settlement, and economic activity. Missouri grew quickly and benefited from such economic development. The state's population steadily increased at a rate about seven times the national average, from about 66,000 in 1820 to nearly 1.2 million inhabitants by the time of the Civil War. Migrants who were part of this population increase contributed to a growing demand for food during their first several years of farming. Newcomers then demanded manufactured goods and luxuries to improve their standards of living in their new homes, driving the region's economy through their production and consumption.[24]

The famous Santa Fe trade began by accident in 1821, when William Becknell, a Missouri trader from the town of Franklin, reached the New Mexico capital with a small group of men. The severe depression that followed the Panic of 1819 in the United States had caused a serious shortage of hard currency, which limited economic activity. Farmers were unable to sell their surplus agricultural goods, and many could not earn the cash to pay their mortgages. Farmers, merchants, and traders—like William Becknell—went in search of markets. Becknell had headed west into Indian country, hoping to sell the goods he carried, which included clothing, tools, kitchen utensils, and household goods. He and his party of five men intended to trade their merchandise for horses and mules and to hunt bison and other animals on the Plains. Becknell and his men encountered a detachment of Mexican soldiers, who informed them that they would be welcomed in Santa Fe. The company quickly crossed to the city, sold their goods in November at a high profit, and returned home with news of their great success.[25]

The news of Becknell's good fortune spread quickly and encouraged further such activity. Josiah Gregg, whose father was a member of Becknell's second expedition to Santa Fe, noted that "the favorable reports brought by the enterprising Captain [Becknell] stimulated others to embark in trade." In May 1822, Becknell's second caravan left for Santa Fe with twenty-one men and three wagons. Other parties left as well, and Gregg estimated that one caravan of fifteen men left Franklin with $4,000 to $5,000 in merchandise. (Caravans left from Franklin until shifting west to depart from Independence in the 1830s.) Early merchants may have earned profits of 100 percent, and in 1824 a caravan of about eighty Americans earned $180,000 in the trade. After the second year of successful trading in 1823, the *Missouri Intelligencer* wrote that it was "gratifying to learn that these enterprising adventurers have made a profitable trip." The traders returned with more than four hundred mules, a "quantity of beaver," and a "considerable" amount of silver, in exchange for the merchandise they had taken across the Plains. But the silver coin that was brought back to Missouri was probably most important, for the specie would help to "impart activity" to the depressed Missouri economy.[26]

The Santa Fe trade greatly encouraged the economic development of central Missouri. The import of livestock, furs, and silver provided vital animal power and hard currency for Missouri's cash-starved economy. The trade brought between $100,000 and $200,000 in silver to the state each year, which helped fuel the frontier economy. The export of merchandise from the towns of western Missouri created new business opportunities or supported existing mercantile shops. James Josiah Webb wrote in *Adventures in the Santa Fe Trade, 1844-1847* that he had purchased most of his goods in St. Louis—spending $1,800 for one trip—but had "outfitted" in

Independence. Here he had spent $100 for a wagon, $112 for oxen, and $100 on other goods. He claimed to have made a 45 percent profit on his trip. No one firm dominated the trade, and many small merchants took part on a semi-regular basis. These traders purchased large quantities of merchandise for their expeditions, and their expenditures contributed significantly to the economy of central Missouri. In 1828, merchants transported $100,000 in goods to Santa Fe; in 1831 they took $250,000 worth to New Mexico. Six years later this amount had doubled, to about $500,000 in merchandise that was bought in Missouri for sale in Santa Fe. Traders brought back to Missouri more than $100,000 a year in hard currency in the 1830s. American merchants in Missouri were so intent upon making money from the Santa Fe trade, reported the *Missouri Intelligencer* in 1831, that medicines sent to New Mexico had directions written in Spanish and were packed in cases solely for export to the southwest. This brisk and widespread business activity, argued historian Dorothy Dorsey, "transformed the region of central Missouri into a veritable hive of industry."[27]

Merchants served an important function for frontier society, serving as middlemen between farmers and wholesalers. They helped rural farmers and settlers market their extra farm production and allowed farmers, in return, to purchase goods that improved their quality of life. Markets created opportunity for farmers, who willingly produced cider and shoes, picked cherries, or hauled firewood in the quest for profit. Midwestern merchants worked as midwives to capitalism, helping bring the market economy to the rural population. They helped "liberate" Western residents from the primitive living conditions of early settlements, argued historian Lewis Atherton. Once a store opened up in their community, farm families and their neighbors no longer had to produce most of the food, clothing, and other items they needed to survive on their own. Storekeepers allowed farmers to escape from the spartan and subsistence stage of initial settlement by marketing agricultural produce. Dewitt Clinton Basey, who lived in the small town of Brunswick on the north bank of the Missouri River, wrote that he could pay off his store debts with bear skins, honey, or beeswax. These items operated as "legal tender" and "you could pay debts with them if you had no money."[28]

By offering credit in exchange for farm goods, merchants allowed the development of a commercial economy in regions where banks or currency were absent or rare. They opened markets for farm crops and accelerated the commercial development of areas from Kentucky to Missouri to Mississippi. Storekeepers helped the western nineteenth-century economy operate because they had access to capital and credit. They transferred western farm goods to eastern markets and in return provided raw materials to artisans and manufactured goods to farmers. Merchants facilitated the flow of agricultural production and finished goods between east and west and helped create a riverine economy along the Missouri River. Furthermore, they promoted rural consumerism by providing the residents of central Missouri with the chance to barter or sell farm goods. This seemingly primitive mercantile system of barter facilitated trade and economic development and helped farmers improve their standard of living. Merchants provided settlers with access to the material goods required for a reasonable comfort level. Farmers desired not only necessities such as tools, spices, and cloth, but items they decided to buy from a store instead of making at home, such as brooms, chairs, utensils, candles, and plates. They also purchased luxuries such as china, gloves, clocks, chocolate, carpets, window glass, and inkstands. Expanded opportunities for commerce allowed residents to improve their economic status. Sarah R. Barnes recalled that her parents sold chickens and surplus crops to stores in St. Louis, crossing the Missouri River in a boat to reach the city. She proudly noted that her parents quickly improved their economic position by taking part in commerce. Her parents earned money to purchase mass-produced food and clothing and were able to buy a large farm and build "a good house and a large barn."[29]

Settlers in central Missouri sold their agricultural products to market towns whenever possible. Often, though, they lived in an area that was not close to a town or did not enjoy easy transportation. In these situations, farmers usually sent their surplus produce to the closest town on an irregular basis, after harvests or after a significant amount of locally produced goods—such as chickens, honey, furs, eggs, or corn—built up. Towns like Franklin, Liberty, or Independence served as trade centers for commercially minded rural farmers, as well as for merchants and Santa Fe traders. They were centers for exchange, encouraged farmers to produce and sell extra crops, and allowed them to benefit materially from their market activity.[30]

In Harrison County in northwestern Missouri, frontier residents took advantage of the opportunity to improve their standards of living by selling farm produce in the nearest market center. In the late 1830s and 1840s, early settlers supplied themselves with most of the farm goods they needed, as farmers away from the river were far removed from the commercial economy farther downstream. Staple foods for these pioneers included cornbread, potatoes, vegetables, and home-produced eggs, milk, and butter. The closest town was Liberty, eighty miles to the southeast. Farmers gathered their surplus crops, loaded up a wagon, and chose someone to make the weeklong round trip. This individual then bartered all the produce for the best possible price. These frontier farmers most wanted tea, coffee, salt, cloth, and dye; they sent honey, beeswax, and raccoon and mink skins in exchange. When the driver returned, the farmers divided their goods and any money left over. However, once the town of St. Joseph was established in 1843, it became much more attractive as a market center, as it was only about fifty miles away. Farmers took their surplus produce there until merchants set up shop in the local town of Betheny. Then, farmers were able to market their crops directly to a nearby merchant. Other stores were also set up in smaller towns in the county. The barter trade in honey and animal skins rapidly faded and farmers began to sell the products of their own labors, rather than those gained from the land around them, to local merchants. Families sold butter, eggs, chickens, ham, bacon, and cattle to merchants and purchased tea, coffee, sugar, molasses, flour, salt, and candles.[31]

Women took an active role in this growing commerce, producing farm goods for sale or credit at local general stores. Sally Dodge Morris, a farm wife in western Missouri, made coats, pants, and vests and gathered honey and nuts to earn mercantile credit to buy corn, pork, potatoes, and beans for her family. Elise Dubach Isley helped her family earn credit and cash by selling field crops, butter, cheese, eggs, and timber in nearby St. Joseph. She was responsible not only for making butter and cheese and caring for chickens, but for also transporting farm goods to town for sale. James Williams recalled taking his mother's produce and chickens to nearby towns for sale, as well. Pauline Stratton, who lived in Cooper County with her family and their slaves, was responsible for directing the production and sale of farm goods that brought in much-needed cash and store credit for her family in the 1850s. She regularly sold eggs, chickens, and butter to merchants in nearby towns, as well as to the occasional traveler or party heading west. In 1856 she sent 24½ dozen eggs and 99 pounds of butter to local stores, earning more than $22. Stratton purchased a set of plates, six tumblers, a set of cups, a pitcher, and a saucer with these earnings. In April 1859 she sold 3 pounds of butter and 4 dozen eggs to cattle drovers heading for California; Stratton also sold 100 chickens and turkey eggs that month as well. These sales earned her family almost $10 in one month. After the Civil War broke out she sold apples, beef, and butter to Union troops. These women and thousands of other farm women played a significant role in the family economy, and their market production helped their families improve their lives by providing access to desired items at local stores.[32]

Mercantile records show that a wide variety of necessities and luxury goods were available for rural Missouri residents. Most of these items could be classified into seven different categories: fabrics, food and drink, hardware, clothes and accessories, household goods, personal items, and miscellaneous. Sugar, spices, alcoholic drinks, and meat were always in demand, as they were necessary frontier goods. While most clothes were made at home, often with fabric acquired from stores, items that were more difficult to make, such as shoes, boots, gloves, and hats, were often bought from stores. Manufactured household goods, such as pots, pans, bowls, utensils, and dishes, were also usually purchased from merchants when possible. Hardware included merchandise used in construction, agriculture, and hunting and comprised goods ranging from nails, shot, and iron to hoes, bridles, and spurs. Personal items consisted of razors, combs, paper, glasses, handkerchiefs, and tobacco products. Most of these things were available in rural central Missouri, depending on location. Some necessities and staples, such as sugar, nails, or shoes, could be bought from merchants in the 1820s and 1830s, while luxury items, such as combs, pitchers, and mass-produced clothing and personal items appeared in large amounts in account books near the end of the antebellum period. Two examples of mercantile businesses illustrate the importance of storekeepers in the spread of commerce in the region.[33]

In 1828, twenty-one-year-old Moses Payne started a general store in Columbia in partnership with his brothers. They opened up the firm J.U. Payne & Brothers just as regular steamboat travel began to tie central Missouri to eastern states and when the town was near the starting point of the Santa Fe trade in the late 1820s. Their firm opened in June 1828 with goods brought west from Kentucky and purchased from a merchant in Versailles, Missouri. The store prospered and at the end of their first year of operation had sales of $17,202.47. Only about 40 percent of these sales were in cash, with the remainder on credit or via barter. In their second year, the Paynes had $46,361.80 in sales, with about a quarter of this amount paid in cash. In 1831 Jacob Payne opened a second store in Fulton with his brother-in-law. He wrote to Moses on December 20, 1831, that store sales were "tolerable," ranging from $50 to $75 a day. The brothers also opened up a store in Rocheport farther west, as the state's population grew and expanded upriver. Moses seems to have been especially attentive to customers: O. Williams wrote to him in July 1832 and requested that he pick up a bill of goods and fill it while on his mid-year trip east to buy goods. Another customer, George W. Ferguson in Rocheport, wrote to Moses to ask him to buy more sole leather for the neighborhood. But Payne did not just work to make his customers happy. He also had to ensure that store goods purchased from wholesalers in New York or Philadelphia made it to Missouri. When shortages of certain items arose, such as blankets, coffee, shoes, and sugar, he also had to buy goods from fellow retailers in St. Louis at higher prices than he would have preferred.[34]

Like all western merchants, the Payne family stores carried a wide variety of items and took payment in a number of ways. They stocked a surprising variety of drugs, including Epsom salts, castor oil, quinine, calomel, sedatives, and even opium. They accepted both cash and bartered goods in payment, as western merchants had to. Customers sometimes used locally made artisan goods to pay their accounts. A shoemaker paid his debts with shoes, a tanner paid with leather, and a hatmaker with hats. A local tinner received $8.50 in credit for six tin buckets and eight coffee pots he made. Often these artisans paid their accounts with finished goods like shoes, gloves, or hats made from raw materials purchased from the Paynes. Moses Payne and his brothers also accepted bacon, pork, furs, skins, hemp, and whiskey in barter for store goods. Whiskey sold better than any other liquor, such as wine, gin, or rum, and was usually in demand in western stores. Whiskey earned thirty cents credit per gallon and was sold back to customers for fifty cents a gallon. Cotton was credited at eight cents a pound and homemade soap at six cents a pound. Records from 1842 and 1843 from another merchant family in central Missouri, the Aulls, show that they took wheat, bacon, hemp, hides, flaxseed, and lard in payment from their customers. Wheat was the most popular crop, with $3,180.59 accepted in these two years, followed by hemp with $1,245.62 in sales, bacon with $994.12, flaxseed with $650.86, lard with $202.69, and hides with $18.45. Most of the wheat—60 percent—was taken for credit or payment during harvest season, from mid-September to November. Such surplus agricultural production was collected by the Aulls and sent to St. Louis and New Orleans for sale.[35]

Like the Paynes, James and Robert Aull migrated west to central Missouri to seek their fortunes. They moved to Lexington, Missouri, in 1825 and opened a retail store. Two years later James established a store in Independence; a year after this, Robert and a partner started another mercantile store in Liberty. In 1830, James opened up a final store in Richmond, Missouri. The brothers and their partners also invested in steamboats, saw and grist mills, and in the Santa Fe trade. Their booming business made them, along with the Payne brothers, well known and wealthy in the region. The Aulls stocked their store in part with local goods bartered by customers and then resold, such as whiskey, salt, beans, tobacco, and vinegar. They also imported hundreds of varied items from eastern wholesalers each year. One 1833 inventory showed six different kinds of blankets for sale, including blue, green, heavy, rose, and broad-striped varieties in one store. They also had mugs, tea pots, cups, and seven different types of plates. Robes, ostrich feathers, silk gloves, trunks, cotton candy, wine, and a bewildering number of different medicines were also available. They exported tobacco, beeswax, furs, honey, hemp rope, and pork to New Orleans, though they only sent four hogsheads of tobacco south in 1828. The Aulls did export sixty thousand to seventy thousand hemp and bale ropes each year, manufacturing them in a small rope-making factory they owned. They also sold foodstuffs to the government for Indian supply or to troops at Fort Leavenworth. Their customers, like those of the Paynes, rarely paid in cash. Customers often paid with barrels of whiskey, beeswax, tallow, sugar, or homespun linen. The Aulls also allowed customers to pay their bills through labor, which included cutting brush for the business.[36]

Customers in the Aull family's Lexington store in the autumn of 1839 purchased basic necessities far more than other items. Salt, sugar, and coffee were popular, as were shoes, hats, and suspenders. Nails, gunpowder, knives, buttons, and fabrics such as calico and linen were also bought on a regular basis. Items that were rare, only appearing once or twice out of nearly one thousand items, were an ink and quill, nutmeg, a spade, a pitcher, and lace. A typical entry, from June 27, listed the sale of twenty-six pounds of flour, a pound of powder, and four combs. Cash payments for store goods were rare and a large majority of transactions were through barter and credit. Up until the late antebellum period, customers rarely bought from the Lexington store many items that could be made or grown at home, including soap, whiskey, candles, butter, tobacco, clothing, and food products. These things seem to have still been produced at home by farm families, who used surplus farm goods for necessities or for the occasional luxury item.[37]

However, entries in the 1854 Lexington store accounts show that local residents were purchasing many more luxury items than had been the case fifteen years before. Customers were making fewer products at home and buying more goods of all types from stores. This consumer shift helps to demonstrate that residents in central Missouri became increasingly involved in the region's market economy. Whiskey, candles, potatoes, brandy, butter, tobacco, maple syrup, rice, combs, and ham appeared as purchases on a regular basis. Necessities such as coffee, sugar, boots, nails, shoes, and gunpowder continued to appear throughout the sample. New and more numerous luxury items, such as table covers, flannel, silk, cups, tea, and paper, also showed up regularly. An average transaction could be for six pounds of Havana coffee (September 14), a pair of shoes (September 30), or for ten pounds of tobacco, two pounds of soda, a flask and whiskey (September 16). Cash payments had increased only slightly since 1839, and these accounted for about 15 percent of overall business. The region operated with about the same limited supply of cash as it had before. Thus, non-cash transactions continued to make up a substantial majority of all transactions throughout the antebellum period.[38]

Merchants such as the Aull and Payne families provided residents in central Missouri with access to mass-produced and manufactured goods made outside the region and helped tie it to the expanding national economy. Customers avidly bought items of all sorts from general stores, paying for their bills with bartered goods, on credit, or through personal labor or even artisan goods. Residents' buying habits changed over time, as the transportation revolution and increasing market development allowed households to participate in the market economy more often. Farm families purchased nonessential and luxury goods in far greater amounts in the 1850s than before. They also produced fewer of the things at home—butter, pork, tobacco, and whiskey—than they had in the 1830s. Thus, farmers chose to produce more for commercial use and less for home consumption. Merchants took farm products in payment for consumer goods and exported them to St. Louis or New Orleans. In exchange, merchants provided access to a world of goods, often the same items customers had previously made on their own farms. This transformation in consumption is evidence for the increasing commercialization of central Missouri in the 1840s and 1850s. This new market behavior contrasts starkly with the more primitive agricultural system that existed before steam transport tied the region to the larger national economy. Starting in the 1830s, farm families along the Missouri River chose to become increasingly involved in the growing commercial economy. In doing so, they improved the quality of their lives as they added goods to their households that made their living more comfortable.

NOTES

1. Gottfried Duden, *Report on a Journey to the Western States of North America* (1829; repr., Columbia: University of Missouri Press, 1980), xi–xiii, 52-57, 66-67, 171, 176, 247.

2. Ibid., 256-57.

3. Richard Lyman Bushman, "Markets and Composite Farms in Early America," *William and Mary Quarterly* 55, no. 3 (1998): 351-74; Daniel Vickers, "Competency and Competition: Economic Culture in Early America," *William and Mary Quarterly*, 3rd ser., 47, no. 1 (1990): 4-12; Christopher Clark, *The Roots of Rural Capitalism: Western Massachusetts, 1780-1860* (Ithaca, NY: Cornell University Press, 1990), 13-18, 84-88, 304-10, 318-29; Christopher Morris, *Becoming Southern: The Evolution of a Way of Life, Warren County and Vicksburg, Mississippi, 1770-1860* (New York: Oxford University Press, 1995), xviii, 11-18; William Lass, *Navigating the Missouri River: Steamboating on Nature's Highway, 1819-1935* (Norman, OK: Arthur H. Clark Company, 2008), 71-72, 57. Numerous recent studies have refuted arguments in Charles Sellers, *The Market Revolution: Jacksonian America, 1815-1846* (New York: Oxford University Press, 1991), that such a change occurred in the antebellum period and encountered substantial resistance. See Craig T. Friend, *Along the Maysville Road: The Early American Republic in the Trans-Appalachian West* (Knoxville: University of Tennessee Press, 2005); Winifred Barr Rothenberg, *From Market-Places to a Market Economy: The Transformation of Rural Massachusetts, 1750-1850* (Chicago: University of Chicago Press, 1992); Kim M. Gruenwald, *River of Enterprise: The Commercial Origins of Regional Identity in the Ohio Valley, 1790-1850* (Bloomington: Indiana University Press, 2002); Daniel Walker Howe, *What Hath God Wrought: The Transformation of America, 1815-1848* (New York: Oxford University Press, 2007.)

4. Willard H. Rollings, *The Osage: An Ethnohistorical Survey of Hegemony on the Prairie-Plains* (Columbia: University of Missouri Press, 1992), 1-8, 20; Stephen Aron, *American Confluence: The Missouri Frontier from Borderland to Border State* (Bloomington: University of Indiana Press, 2006), xvi–xvii, 9-13, 41-50, 67, 104-5, 150; Carl J. Ekberg, *Colonial Ste. Genevieve: An Adventure on the Mississippi Frontier* (Gerald, MO: Patrice Press, 1985),

34-44; William E. Foley, *A History of Missouri, 1673-1820* (Columbia: University of Missouri Press, 2000), 16, 59; Nicolas de Finiels, *An Account of Upper Louisiana,* ed. Carl J. Ekberg and William E. Foley (Columbia: University of Missouri Press, 1989), 1-10, 62-70. 76-77; Louis Houck, *A History of Missouri: From the Earliest Explorations and Settlements until the Admission of the State into the Union,* vol. 2 (Chicago: R.R. Donnelley & Sons, 1908), 238, 256-58.

5. Diane Mutti Burke, "On Slavery's Borders: Slavery and Slaveholding on Missouri Farms, 1821-1865" (PhD diss., Emory University, 2004), 4-7, 71-72; Friend, *Along the Maysville Road,* 114-18.

6. Timothy M. Mahoney, *River Towns of the Great West: The Structure of Provincial Urbanization in the American Midwest, 1820-1870* (Cambridge, UK: Cambridge University Press, 1990), 44-49; Friend, *Along the Maysville Road,* 105; Jacob Lanius Diary, July 21 and December 17, 1835, October 13 and December 20, 1838, June 22 and 23, 1839, Western Historical Manuscripts Collection, University of Missouri, Columbia (hereafter cited as WHMC).

7. Gruenwald, *River of Enterprise,* 28; R. Douglas Hurt, *Agriculture and Slavery in Missouri's Little Dixie* (Columbia: University of Missouri Press, 1992), 64-66; Friend, *Along the Maysville Road,* 105, 110-19, 124.

8. Timothy Flint, *Recollections of the Last Ten Years in the Valley of the Mississippi* (1826; repr., Carbondale and Edwardsville: Southern Illinois University Press, 1968), xiv–xvi, xxii, 76-78.

9. Flint, *Recollections of the Last Ten Years,* 78-80; Thomas Beckwith, "Early Customs," n.d., typescript collection no. 995, WHMC.

10. Lewis Atherton, *The Frontier Merchant in Mid-America* (Columbia: University of Missouri Press, 1971), 45-47; Ann Smart Martin, *Buying Into the World of Goods: Early Consumers in Backcountry Virginia* (Baltimore: Johns Hopkins University Press, 2008), 13-14.

11. Atherton, *Frontier Merchant,* 45-48; Charles J. Farmer, *In The Absence of Towns: Settlement and Country Trade in Southside Virginia, 1730-1800* (Lanham, MD: Rowman and Littlefield, 1993), 139-42; Joseph T. Rainer, "The 'Sharper' Image: Yankee Peddlers, Southern Consumers, and the Market Revolution," in *Cultural Change and the Market Revolution in America, 1789-1860,* ed. Scott C. Martin (Lanham, MD: Rowman and Littlefield, 2005), 89-97, 107-108; Martin, *Buying Into the World of Goods,* 45-46.

12. R. Douglas Hurt, "Seeking Fortune in the Promised Land: Settling in the Boon's Lick Country, 1808-1825," *Gateway Heritage* 13, no. 1 (1992): 8-9; Andrew R. L. Cayton and Peter S. Onuf, *The Midwest and the Nation: Rethinking the History of an American Region* (Bloomington: Indiana University Press, 1990), 30-36; James E. Davis, *Frontier Illinois* (Bloomington: Indiana University Press, 1998), 104-5, 171; Lass, *Navigating the Missouri,* 17, 91; Burke, "On Slavery's Borders," 5, 12, 71-72.

13. George Rogers Taylor, *The Transportation Revolution, 1815-1860* (New York: Harper Torchbooks, 1951), 15-16, 56; Stuart F. Voss, "Town Growth in Central Missouri," pt. 3, *Missouri Historical Review* 64, no. 3 (1970): 323; Cayton and Onuf, *The Midwest and the Nation,* 39; Perry McCandless, *A History of Missouri, 1820-1860* (Columbia: University of Missouri Press, 2000), 31, 137-39; Lisbon Basye Diary, March 18, 25, May 31, 1852, State Historical Society of Missouri, Typescript Collection, vol. 1, no. 4, WHMC.

14. Erik F. Haites, James Mak, and Gary M. Walton, *Western River Transportation: The Era of Early Internal Development, 1810-1860* (Baltimore: Johns Hopkins University Press, 1975), 18-20; Donald T. Zimmer, "The Ohio River: Pathway to Settlement," in *Transportation and the Early Nation: Papers Presented at an Indiana American Revolution Bicentennial Symposium* (Indianapolis: Indiana Historical Society, 1982), 64-65, 74; Lass, *Navigating the Missouri,* 88, 91-94.

15. Taylor, *The Transportation Revolution*, 3-9, 29, 32-47, 396-98; Paul Johnson, *The Early American Republic, 1789-1829* (New York: Oxford University Press, 2006), 55-56, 64-67; Mark Wyman, *The Wisconsin Frontier* (Bloomington: University of Indiana Press, 1998), 128-29; McCandless, *History of Missouri*, 145-150; Howe, *What Hath God Wrought*, 220-21.

16. Louis C. Hunter, *Steamboats on Western Rivers: An Economic and Technological History* (New York: Octagon Books, 1969), 13, 21, 38, 47; Zimmer, "The Ohio River," 68; *Missouri Intelligencer*, May 28, 1819, May 7, 1821; Dorothy Dorsey, "The Panic and Depression of 1837-1843 in Missouri," *Missouri Historical Review* 30, no. 2 (1936): 134; David Dary, *The Santa Fe Trail: Its History, Legends, and Lore* (New York: Penguin Books, 2000), 65.

17. Taylor, *Transportation Revolution*, 63-64; Cayton and Onuf, *The Midwest and the Nation*, 36; Haites, Mak, and Walton, *Western River Transportation*, 16-20; James Neal Primm, *Lion of the Valley: St. Louis, Missouri, 1764-1980* (St. Louis: Missouri Historical Society Press, 1998), 134-35; Davis, *Frontier Illinois*, 169-70; Zimmer, "Ohio River," 134; McCandless, *History of Missouri*, 137; Johnson, *The Early American Republic*, 65-66; Christopher Clark, "The Consequences of the Market Revolution in the American North," in *The Market Revolution in America: Social, Political and Religious Expressions*, ed. Melvyn Stokes and Stephen Conway (Charlottesville: University of Virginia Press, 1996), 23-25, 30.

18. Hurt, *Agriculture and Slavery*, 65-66; Primm, *Lion of the Valley*, 134-35; July 21, 1835, Letters of Frederick Steines, WHMC.

19. Stuart F. Voss, "Town Growth in Central Missouri, 1815-1860: An Urban Chaparral," pt. 1, *Missouri Historical Review* 64, no. 1 (1969): 65; McCandless, *History of Missouri*, 131.

20. Voss, "Town Growth in Central Missouri," pt. 3, 323; Voss, "Town Growth in Central Missouri," pt. 1, 65-67, 76-80; Walter A. Schroeder, "The Spread of Settlement in Howard County, Missouri, 1810-1859," *Missouri Historical Review* 63, no. 1 (1968): 15-19; Hurt, "Seeking Fortune in the Promised Land," 9-12; Jonas Viles, "Old Franklin: A Frontier Town of the Twenties," *Mississippi Valley Historical Review* 9, no. 4 (1923): 269-75; *Missouri Intelligencer*, May 2, 1828.

21. Hurt, "Seeking Fortune in the Promised Land," 11; Eldon Hattervig, "Jefferson Landing: A Commercial Center of the Steamboat Era," *Missouri Historical Review* 74, no. 3 (1980): 277-78; Stephen G. Hyslop, *Bound for Santa Fe: The Road to New Mexico and the American Conquest, 1806-1848* (Norman: University of Oklahoma Press, 2002), 109; McCandless, *History of Missouri*, 132.

22. Josiah Gregg, *The Commerce of the Prairies* (1844; repr., Lincoln: University of Nebraska Press, 1967), 20-22; Francis Parkman, *The Oregon Trail* (1849; repr., New York: Library of America/Viking Press, 1991), 9-13.

23. *Niles' Register*, January 2, 1819; Raymond D. Thomas, "Missouri Valley Settlement —St. Louis to Independence," *Missouri Historical Review* 21, no. 1 (1926): 40; "Farming in Missouri, &c," *Cultivator* 4 (1849): 302-3. This journal was published in Albany, New York, and a copy of this article can be found in collection 799, folder 2, WHMC.

24. Johnson, *The Early American Republic*, 67; Davis, *Frontier Illinois*, 104-5, 113, 133-34; Cayton and Onuf, *The Midwest and the Nation*, 29, 42; Malcom J. Rohrbough, *The Trans-Appalachian Frontier: People, Societies, and Institutions, 1775-1850* (Belmont, CA: Wadsworth Publishing, 1990), 76; Ray Allen Billington, *Westward Expansion: A History of the American Frontier* (New York: Macmillian, 1960), 468-69; McCandless, *History of Missouri*, 31-35, 119.

25. Hyslop, *Bound for Santa Fe*, 33-37, 40-43; Lewis E. Atherton, "The Santa Fe Trader as Mercantile Capitalist," *Missouri Historical Review* 77, no. 1 (1982): 3; David J. Weber, *The Mexican Frontier, 1821-1846: The American Southwest under Mexico* (Albuquerque: University of New Mexico Press, 1982), 125, 128-29; McCandless, *History of Missouri*, 128-30.

26. McCandless, *History of Missouri,* 119, 128-31; Hyslop, *Bound for Santa Fe,* 40-50; Gregg, *Commerce of the Prairies,* 6-10; Authorene Wilson Phillips, *Arrow Rock: The Story of a Missouri Village* (Columbia: University of Missouri Press, 2005), 35-40; *Missouri Intelligencer,* October 28, 1823; Dary, *The Santa Fe Trade,* 84-85.

27. James Josiah Webb, *Adventures in the Santa Fe Trade, 1844-1847* (1931; repr., Lincoln: University of Nebraska Press, 1995), 23-28, 42-45, 127-29; McCandless, *History of Missouri,* 128; F. F. Stephens, "Missouri and the Santa Fe Trade," *Missouri Historical Review* 11, no. 3 (1917): 289-312; *Missouri Intelligencer,* April 2, 1831; Dorsey, "The Panic and Depression," 133-35.

28. Lewis E. Atherton, "The Services of the Frontier Merchant," *Missouri Valley Historical Review* 24, no. 2 (1937): 156-63; Gruenwald, *River of Enterprise,* 4; David Blanke, *Sowing the American Dream: How Consumer Culture Took Root in the Rural Midwest* (Athens: Ohio University Press, 2000), 67; Dewitt Clinton Basey, "Early Recollections of Brunswick," n.d., typescript collection no. 995, WHMC.

29. Atherton, " Services of the Frontier Merchant," 156-63; Gruenwald, *River of Enterprise,* xii, 4, 28-31, 42, 100, 117; Blanke, *Sowing the American Dream,* 72; Morris, *Becoming Southern,* 12-15; Martin Bruegel, *Farm, Shop, Landing: The Rise of a Market Society in the Hudson Valley, 1780-1860* (Durham, NC: Duke University Press, 2002), 56, 162; John A. Ramage, *John Wesley Hunt: Pioneer Merchant, Manufacturer, and Financier* (Lexington: University Press of Kentucky, 1974), 21, 29; Jack Larkin, *The Reshaping of Everyday Life, 1790-1840* (New York: Harper and Row, 1988), 130-45; Sarah R. Barnes Papers, WHMC.

30. Schroeder, "Spread of Settlement in Howard County," 15-20; Hurt, "Seeking Fortune in the Promised Land," 9-15.

31. Ethel Grant Inman, "Pioneer Days in Northwest Missouri—Harrison County, 1837-1873" *Missouri Historical Review* 22, no. 3 (1928): 314-15.

32. Sarah J. Gregory, "Pioneer Housewife: The Autobiography of Sally Dodge Morris," *Gateway Heritage* 3, no. 4 (1983): 25-27, 32-33; Elise Dubach Isley, *Sunbonnet Days, by Elise Dubach Isley, as told to her son, Bliss Isley* (Caldwell, ID: Caxton Printers, 1935), 65, 86, 94; Pauline Stratton Diary, February 16, March 10, early June (no exact date), April 10, May 1, October 5, December 24, 1856, April 22, 1859, WHMC; James Williams, *75 Years on the Border* (Kansas City, MO: Press of Standard Printing Company, 1912), 2-5, 59-61.

33. Farmer, *In the Absence of Towns,* 159-67.

34. Mary Alice Kennedy, "The Business Career of Moses U. Payne, 1828-1870" (master's thesis, University of Missouri, Columbia, 1944), 5-16, 22-26, 33-36; collection description for C 983, Payne-Broadwell Family Papers, WHMC; Atherton, *Frontier Merchant,* 146; J. M. and A. M. Payne Day Book, 1830-1831, vols. 3 and 4, Payne-Broadwell Family Papers, WHMC; Jacob Payne to Moses Payne, December 20, 1831, folder 6, Payne-Broadwell Family Papers, WHMC; O. Williams to Moses Payne, July 1832 (exact date illegible), folder 7, Payne-Broadwell Family Papers, WHMC; bill from Jacob Payne to Moses Payne, December 8, 1832, folder 7, Payne-Broadwell Family Papers, WHMC; MacKay Morton to Moses Payne, August 5, 1854, folder 18, Payne-Broadwell Family Papers, WHMC.

35. Kennedy, "Business Career," 32-35, 38-41, 47-50; Aull Family Business Records, vol. 25, WHMC. The mercantile records for the Payne family are fragmentary and the author was unable to find estimates or exact numbers for farm goods used by customers to pay their accounts. Here the Aull Family records are useful.

36. Lewis E. Atherton, "James and Robert Aull—A Frontier Missouri Mercantile Firm," *Missouri Historical Review* 30, no. 1 (1937): 27-28, 31, 40-41, 46-47; Atherton, "Services of the Frontier Merchant," 164; Aull Family Business Records, vol. 4, WHMC. The total value of the inventory was $8,777.74.

37. June 10 to July 10, Daybook of Store, 1839-1840, Aull Family Business Records, vol. 1, WHMC. Also, see Martin, *Buying Into the World of Goods*, 53-56, for parallel activity in Virginia in 1771.

38. September 1 to September 30, 1854, Aull Family Business Records, vol. 7, WHMC.

Chapter 4

"Anything . . . That Would Pay"

Yeoman Farmers and the Nascent Market Economy on the Antebellum Plantation Frontier

Gary T. Edwards

Noting the effects of cold weather during the spring of 1843 and its subsequent delay on the task of seasonal plowing, the southwestern Tennessee planter Howell Taylor observed that his neighbors in Fayette County took this as an opportunity to fret. "The people complain very much of hard times, but it is mostly their fault," he concluded. Taylor's diagnosis reflected his view of a frivolous use of credit, as he indicated that some of his neighbors "have been going into debt year after year as though they thought pay day would never come." However, if the accumulation of capital prevented bankruptcy and the subsequent loss of farming independence, it occasionally symbolized the evil power brokers, according to Jacksonian rhetoric: the monied interests of the banking class. Representative of this view, Andrew Mitchell of Hardeman County, Tennessee, expressed his disdain for those who opposed the principles of Jacksonian Democracy, particularly the national leadership of the Whig Party. Writing in 1838, he fearfully prophesied a Whigish future he hoped would never materialize. "Mr. [Henry] Clay's plan of construing the constitution would soon involve all the working classes in vassalage to capitalists," he warned. Last, indicative of the yeomen's plight, James E. Dickinson of Madison County, Tennessee, recalled that common folk approached America's changing economic environment with a utilitarian attitude. He based his observations on real experiences accumulated on his family's eighty-one-acre farm. "The poor class which was in the majority," Dickinson declared, "all [did] anything they could get to do that would pay." As one might expect, the yeomen may not have been giants of capitalism, but Dickinson suggests they possessed few reservations concerning the use of capital within a context of necessity. All the preceding comments reflect the multifaceted nature of antebellum America's capitalistic economic transition—a market revolution, which frightened some inhabitants, bankrupted others, but challenged virtually all of them.[1]

Throughout the history of the antebellum South, it seems as if small landowning family farmers—the yeomanry—have been the forest that we could not see for the trees. The yeomen were everywhere and nowhere at the same time. Standing in as a backdrop for plantation culture, they offer necessary social context but little personal content. Their very presence complicates facile reductionism about the Old South based solely on a dialectic of power and paternalism (such as with master and slave). Still, our evaluation of them is often reduced to a common sense dialectic based on human striving and thriving. When we assume that we know everything about them because their lives seemingly consisted of a simplistic formula of habitual labor, it is often surprising to discover the dearth of evidence that would confirm our conclusions about such a large class of people. This essay adds to that body of evidence and seeks to modify previous assumptions that antebellum yeomen were fixated on subsistence to the exclusion of any risks. The idea that antebellum yeomen possessed an attitude that embraced subsistence agriculture and rejected the market revolution, instead of balancing between the two, continues to exert some influence. A generation ago Paul Gates bluntly articulated this view in *The Farmer's Age* when he wrote: "the failure of a cotton crop meant disaster to a small farmer." More recently, some scholars suggested that antebellum yeomen viewed self-sufficiency and market participation as antagonistic choices between two ways of life. "To say yes [to the market]," they concluded, "meant that providing food and clothing for the family took second place to the production of a money crop, usually cotton." This interpretive dichotomy between agricultural subsistence and economic risk, although a useful framework, may be too simplistic to appreciate the full range of complexity that defined the family farm during an age of blossoming market capitalism. Yeomen, particularly in the plantation South, grappled with these polarizing economic strategies yet ultimately rested within a balanced area where the contrasting ideologies intersected.[2]

Set in the cotton frontier of western Tennessee, this study brings into focus an imperfectly understood class living in an understudied region. Focused on five rural counties (Fayette, Hardeman, Haywood, Madison, and Tipton), it investigates the heart of antebellum Tennessee's cotton agriculture and enslaved population. It ushers into view an agricultural transformation that occurred in a relatively brief span of time. For instance, during the 1830s the region's most popular citizen, David Crockett, based much of his fame upon his prowess as a hunter of western Tennessee's copious bear population. By the 1850s, if still alive, Crockett would have found his old hunting grounds in northwestern Tennessee unsuitable and the cotton fields of southwestern Tennessee unrecognizable. The sight of thousands of enslaved laborers and the sound of new locomotives transporting tons of cotton toward Memphis signaled the culminating effects of the Jacksonian market revolution. Southwestern Tennessee has been overlooked as a significant case in point of America's distinctive development in the nineteenth century. Its interpretive significance potentially rivals the plantation country of the Carolinas—a locale that has received an abundance of scholarly attention—while offering innovative ways of understanding the yeomanry of the slave South. The yeomanry of southwestern Tennessee represent equal or greater potential and can be an instructive example through which the progressive development of a mature plantation society can be evaluated against the national backdrop of a nascent market economy. Finally, as a class of agriculturalists, the yeomen also marched to an economic cadence similar to their plantation neighbors in fundamental ways. But historical understandings of those unique rhythms have been in flux. In that vein, our understanding of the economic culture and behavior of the planter class has been modified by scholarship over the last twenty years. A reconsideration of the ideological, cultural, and economic motivations underlying the strategies adopted by the yeomen and landless farm laborers alike is therefore in order.[3]

The agricultural population of antebellum southwestern Tennessee existed between the polarizing interests of farming to produce food and farming to produce capital. In light of that idea, the purpose of this essay is to evaluate a portion of the yeomanry's engagement with the market revolution in antebellum southwestern Tennessee's cotton belt. Gavin Wright's well-worn phrase ("safety-first") neatly structures the yeomen's world around the dual concepts of necessity and surplus. However, the critical component was the degree of risk that individual yeomen accepted when spring planting compelled them to choose how much land to sow in grain and how much in cotton. Richard Bushman's concept of composite farming is an amplification of "safety-first," as it recognized the secondary but growing importance of profit as farmers found themselves enmeshed in a transitory economy. Composite farming is a logical synthesis that reflects the practicality of simultaneously growing what is necessary and selling or trading what is not. Certainly, it is a reflection of the notion that analytical distinctions are more important to historians of the yeomanry than they probably were to the yeomen who practiced them as a way of life. Thus if antebellum southern yeomen leaned toward a "safety-first" agricultural mentality, it was still nevertheless quite compatible for yeomen to simultaneously advocate a capitalistic tendency that could be referred to as "profit-second." Such a model blends the symbiotic relationship between household and market production while also complementing an interpretation that allows for agricultural change to occur at a gradual or evolutionary pace rather than at a watershed or revolutionary moment in time. In other words, it further enhances our understanding of southwestern Tennessee's yeomen as living in the midst of a protracted period of significant economic transition.[4]

The words of the yeomen themselves reflected this sense of duality and priority. W. S. Baxter, the son of a Fayette County yeoman farmer, recalled that his father engaged in "farming for a living and to make money." The distinction between then and now is self-evident: antebellum farming could yield a livelihood while bypassing the accumulation of capital almost entirely. Modern farming, on the other hand, is first and foremost a quest for monetary profit by which a livelihood is subsequently obtained after the fact. Baxter's precise categorization suggests that yeomen probably viewed farming as a lifestyle that defined one's identity. "Making money," as Baxter differentiated, remained incidental to the more important process of "making a living," but was not necessarily vital in the modern sense. Indeed, Baxter's dualism reveals an affinity with James Dickinson's utilitarianism. Both yeomen's recollections underscore the idea that common families in the cotton belt already farmed for safety (a living) and profit (money), prior to the Civil War.[5]

Precisely who were these yeomen, like Baxter and Dickinson, who farmed for a living and to make money? Historians do not agree. Recent scholarship indicates a trend toward an elastic definition that incorporates the broadest range of potential yeomen and the particular choices they faced. In an attempt to maintain continuity with previous scholarship, this study defines an antebellum southwestern Tennessee yeoman as a landowning, self-working farmer, owning no more than 150 improved acres (land ready for cultivation) and no more than nine slaves. These variables are fluid enough to encompass the majority of the white population while clearly excluding the minority of the plantation agriculturalists. Thus this use of *yeoman* is sufficiently broad to allow for comparison with other studies while precise enough to incorporate self-working families.[6]

Yeomen, broadly defined, comprised the bulk of southwestern Tennessee's farming population. The majority of slaveholders in the five-county sample possessed fewer than ten slaves, and the majority of farms, with the exception of those in Fayette, consisted of fewer than one hundred acres. Even in the plantation belt of southwestern Tennessee, family farms peppered the landscape as yeomen tilled their acreage with the benefit of a few bondsmen or nothing more than the collective resilience of their family's labor. With more farms than the other counties, Madison best represented the statistically dominant yet socially taciturn presence of yeomen families in the cotton belt. Thus a representative sample from Madison has been singled out for closer examination. As tables 1 and 2 indicate, yeomen declined in their percentage of the farming population. Their diminution, in part, reflected growth among planters and tenants, as well as a drop in white population due to emigration during the 1850s. Despite their numerical decline (a common phenomenon that decade), these data corroborate much of what we know about the yeomanry elsewhere while reinforcing their statistical prominence in Tennessee's cotton belt.[7]

Any time the phrases "capitalist transformation" or "market revolution" are employed as interpretive constructs for antebellum America, historians argue over the definition of *capitalism*.[8] Ideological and teleological preferences ultimately prevented any useful consensus and, in fact, left many to conclude that the entire debate is caught in a repetitive loop that commences with competing definitions, which reinforce contrary hypotheses. For the purpose of this essay, *capitalism* shall be limited to an understanding of human relationships that revolve around production for exchange, particularly exchange involving either capital or commodities

Table 1. Farms and Plantations in Madison County, Tennessee (Districts 5, 7, 8), 1850

Improved Acres Owned	No. Farms	% All Farms	Avg. No. Slaves
Tenant Farmers	32.0	15.8	1.2
1-24	7.0	3.5	0.6
25-49	39.0	19.3	0.5
50-99	57.0	28.2	1.5
100-150	26.0	12.9	6.2
Yeomen Totals	129.0	63.9	1.8
151-199	10.0	4.9	12.5
200-299	6.0	3.0	18.5
300-499	19.0	9.4	28.6
Planter Totals	35.0	17.3	22.3
500+	6.0	3.0	65.0
Great Planter Totals	6.0	3.0	65.0
Total	202.0	100.0	

SOURCE: Seventh U.S. Census, Population, Agriculture, and Slave Schedules, Madison County, Tennessee, 1850.

that may be recorded in a monetary framework. While this may blend a classical Marxist understanding of production for exchange (which always involves money), it is this blending that best fits the paradigm of a period of economic transition and best reflects on the choices of composite farmers. This does not preclude the importance of other forms of exchange, which may have altered behavior over time and encouraged the yeomanry to be more "capitalistic."[9]

If the yeomen of antebellum southwestern Tennessee were becoming more market oriented and capitalistic, albeit incrementally and in association with household need, we may possibly discern the collective ingredients that fostered localized market revolution as well as the various degrees of capitalistic involvement on the part of yeomen collectively. Many studies have emphasized the primacy of trading connections (domestic and foreign), transportation, and a mentality that reflected a pursuit of profit as vital ingredients that ushered in the beginnings of capitalist transformation. Scholars have noted this transformation blossomed in the American South after the War of 1812. In southwestern Tennessee, this potent combination of ingredients fused during the 1850s—the decade that witnessed

Table 2. Farms and Plantations in Madison County, Tennessee (Districts 5, 7, 8), 1860

Improved Acres Owned	No. Farms	% All Farms	Avg. No. Slaves
Tenant Farmers	34.0	20.5	1.1
1-24	5.0	3.0	0.6
25-49	25.0	15.1	1.3
50-99	40.0	24.1	1.8
100-150	20.0	12.0	7.2
Yeomen Totals	90.0	54.2	2.6
151-199	11.0	6.6	12.4
200-299	8.0	4.8	19.4
300-499	12.0	7.2	30.6
Planter Totals	31.0	18.6	22.2
500+	11.0	6.7	58.1
Great Planter Totals	11.0	6.7	58.1
Total	166.0	100.0	

NOTE: Overall, Madison's white population dropped 11 while the sample's dropped 18 percent. Eighth U.S. Census, Population, Agriculture, and Slave Schedules, Madison County, Tennessee, 1860.

the transformative power of the railroad. Afterward, agriculture would never be quite the same in the South. Combined with a seemingly insatiable demand for cotton on both national and international markets, even in the face of burgeoning productivity, yeomen contemplated increased participation in the growth they observed around them. Likewise, degrees of subsequent yeomen involvement in artisanship, livestock usage, crop selection, and slave ownership conveyed relevance and are indicative of yeomen capitalistic strategies.[10]

Any study that seeks to understand the market orientation of antebellum yeomen must acknowledge the significance of landless inhabitants in a society predicated on landownership. Yeomen knew they were better off than those without property, yet landless citizens constituted a highly visible minority across southwestern Tennessee. Representative of the region, 35 percent of all families in Madison County owned no real estate in 1850. However, hidden within that substantial percentage were numerous artisans and professionals. Blacksmiths, carpenters, attorneys, and academy teachers were often cited in the census as landless. Their failure to possess real estate was not necessarily an impediment to economic independence. Skill and advanced education provided options that mitigated the circumstances accompanying landlessness. As table 3 indicates, the majority of the landless consisted of those who earned a livelihood through the soil without the benefit of ownership.[11]

The impoverished majority of landless agricultural laborers and tenants lacked the time, and usually the inclination, to record the daily events of their lives. Statistics gleaned from the census records of two counties yield modest insight. In 1850, 19 percent of Madison County's families engaged in an agricultural occupation owned no real estate. In neighboring

Table3. Landless Population in Madison County, Tennessee, (Districts 5, 7, 8), 1850 and 1860

	1850		1860	
Category	Number	Percent	Number	Percent
Farmers/Laborers	52	47.7	41	46.1
Tenants	32	29.4	34	38.1
Artisans	16	14.7	10	11.3
Professionals	9	8.2	4	4.5
Total	109	100.0	89	100.0

SOURCE: Seventh and Eighth U.S. Census, Population and Agriculture Schedules, Madison County, Tennessee, 1850, 1860.

Fayette County the number was 27 percent. Ten years later, 20 percent of Madison's farming families remained without land, and in Fayette the figure moderated to 23 percent. As these figures suggest, a rough estimation of landless farming families throughout the cotton region was approximately one in five. However, during the late antebellum period, the white population experienced tremendous fluctuations due to emigration. Nevertheless, the overall percentage of landless farmers remained reasonably consistent during the decade preceding the Civil War.[12]

Tenant farmers comprised the pool of potential yeomen and thus constituted the most significant segment of the landless farming population.[13] Generalizations elude application to such a mysterious group, but it is reasonable to conclude that the lack of land ensured a marginal existence. Regional tenant farms usually contained between twenty and forty acres. Landlords often used less desirable ground for such transactions and saved the prime acreage for themselves. Quite literally, the land may have been twenty to forty "hard" acres. Typical of antebellum tenant farming families across the region, Burrell and Nancy Richardson raised eight children on their twenty-five rented acres. They concentrated heavily on corn and wheat, versatile crops that could feed both their large family and their small number of livestock. There probably was little choice or reflection on the part of Burrell Richardson in this regard. With so many mouths and so few acres, the maximum amount of food was necessary. Despite this fact, the Richardson farm also produced one entire bale of cotton. However, a similar imperative emerged here as well, since the raw cotton from a single bale could have also been consumed by the large family's clothing needs. In the absence of home consumption, Burrell possibly traded his cotton at a local country store, if the price was good that year. If so, he now possessed store credit, but Nancy undoubtedly still required cloth for the forthcoming year. Consequently, Richardson may have been compelled to convert his cotton credit into manufactured cloth. Thus, one way or another, tenant farmers probably consumed all of their meager produce from one season to the next.[14]

A central question concerning tenancy revolves around its utility as a steppingstone into the yeoman class. Undoubtedly, Burrell Richardson's case suggests the perpetuation of poverty unless he altered some of the variables in his agricultural lifestyle. One logical scenario for any tenant wishing to improve his future required the rental and cultivation of more arable land. Two cases are instructive of the progression of tenancy in southwestern Tennessee. With a family comparable in size to the Richardsons, Mark Mangrum rented thirty-five acres and produced six bales of cotton in 1850. This arrangement did not promote stability for the Mangrum family, as they apparently moved sometime before the next census. On the other hand, twenty-seven-year-old William R. Baker lived on twenty rented acres with his much smaller family and produced one bale of cotton. However, for the Bakers, this foundation led to their establishment in the yeoman class. In 1860, Baker owned fifty improved acres, which his seventeen-year-old and fourteen-year-old sons helped him cultivate. With a balanced mixture of grain crops, he now harvested four bales of cotton, possibly to pay the taxes and debt owed on his property. Considering the limitations of what can be concluded from a decennial census with no record from the other nine years, we can be less certain why Mangrum failed to own land where Baker succeeded. If tenancy represented a steppingstone for some, it was an unstable launching point. Where the Bakers experienced opportunity, others experienced frustration. As another antebellum tenant farmer from Tennessee remembered in exasperation, "a renter had no chance to save anything."[15]

Despite the difficulty of ownership, southwestern Tennessee farmers cleared, cultivated, and enclosed more land in the 1850s—most likely in response to the profitability of cotton. This kind of improved acreage suggested more intensive cultivation, a hallmark of commercial agriculture. Overall, the percentage of improved soil in the region exceeded the 30 percent average found in much of the Cotton South (especially Fayette—51 percent—and Madison—44 percent). However, the majority of this productive increase probably came from enslaved plantation laborers. As tables 4 and 5 demonstrate, the greatest growth occurred in the two wealthiest deciles. Statistically, the top 20 percent of inhabitants consisted almost entirely of planters and possibly some slave-owning yeomen. The remaining 80 percent, the majority of the yeomanry combined with all the various categories of landless agriculturalists, declined in their share of the percentage of acreage relative to their more prosperous neighbors. In farm value, the difference was even more pronounced, as the wealthiest deciles reflected significant increase. As a result, the plantation minority now controlled the majority of the region's most valuable farm land. If the yeomen were to grow or expand economically, they would have to do so with proportionally less of the region's land. Apparently, they did precisely that. In 1850, only 13 percent of yeomen farms improved at least one-half of their total acreage. A decade later, this percentage dramatically increased. In 1860, 39 percent of yeomen farms held at least 50 percent of their land as improved acreage. James Dickinson's family reflected this trend. In 1850 they owned seventy acres (thirty improved). In 1860 they owned eighty-one acres (forty improved). In most respects, their farm maintained its 1850 level of subsistence production—with one glaring exception. Their cotton crop mushroomed from three to eight bales. Thus, while the statistical dominance of planters remains indisputable, the more important fact about the yeomen is their relative growth from 1850 to 1860. Moving beneath the "historical radar," families like the Dickinsons cleared and enclosed more land for the

Table 4. Southwestern Tennessee Farms and Improved Acreage, 1850-1860

	1850			1860		
County	Farms	Acreage	% Improved	Farms	Acreage	% Improved
Fayette	1,172	159,430	44.6	942	184,624	51.1
Hardeman	1,027	107,022	26.4	866	111,888	33.9
Haywood	967	93,619	32.1	1,004	138,026	39.1
Madison	1,408	115,872	36.5	1,479	160,401	43.7
Tipton	631	48,176	26.6	673	65,570	32.5

SOURCE: Seventh and Eighth U.S. Census, Agriculture Schedules, Fayette, Hardeman, Haywood, Madison, and Tipton Counties, Tennessee, 1850, 1860.

Table 5. Improved Acreage and Farm Value Distribution among Landowners and Tenants, Madison County, Tennessee, 1850-1860

	1850		1860		
Deciles	Class Acreage	% of Total Farm Value	% of Total Acreage	% of Total Farm Value	% of Total
1-2	Planters	55.3	65.3	60.5	68.3
3-7	Yeomen	36.9	33.0	33.2	28.3
8-10	Tenants	7.8	1.7	6.3	3.4

SOURCE: Seventh and Eighth U.S. Census, Agriculture and Population Schedules, Madison County, Tennessee, 1850, 1860.

cultivation of cotton. They adjusted their farming choices in response to a changing economic environment.[16]

Undoubtedly, transportation had always been a precarious necessity for the market aspirations of all agriculturalists since the initial settlement of the region. Prior to the infiltration of the railroad, the transportation of marketable crops beyond the local county seat often proved especially inconsistent. Before 1850, there is little evidence of regional exports from southwestern Tennessee for items other than cotton. Ample evidence exists demonstrating dedicated efforts undertaken by planters to ensure their profitable fiber arrived in Memphis, New Orleans, and eventually the textile mills of Great Britain. During the frontier era, this process depended on a flotilla of shallow-draft steamboats that plied the Hatchie, Forked Deer, and Wolf rivers during the winter and early spring. Cotton had to be hauled to various receiving points along the respective rivers to await seasonal precipitation and the subsequent rise of water levels sufficient for navigation. Far from efficient, this method required both vigilance and patience, as crop transportation demanded careful coordination with unpredictable weather cycles.[17]

Despite the option of boat travel, transport by wagon remained in use throughout much of the antebellum period. Planters could exercise more control over this process, if they wished, by contracting younger male relatives or even hauling their crop to Memphis themselves. However, the journey from the cotton fields of eastern Madison and Hardeman counties to Memphis required three to four days each way. Additionally, the cost of horsepower as well as manpower would cut deeper into the profit than water transportation did.[18]

In light of these early problems with cotton transport, most planters enthusiastically embraced the greater efficiency and reliability of the railroad. During the decade prior to the Civil War, rail construction boomed as hundreds of miles of new lines crisscrossed western Tennessee before ultimately converging on the Mississippi River at Memphis. Representative of the excitement of this period, J. B. Maclin informed his employer in North Carolina of the railroad's progress from Memphis to the Haywood County seat in Brownsville. Maclin's correspondence clearly indicated that a completed railroad might bring many wonderful conveniences into the community, but its utility as a means of export seemed to take precedence. Writing before spring planting in 1854, he noted with anticipation that an effort would be made to complete the line "in time to carry off the next year's crop." Overall, planters had the most to gain from this relatively smooth and reliable transportation. But once in place, the railroad became a force that yeomen reckoned with as well.[19]

While the railroad undoubtedly positioned the region's economy for potential transformation, some southwestern Tennessee yeomen could also make strides toward the larger market revolution through their supplemental skill as artisans. Although identified as yeomen, these farmers worked a trade while maintaining a family farm. Carpenters, tanners, brick masons, and blacksmiths all offered a vital service that could be profitably exchanged among other yeomen and planters alike, although larger plantations typically possessed slave artisans who often provided these services.[20] Many yeomen remembered that their fathers divided their time between two occupational pursuits. A. J. Derryberry recalled that his father "worked at [the] carpenter's trade" when he was not engaged in farming. In addition to working their family farm, James Dickinson's father also found employment as a "mechanic" and "often made spinning wheels and looms and wagons." In light of Dickinson's prior comment that yeomen all "did anything that would pay," his father's supplemental income as a mechanic is important for two reasons. First, this significant information is altogether obscured by the census, which identifies the elder Dickinson only as a farmer. Thus it is suggestive of other similarly skilled farmers hidden within the decennial records. In fact, any yeomen who successfully managed to acquire and hold a family farm probably succeeded because he shared Dickinson's view of diversified labor—particularly if it would pay. Second, it also points to the existence of a vibrant local exchange economy among other yeomen families who desired Dickinson's spinning wheels, looms, and other items. This, of course, suggests a more insular economy, less affected by external market forces and more responsive to families' bartering for essentials.[21]

While the evidence pertaining to antebellum yeomen/artisans in southwestern Tennessee is impressionistic, recent scholarship on artisans in other regions suggests that such men may have viewed themselves as "planters in the making" rather than permanently bound to a lifestyle of arduous handwork. Certainly, the Old South was not without its share of popular examples of fortunes made from self-employed artisans who eventually accumulated enough capital to purchase slaves and rise through the ranks of the planter class. This formula for success was tied to a fortuitous moment in time when the artisans of the antebellum South still counted on relatively cheap land and enslaved labor and the absence of significant competition from northern manufacturing. Proportionally, these variables changed during the late antebellum era as the odds leaned against the southern artisan's quest to "make" himself into a planter.[22] Southwestern Tennessee was not without its own examples of this phenomenon. Martin Cartmell migrated to Madison County in the 1820s and used his skill as a saddler to accumulate capital and moderately priced frontier land. By the time of his death during the Civil War, he was acknowledged to be one of the wealthiest planters in his community. Typically, such success may have been noteworthy precisely because it was rather exceptional.[23]

However, for the majority of yeomen, any capitalistic or market aspirations are best measured within the context of a life from the soil. In this regard, the most common method for the yeomanry of the Old South to accumulate any profitable surplus may have been through raising livestock. All agriculturalists possessed some livestock as a matter of necessity; over time, this survivalist mandate made it easier for them to increase the number of animals past the point of family need. Nevertheless, the degree of relative ease and efficiency by which yeomen turned swine, cattle, and even sheep into surplus income remains a topic of continual debate.[24]

Certainly there were specific benefits peculiar to the nineteenth-century approach to raising livestock. The fundamental distinction pertained to the existence of the open range, which required that farmers enclose their fields rather than their animals. Thus cattle and hogs foraged and browsed extensively in any open pasture or unenclosed forest. This system turned out to be especially advantageous for raising hogs, which survived as omnivorous browsers on a diet of nuts, roots, wild fruit, and almost anything else within reach. In large part, this adaptability explains why swine were the preferred source of meat. Cattle depended more on the region's limited supply of available pasture; consequently, any raised on the open range were typically considered to be of a lesser quality. Thanks to the marksmanship of David Crockett and others, few large predators remained in southwestern Tennessee by the late antebellum period. Livestock roamed the woods and fields in relative safety until farmers herded them together for sale or slaughter. Occasionally this was preceded by a brief period of fattening select animals on a diet of corn, although yeomen understood that feeding hogs too much grain inflated their cost beyond the point of profitability. If possible, yeomen avoided transforming bushels of corn into slabs of bacon. As one visitor to the region marveled, "with little feeding and less care . . . [hogs] live . . . independent of their owner."[25]

Unique drawbacks accompanied raising livestock in an open-range system. While wild predators no longer posed any threat, slaves and poor whites frequently roamed the edges of the open range when motivated by hunger. Perhaps the most consistent problem pertained to the aggravation associated with protecting one's own fields from the ravenous herds by constructing and maintaining rail fencing. Even then, a meticulous farmer could successfully protect his herd in every respect only to suffer the ravages of periodic epidemics. The open range facilitated a more rapid spread of livestock disease. Evidence suggests hog cholera reduced the swine population in one Madison County neighborhood by two-thirds in the summer of 1859.[26]

All farmers in antebellum southwestern Tennessee continued to raise livestock out of necessity; but the statistical evidence does not suggest that this activity significantly increased as a source of income production during the last decade before the Civil War. While the value of live and slaughtered stock increased, the herds themselves decreased overall. Of the five counties sampled, the most substantial increase occurred in the number of sheep in Fayette and Tipton. Otherwise, stock populations tended to be either stable or in decline. Since the region was never poised to become a major wool producer, the more striking statistic was the significant drop in every county's swine population. The number of hogs is quite suggestive, since swine were the primary source of domesticated meat. Obviously, a declining human population would not require a larger hog population. Only Fayette County experienced a net loss in human population (9 percent) during the 1850s; however, its swine population decreased even more dramatically (21 percent). See table 6.

These data present an especially intriguing question: if open-range livestock raising was such an appealing method to achieve prosperity,

Table 6. Southwestern Tennessee Livestock Values and Population, 1850-1860

	Livestock Value	Slaughtered Stock Value	Swine	Cattle	Sheep
1850					
Fayette	$640,697	$125,829	52,108	10,826	8,382
Hardeman	$502,334	$107,119	45,823	8,566	9,819
Haywood	$399,428	$97,690	42,030	7,204	16,977
Madison	$629,786	$126,730	56,981	10,718	14,564
Tipton	$315,107	$54,438	31,014	5,947	3,222
1860					
Fayette	$1,171,945	$224,574	41,124	10,755	11,269
Hardeman	$830,457	$198,116	33,586	6,803	7,604
Haywood	$973,750	$217,361	29,264	5,884	16,881
Madison	$1,044,553	$260,837	48,645	10,087	11,055
Tipton	$640,992	$118,251	27,302	6,867	5,417

SOURCE: Seventh and Eighth U.S. Census, Agriculture Schedules, Fayette, Hardeman, Haywood, Madison, and Tipton Counties, Tennessee, 1850, 1860.

particularly for common farmers, what can explain the dramatic decline in livestock numbers? A plausible answer involves an interpretation that views antebellum herding as a transitional endeavor and more of a means to establish oneself with land rather than as a permanent occupation. In addition to the documented drop in livestock, several other factors reinforce the likelihood of this interpretation. The people who most favored herding may have moved west during the 1850s, taking their herds with them, in order to find areas with relatively more open land. The rising price and overall strength of the cotton market, especially by the middle of the decade, coupled with the efficiency of the railroad may have encouraged more emphasis on cultivation. Certainly the regional increase in overall improved acreage would suggest this. Simultaneously, improved acreage meant enclosed acreage, which in turn translated into less open range for livestock. The planters and yeomen who remained in southwestern Tennessee during the late antebellum era raised less livestock while enclosing more land for the purpose of cultivation. Therefore, if herding had progressed in this manner to 1850, then it very well may have been a capitalistic means that helped persisting yeomen in becoming settled cultivators of the soil.[27]

While the necessity of keeping livestock could translate into productive capital, nothing equaled the potential income that accompanied cotton. Southwestern Tennessee yeomen took advantage of the regional climate and soil to raise various amounts of the fiber, depending on a wide variety of factors: weather, yield, price, ginning, marketing, transportation, family need, and slave ownership all influenced the decision to cultivate cotton. However, the pivotal variable turned upon the degrees of risk associated with this crop. The "risk" of cotton cultivation was not just a simple dichotomy between market and household. Frank Owsley famously wrote that "relatively few of the plain folk . . . seem to have had a desire to become wealthy." Ironically, such a view could imply that yeomen refrained from growing cotton because it could either ruin them or make them rich. The entire notion of risk and yeoman crop selection—especially cotton—needs to be evaluated in context. Corn has frequently been exalted above cotton by scholars who marveled at its versatility. Still, just because cotton could not be eaten by the farmer or his livestock, it did not necessarily mean that a low price or yield would ruin a yeoman. After all, cotton served a basic need for antebellum farmers, who still produced much, in some cases all, of their own raw fiber and finished clothing. Unless they abandoned household production, yeomen maintained an equilibrium between the two extremes of ruin and riches. A meticulous exploration of yeomen's cotton cultivation can potentially illuminate our understanding of the yeomen's sense of identity with the cotton South.[28]

Across southwestern Tennessee, both the ubiquitous presence of expansive cotton fields beside the planter's mansion and the diminutive cotton patches beside the yeoman's cabin testified to the relative importance of that crop's cultivation. Table 7, for Madison County, demonstrates that cotton was commonly grown across the entire socioeconomic spectrum in southwestern Tennessee. Replicating a common trend in the Old South, the wealthiest 20 percent controlled around 75 percent of the harvest. Conversely, the poorest 20 percent of farmers in 1850 and 1860 did not raise a single bale. This left the yeomen's (and tenants') share at one-fourth (1850) to one-fifth (1860) of the harvest. Data of this kind are seldom appreciated. Often, the relevance is dwarfed by the dominating share of planters. This is precisely where the yeomen become the metaphorical forest that cannot be seen for the trees. Despite the commonality of cotton cultivation among them, the yeomen's share appears insignificant. But in regard to the yeomen's economic standing, their percentile contribution is not as important as the fact that their small harvests increased during the decade and potentially transformed their lives with one or two good crops. Furthermore, relatively few studies document the yeomen's percentile con-

Table 7. Distribution of Cotton Harvest by Class in Madison County, Tennessee, 1850-1860

Deciles	Class	Percentage of Harvest	
		1850	1860
1-2	Planters	72.1	76.7
3-7	Yeomen	26.6	19.3
8-10	Tenants/Laborers	1.3	4.0

NOTE: 1850 figures divide the county's population into ten precise wealth deciles. The figures for 1860 are taken from the micro-sample consisting of Civil Districts 5, 7, and 8, which comprised a representative cross-section of 11 percent of Madison County's population. Seventh and Eighth U.S. Census, Population and Agriculture Schedules, Madison County, Tennessee, 1850, 1860.

tribution to regional cotton harvests. For example, a study of antebellum Mississippi placed the yeomen's contribution no higher than 7 percent. Madison County's yeomen families contributed substantially more but for reasons that cannot be ascertained with precision at present. Certainly this is an exhortation to future scholars to provide comparative data from other regions.[29]

When yeomen contemplated whether or not they should plant cotton every spring, they calculated the combined risks associated with local weather patterns and climate, which no farmer could control. Most years southwestern Tennessee's weather nicely complemented the growth of cotton. The crop usually performed best with ample rain after spring planting followed by proportionally less precipitation till the heat of late summer ushered in a dry period for harvest. The occasional April frost threw this entire cycle off balance. In those seasons, replanting posed an additional risk because of the loss of valuable time needed to plant other crops. Likewise, such a late start meant a later harvest, which would be more vulnerable to an early autumn frost at the conclusion of the cycle. This was a pervasive problem across the region as all agriculturalists, especially in Madison and Haywood counties, understood that they literally lived on the northern fringe of the Cotton South. Documentary evidence on the 1853 cotton crop suggested that early frost resulted in a 22 percent loss of the anticipated harvest. Nevertheless, such a risk was most certainly relative to both the number of acres allocated to cotton and the specific cash needs of the respective farmer during a given season.[30]

Another seemingly capricious variable associated with cotton cultivation was profitability.[31] Obviously this was most affected by the yield per acre and the market price per pound, after the yeoman accounted for the limitations of his available labor supply. Antebellum cotton yields remain shrouded in mystery, as decennial census data only recorded the size of the harvest. Likewise, soil quality exerted tremendous influence over the final product, and it displayed wide variation even in the same county. Thus any estimation of yields will necessarily be rather broad. Anecdotal evidence reveals that a cotton yield of 1,200 pounds (three bales) to the acre was common in Fayette County, with rumors of 2,100 pounds in isolated but undoubtedly fecund subregions. However, just thirty miles northwest, yields around the town of Jackson averaged around 250 pounds, with documentation of a 400-pound yield. The price of cotton varied widely during the late antebellum era. Between 1849 and 1851 it fell from 11 to 7 cents a pound, then climbed to 15 cents by 1857 and remained high despite the heavy crops leading up to the war. Thus for one bale of cotton, yeomen could expect its value to range from $28.00 to $60.00 during the 1850s. With this income, yeomen paid off past debt, procured present subsistence, or saved to buy future acreage. During an era when common laborers earned one dollar a day, cotton was indeed profitable for yeomen, albeit in a circumscribed manner, as befitted the family needs on a composite farm.[32]

When considering the profitability of homegrown cotton, one must remember that it also supplied part or virtually all of some families' annual clothing needs. Although increasingly less common in the late antebellum North, spinning wheels and looms maintained a highly visible presence in the households of southern common folk. The wives and daughters of many yeomen exerted tremendous effort to transform raw fiber into fabric and then "homespun" clothing. Westley Sheets of Hardeman County testified that his mother "spun the thread and dyed it and wove the cloth for the family needs . . . suits, blankets, and carpets and did all the knitting." Evidence suggests that yeomen families could realistically raise enough cotton themselves to take on this chore if household labor proved equal to the task. For a family of eight, this roughly translated into one bale of cotton. Thus, if a family produced the first bale, they could fashion a minimalist wardrobe; the second and third bales could help them establish good credit at the country store. Small yeomen families who made four or five bales possibly viewed this modest surplus as a monetary cushion. Yeomen families who managed a cotton harvest of more than five bales, especially without slave labor, placed themselves on the threshold of meaningful economic change. This was uncommon but not unprecedented as yeomen families increased their commitment to cotton on the eve of the Civil War.[33]

Table 8 reflects the vitality of yeomen cotton cultivation. Even on farms without slave labor, production increased by two whole bales (55 percent). As might be anticipated, farms with enslaved labor grew more cotton in proportion to their larger number of slaves and more urgent necessity for capital. This trend generally held across all portions of the Old South

Table 8. Cotton Production of Yeomen Slaveholders and Nonslaveholders (Districts 5, 7, and 8), Madison County, Tennessee, 1850-1860

	1850		1860	
Slaves Owned	Cotton Bales Per Farm	% Growing Cotton	Cotton Bales Per Farm	% Growing Cotton
0	3.6	77	5.6	82
1-4	5.8	89	7.3	81
5-9	13.6	91	15.3	88

SOURCE: Seventh U.S. Census, Population, Agriculture, and Slaves Schedules, Madison County, Tennessee, 1850.

where cotton predominated. The most interesting group consists of nonslaveholding yeomen who raised cotton, particularly more than five bales. However, some patterns emerge through an examination of household level data across all these groups.[34]

Among slaveowning yeomen, roughly 10 percent did not raise cotton, while nearly 20 percent of the smallest slaveholders did not in 1860. Although an anomaly, this small group's decision demands some attempt at an explanation. Overall, the majority of this group shared two things in common: few or no children in the family combined with a majority of young female slaves. The decision to abstain from cotton cultivation was most often related to issues of insufficient labor. However, one example is exceptional. John Williams, a forty-one-year-old yeoman with a wife, seven children, and five slaves, farmed sixty acres without harvesting any cotton. Instead his farm produced 1,500 bushels of corn and 150 of wheat, far exceeding the typical grain crop of most yeomen farms. His situation in 1850 remains curious, as three of his slaves were males between the ages of fourteen and twenty-three and undoubtedly capable of all the labor required to raise a profitable cotton crop. Instead, Williams focused on the largest possible grain crop—unusual behavior for a slaveowning yeomen. However, the best rejoinder to Williams' "safety" in 1850 is revealed by his "profit" in 1860. With an enlarged farm (one hundred improved acres) and labor force (eight slaves), he raised only 700 bushels of corn—still more than he needed. But his wheat crop yielded 236 bushels and his cotton produced 43 bales—an astonishing harvest even for a slaveowning yeoman. In fact, Williams produced more wheat and cotton than any yeoman in the statistical sample. Thus, while Williams was the most successful slaveowning yeoman in his neighborhood, he also demonstrated that slaveowners needed to earn capital.[35]

Among nonslaveowning yeomen, approximately 20 percent did not harvest cotton during the 1850s. Several were artisan-yeomen with tiny farms (fifteen to twenty acres) who profited more from their craft than their soil. In addition to the absence of slaves, the household in this group exhibited commonality in containing a preponderance of young children and older grandparents. Essentially, a lack of masculine labor (black or white) and land necessary for the most productive levels of arduous farm work proved the most common attributes throughout this group.[36]

The most interesting and seldom examined segment of the yeomanry are nonslaveholders who managed to cultivate modest yet impressive amounts of cotton. In the Madison County sample, 19 percent of nonslaveowning yeomen raised more than 5 bales in 1850. This grew to 51 percent in 1860; reflecting the fact that the average family harvest now stood at 5.6 bales. The maximum harvest for nonslaveholders, in either census, was 12 bales (7 percent of all nonslaveowing yeomen attained this in 1860). Certainly, hidden within the census data are relations of slaveowning kin and neighborly assistance that might explain how some farmers raised much more cotton than necessary. Nevertheless, most of these yeomen families shared one significant variable: multiple adolescent and adult males capable of significant agricultural labor. In the absence of slaveownership, these families relied on a transcendent method and raised their own laborers, just as they raised everything else they needed. Obviously, labor of this kind was ephemeral, as families could not take advantage of such assistance indefinitely. This natural drawback most likely presented a ten-year (at most) window of opportunity as families used the agricultural labor of sons before they established independence via marriage.

One example illustrates the larger pattern. Caleb and Anna Watson, a forty-seven-year-old couple with ten children, harvested twelve bales of cotton on seventy-five improved acres in 1850. The most revealing statistic about the Watsons was their five oldest children: all sons, ranging from twenty-two to fourteen years old. The six Watson men, through balanced and purposeful effort, could realistically harvest a cotton crop that size and meet the minimum requirements for family subsistence. However, the Watsons also exemplified another common feature of yeomen life: migration. Apparently, by 1860, they had left the county. As a farming family, the Watsons were unique but they demonstrated what was possible, if only briefly.[37]

Ultimately, this effort all would be void if yeomen could not arrange the ginning and transporting of their crop to a location where they could best take advantage of the regional market price. If possible, yeomen in southwestern Tennessee probably avoided relying on cotton factors based out of New Orleans and the associated problems with complex transportation arrangements and the purchase of expensive insurance. Country stores often served the twofold purpose of ginning and accepting cotton as payment for last year's bill. The front porches of these stores served as public meeting places, where the news from local and national papers, the market price in New Orleans, and the anticipated demand in Liverpool were certainly conversational topics. Yeomen possessed a clear idea of exactly what their cotton, corn, wheat, and pork were all worth. Likewise, they realized that they might make more without the additional "middle man" in the guise of a country store owner. But the yeomen always returned to the utilitarian rationale of the composite farmer. They realized that wanting more profit from a stranger in New Orleans made less sense than acquiring what they needed from the neighbor who stood in front of them.[38]

One additional variable, perhaps the most important of all, that distinguished southern agriculture during the nineteenth century was the institution of slave labor. Arguably, slavery constituted the singular feature that set apart the American South as truly distinctive.[39] Slavery and slaveowners exert tremendous influence over the question of yeomen capitalism and market production. Naturally, in the plantation region of antebellum southwestern Tennessee, yeomen recognized that their most successful neighbors were slaveowning cotton planters. It is reasonable to suggest that yeomen may have measured their own success, in part, in relation to the economic standard set by planters with their numerous bondsmen. Any southern yeoman who aspired to great wealth probably aspired to be the owner of slaves as well. However, in southwestern Tennessee, as in the majority of the late antebellum South, slave ownership was becoming more concentrated (in conjunction with land ownership and cotton production). Thus, the ambitions of small slaveowners who desired more were certainly constrained by the increased value of human property. At the same time, slaveownership was especially precarious for yeomen. From one harvest to the next, disease, disaster, and debt could seize all or part of their meager enslaved labor pool. Understanding the fickle nature of success, the mentality of small slaveholders probably rested on a razor's edge between home consumption and market production.[40]

Scholars have argued at length as to whether or not plantation slavery qualified as capitalism. Much of the debate hinged on the importance of free wage labor and the complexity surrounding the organic nature of social relations between masters and slaves. While the majority of yeomen families did not own slaves, a beneficial comparison exists between those families who purchased labor and those who remained, for whatever reasons, more self-reliant. However, there can be no mistake that the acquisition of slave labor was clearly a "capitalistic" investment that compelled yeomen to seek a financial return in capital.[41]

From a purely economic point of view, one slave represented a tremendous financial risk, and acquiring a slave was the boldest financial

Table 9. Gender and Age Composition of Yeomen Slaveholding (Districts 5, 7, 8), Madison County, Tennessee, 1850 and 1860

Number of Slaves	Percent Adult Male 1850	1860	Percent Adult Female 1850	1860	Percent Children 1850	1860	Percent Female 1850	1860
1	35	25	30	25	35	50	65	75
2	31	50	38	19	31	31	56	38
3	29	38	29	38	42	24	50	50
4	18	25	40	31	42	44	57	50
5	40	14	26	33	34	53	60	67
6	27	29	23	42	50	29	53	50
7	14	20	29	26	57	54	62	52
8	25	27	13	28	62	45	50	40
9	40	55	30	22	30	23	48	33
Total	28	29	28	34	44	37	54	47

SOURCE: Anyone over the age of fifteen was counted as an adult based both on likely consumption of food and production of work. Seventh and Eighth U.S. Census, Population and Slaves Schedules, Madison County, Tennessee, 1850, 1860.

decision yeomen contemplated. The initial purchasing price, future debt payments, taxes, and the subsequent daily needs of the slave all exacerbated the uncertainty of the action as a business venture. This leads to the seldom examined point of the correlation between gender, age, and number of slaves held by yeomen. While few studies have explored this topic, there is a connection between the number of slaves and their subsequent ability to relieve respective yeomen families from most common forms of labor. This, of course, was the fundamental distinction between yeomen who worked with slaves and planters who managed them. It was also, at least in the southwestern Tennessee sample, suggestive of why it might be plausible for a yeoman family to own as many as nine slaves before being largely relieved from common farm labor.[42] See table 9.

As indicated by this sample, yeomen slaveowners benefitted from their position as masters, but it was within the specific natural limitations of the kind of laborers they usually possessed. Throughout the final decade of the antebellum era, the majority (72 percent in 1850; 71 percent in 1860) of yeomen's slaves were women and children. Labor allotments usually suggested that women counted as 75 and children as 25 percent of the labor typically be extracted from one adult male slave. Consequently, even yeomen owning up to nine usually did not have enough slaves to relieve their family from the necessity of labor. An unusual example illustrates the point. Barnes Dickinson (James's uncle and neighbor) owned seven slaves on his 100-acre farm. These two variables typically pointed toward a highly productive yeoman operation. However, Uncle Barnes owned a fifty-three-year-old woman and four children under the age of eleven. His primary "working hands" were two remaining adult women. Thus 100 percent of his slaves were women and children. This combination, only somewhat beneficial, could not relieve his family from common labor or supply them with significant profit—yet.[43]

The unusual gender/age composition of Barnes Dickinson's human property begs the question: why were 70 percent of yeomen's slaves women and children? The most plausible hypothesis points toward a strategic yet blunt economic choice. Young enslaved children cost less than young enslaved adults. Enslaved women offered the possibility of future enslaved children. Enslaved men offered no such future possibility. In that light, yeomen slaveownership patterns may best be interpreted as a calculated, long-term, financial investment. If that is the case, then Dickinson's enslaved property offered more profit in the future than labor in the present.

If the preponderance of women and children compelled yeomen to labor beside their slaves, it did not entirely hinder their pursuit of profitable expansion. However, the risk was acute, as studies of other regions suggested that small slaveholders were as likely to lose their slaves during the 1850s as they were to acquire more. In some cases, slaveownership was obtained through the sale of a portion of valuable improved acreage. Likewise, the reduction of an already small farm, in order to gain labor, posed its own risk.[44]

Two cases in point are illustrative. A nonslaveowning yeoman, Franklin Holloway, owned fifty improved acres in 1850. By 1860, he acquired two slaves, but his farm shrank to twenty-eight acres while his corn and cotton crop reflected no increase. If Holloway's case suggested that becoming a slave owner did not automatically translate into success, James Polk Hogan's reflected the necessity of combining slave labor to pre-existing family labor. Despite the presence of six slaves on his father's farm, Hogan emphasized that during his youth he "plowed, hoed . . . [and] done the same work the negroes did and at the same time and place they did."[45]

The yeoman families of Tennessee's cotton belt engaged in America's mid-nineteenth-century market revolution, as they perceived it, via their daily pursuit of composite farming. Some did well in the quest for subsistence, like the Caleb and Anna Watson family, and used their surplus to finance a move to Arkansas or perhaps Texas. Others, like Franklin Holloway, sold land as a deposit to purchase slaves and discovered the tenuous line between success and failure. Others languished in tenancy from year to year, incapable of acquiring yeomen status. For some yeomen, supplemental activities as artisans provided modest levels of market involvement.

However, like James Dickinson's spinning wheels, artisanship often reflected bartering between parties who still produced the majority of their subsistence. Likewise, yeomen possessed small herds of swine and cattle. Although vital for family survival, dwindling numbers and a shrinking open range suggested livestock's declining significance. Despite all this, the greatest level of market participation for southwestern Tennessee's yeomen remained rooted in their ownership of land and their personal comprehension of how to make it productive. Their actions were predicated on understanding the two greatest economic changes sweeping the regional and national economy in the 1850s: the rapid expansion of the railroad and the exceptional market for cotton. Thus, ironically, despite the insularity of their family farms they nevertheless responded to the same economic stimuli that shaped the world of the planters.

In this regard, three specific areas reflected the yeomen's choice to participate in the national market economy from their own farms. First, they improved a higher percentage of their acreage throughout the decade. Second, they apparently validated their investment in a methodical manner: increasing their average cotton production 55 percent over the decade. Most yeomen families required no more than a bale or two for minimal clothing needs. The average 1860 harvest of 5.6 bales was insignificant compared to the harvest realized by planters but a great surplus for nonslaveowning yeomen families who produced at that level or beyond. Yeomen could not ignore this type of potential agricultural profit. Third, the small number of yeomen slaveowners positioned themselves for long-term growth and greater participation in the cotton economy. In owning a majority of women and children, yeomen started their climb as masters on the lowest rung of the ladder and acquired the cheapest slaves in the market.

Overall, the yeomen of southwestern Tennessee embraced the mentality of the cotton South in which they lived and adapted in a manner that yielded both familial safety and financial profit. As Daniel Thorner concluded about peasant economies, "we are sure to go astray . . . if we suspect capitalism wherever the peasants show evidence of being 'market' oriented. It is much sounder to take it for granted . . . [that they] had a double orientation towards both [market and subsistence]."[46] If Thorner is correct, yeomen balanced their approach to the market revolution while looking for an opportunity to do any of those "things that paid."

NOTES

1. The lengthy historical argument over whether or not there was actually some kind of "market revolution" in America between 1787 and 1860 may finally be resolved—although the meaning, significance, and impact of this "revolution" remains an open question. The best recent summary over this debate and historians' usage of the term

market revolution is found in Harry Watson, *Liberty and Power: The Politics of Jacksonian America* (New York: Hill and Wang, 2006), 255-63. Andrew Mitchell to Plasebo Houston, October 17, 1838, Mary Hunter Kennedy Papers, Southern Historical Collection, University of North Carolina, Chapel Hill; Sarah Alexander Cooley Cottle, comp., "With Pen in Hand: The Story of a Southern Planter Based on His Diary and Letters" (1991), 72-73, Mississippi Valley Collection, University of Memphis Library, Memphis, TN; James E. Dickinson, Tennessee Civil War Veterans Questionnaires, Tennessee State Library and Archives, Nashville, TN (hereafter cited as TSLA).

2. Paul W. Gates, *The Farmer's Age: Agriculture, 1815-1860* (New York: Holt, Rinehart, and Winston, 1960), 138; William J. Cooper Jr. and Thomas E. Terrill, *The American South: A History*, vol. 1, 3rd ed. (Boston: McGraw Hill, 2002), 188.

3. I selected these five contiguous counties in the extreme southwestern corner of Tennessee as representative of the cotton plantation region due to the combination of their significant cotton harvests and enslaved populations. I omitted Shelby County (Memphis) to preserve the rural focus. However, Memphis' phenomenal growth during the 1850s exerted unprecedented economic force over western Tennessee. Previous studies of antebellum Tennessee typically examined counties across all three of the state's major regions (eastern, middle, and western). Most studies that discussed the western third typically relied on Fayette and Haywood. However, those counties contained a majority of enslaved inhabitants, whereas western Tennessee, overall, did not. This study singled out Madison County for special attention because of its regional representativeness: 47 percent of its population was enslaved in 1860 and it contained more farms than any other county in the area. Madison is the most emblematic of the yeomanry within the state's cotton belt. Last, its geographic location on the northern fringe of the cotton South offers the possibility of commentary about yeomen who risked the most unpredictable variable of all: weather. On defining Tennessee's cotton belt, see Lewis C. Gray, *History of Agriculture in the Southern United States to 1860* (Washington, DC: Carnegie Institution of Washington, 1933), 2:873.

4. The "safety-first" thesis is cogently explained in Gavin Wright, *The Political Economy of the Cotton South: Households, Markets, and Wealth in the Nineteenth Century* (New York: W.W. Norton, 1978), 62-74. In addition to "composite farming," Richard Lyman Bushman also suggested that the interpretive framework that seeks a pivotal turning point in nineteenth-century agriculture should be discarded in favor of a view that reconciles the concept of long-term change. See Bushman, "Markets and Composite Farms in Early America," *William and Mary Quarterly* 55 (July 1998): 351-74.

5. W. S. Baxter, Tennessee Civil War Veterans Questionnaires, TSLA.

6. The precise definition of an antebellum yeoman is incredibly varied. Beginning with Frank Owsley, historians generally agree that yeomen must own land. The main disagreement about class identity is the lack of consensus on the economic ceiling, especially the number of slaves owned. At what point does a yeoman graduate to the next social class? Owsley suggested plain folk could own one to ten slaves. Bill Cecil-Fronsman labeled the yeomanry "common whites" as long as they did not own more than ten slaves. According to Steven Hahn, the yeomen of Georgia's upcountry owned no more than five slaves and less than 200 improved acres. Lacy Ford concurred in his study of South Carolina and determined the criteria to be no more than five slaves as well. Breaking the pattern altogether, Charles Bolton's study of North Carolina and Mississippi defined yeomen as landowners with land valued under $5,000. Allan Kulikoff suggested that yeomen could be viewed primarily in terms of class as a group who shared a lifestyle that valued household production and used family labor. Edward Baptist's study of Florida's plantation society omitted *yeomen* and employed the term *countrymen* because antebellum Floridians used it themselves. Baptist set the upper

limit of slave ownership at ten, but he carefully pointed out the fluidity of that limitation. Stephanie McCurry also set the defining variables as the ownership of no more than 150 improved acres and nine slaves (the same used in the present study) in the South Carolina Low Country. McCurry's rationale, in part, is based on her examination of the age and gender of yeomen slaves and the subsequent likelihood that such a combination would relieve individual family members from the necessity of manual labor. Recently, Stephen A. West used Lacy Ford's definition (no more than five slaves) but also argued that owning even one slave instilled South Carolina yeomen with a greater sense of political identity with the planter class. Acknowledging that a few yeomen existed who owned as many as ten or more slaves , Carl R. Osthaus persuasively argued that the personal ethic of a "self-working farmer" is what truly defined a yeoman. Finally, Samuel C. Hyde Jr. exerted considerable effort toward resolving the confusing question of identity. He constructed a precise transitional category he called "middling farmers." Economically above plain folk but not yet planters, "middling farmers" owned between 100 and 150 improved acres and six to nine "working slaves." Hyde defined "working slaves" as anyone between the ages of thirteen and fifty, while females counted as three-fourths of a hand. In theory, a farmer could own more than five slaves and maintain yeoman status, depending on the age and gender of the slaves. Hyde's extensive data from Louisiana and Mississippi depicted "middling farmers" as comprising no more than 1 percent of the population. See Owsley, *Plain Folk of the Old South* (Baton Rouge: Louisiana State University Press, 1949), 8-9; Bill Cecil-Fronsman, *Common Whites: Class and Culture in Antebellum North Carolina* (Lexington: University Press of Kentucky, 1992); Steven Hahn, *The Roots of Southern Populism: Yeoman Farmers and the Transformation of the Georgia Upcountry, 1850-1900* (New York: Oxford University Press, 1982), 27-33; Ford, *Origins of Southern Radicalism: The South Carolina Upcountry, 1800-1860* (New York: Oxford University Press, 1988), 71; Bolton, *Poor Whites of the Antebellum South: Tenants and Laborers in Central North Carolina and Northeast Mississippi* (Durham, NC: Duke University Press, 1994), 11; Kulikoff, "The Transition to Capitalism in Rural America," *William and Mary Quarterly* 46 (Jan. 1989): 141; Baptist, *Creating an Old South: Middle Florida's Plantation Frontier before the Civil War* (Chapel Hill: University of North Carolina, 2002), 39; McCurry, *Masters of Small Worlds: Yeoman Households, Gender Relations, and the Political Culture of the Antebellum South Carolina Low Country* (New York: Oxford University Press, 1995), 48-56; West, "Minute Men, Yeomen, and the Mobilization for Secession in the South Carolina Upcountry," *Journal of Southern History* 71 (Feb. 2005): 75-104; Osthaus, "The Work Ethic of the Plain Folk: Labor and Religion in the Old South," *Journal of Southern History* 70 (Nov. 2004): 745-82; and Hyde, "Plain Folk Reconsidered: Historiographical Ambiguity in Search of Definition," *Journal of Southern History* 71 (Nov. 2005): 803-30.

7. Published census data coalesces all farms between 100 and 499 acres. Without investigating the data farm by farm, the percentage of farms below 150 acres is unknowable. Still, most farms in southwestern Tennessee contained less than 150. Fayette represented a true "plantation county": 51.4 percent of its farms contained more than 200 acres; no other county in the state held as many plantations over 1,000 acres or possessed such a high ratio of slave to free inhabitants (2:1). Eighth U.S. Census, Fayette County, Tennessee, 1860.

8. Modern historians have argued about the timing of this transition while simultaneously parsing the terminology of capitalism itself. What, if any, indications suggest that this transition toward a more capitalistic tendency had already begun during the antebellum phase? Perhaps the most critical appraisal of historians' use of excessively broad and even conflicting definitions of capitalism is Michael Merrill, "Putting 'Capitalism' in Its Place: A Review of Recent Literature," *William and Mary Quarterly* 52 (April 1995):

315-26. It is also well established that antebellum northern farmers had become increasingly enmeshed in more capitalistic endeavors; however, southern farmers appeared to have held on to their dualistic approach into the twentieth century. See Jeremy Atack and Fred Bateman, *To Their Own Soil: Agriculture in the Antebellum North* (Ames: Iowa State University Press, 1987), and Bushman, "Markets and Composite Farms in Early America," 373-74.

9. Unlike Europe, America never emerged from a feudal economy, but it clearly developed into a modern capitalist economy. Debate has turned on what it was before: noncommercial, pre-capitalist, capitalist, or a frontier economy slowly connecting to market forces? Carl Degler set the debate on its modern track with his remark that capitalism "came in the first ships" (*Out of Our Past: The Forces That Shaped Modern America* [New York: Double Day, 1959), 1). Three path-breaking articles written during the 1970s (by Michael Merrill, James Henretta, and Christopher Clark) questioned Degler's assertion. Possibly the most articulate overview of this larger debate—including the influential trio of articles—is Kulikoff, "The Transition to Capitalism in Rural America." Gordon S. Wood synthesized the "transition" question in "Was America Born Capitalist?" *Wilson Quarterly* 23 (Spring 1999): 36-46.

10. Charles Sellers launched much of this discussion on the vital ingredients and larger significance of the market revolution. A contrasting view is found in the work of Daniel Walker Howe. See Sellers, *The Market Revolution: Jacksonian America, 1815-1846* (New York: Oxford University Press, 1991), and Howe, *What Hath God Wrought: The Transformation of America, 1815-1848* (New York: Oxford University Press, 2007).

11. Many studies confirm that roughly one in three families owned no real estate. See J. William Harris, *Plain Folk and Gentry in a Slave Society: White Liberty and Back Slavery in Augusta's Hinterlands* (Middleton, CT: Wesleyan University Press, 1985), 78; McCurry, *Masters of Small Worlds*, 52-53; Hahn, *Roots of Southern Populism*, 20-23; and Ford, *Origins of Southern Radicalism*, 48. Robert Tracy McKenzie found that landless Tennesseans possessed an even chance of becoming landowners during the 1850s, see *One South or Many? Plantation Belt and Upcountry in Civil War–Era Tennessee* (Cambridge, UK: Cambridge University Press, 1994), 79.

12. Seventh U.S. Census, Fayette and Madison County, Tennessee, 1850; Eighth U.S. Census, Fayette and Madison County, Tennessee, 1860; Owsley, *Plain Folk of the Old South*, 214.

13. The antebellum census did not identify tenants. The most direct method of identification (and the one used in this study) asserts that tenants consisted of farmers listed on both the agricultural and population schedules who did not possess real estate. By comparison of these two sources, anyone who farmed but did not own any land almost certainly was a tenant. For the various methods used to identify tenants, see Frederick A. Bode and Donald E. Ginther, *Farm Tenancy and the Census in Antebellum Georgia* (Athens: University of Georgia Press, 1986).

14. In North Carolina and Georgia, tenancy and sharecropping rental normally consisted of one-third the grain and one-fourth the cotton harvest, respectively. See Joseph D. Reid, "Antebellum Share Rental Contracts," *Explorations in Economic History* 13 (Jan. 1976): 69-83; and Hahn, *Roots of Southern Populism*, 64-70. Seventh and Eighth U.S. Census, Population Schedule, Agriculture Schedule, Madison County, Tennessee, 1850, 1860.

15. Across several counties in Tennessee, the majority of tenants in 1850 had moved by 1860. See Donald Winters, *Tennessee Farming, Tennessee Farmers: Antebellum Agriculture in the Upper South* (Knoxville: University of Tennessee Press, 1994), 101-02. Seventh and Eighth U.S. Census, Agriculture Schedule, Population Schedule, Madison County, Tennessee, 1850, 1860; William Beard, Tennessee Civil War Veterans Questionnaires, TSLA.

16. This distribution of wealth appeared common across Tennessee. Winters' eight-county sample (including Fayette and Haywood) reflected a comparable proportion. See *Tennessee Farming*, 109. On the importance of improved acreage as an interpretative variable, see John Majewski and Viken Tchakerian, "The Environmental Origins of Shifting Cultivation: Climate, Soils, and Disease in the Nineteenth-Century U.S. South," *Agricultural History* 81 (Fall 2007): 522-49.

17. *West Tennessee Whig*, January 19, 1854; Robert H. Cartmell Papers, February 5, 1855, TSLA; and James H. Edmondson, "Denmark, Tennessee: The First 150 Years," *West Tennessee Historical Society Papers* 34 (1980): 90-91.

18. John Johnston, "Addendum to Memoirs," 1928, Confederate Collection, TSLA.

19. J. B. Maclin to R. H. Morrison, February 16, 1854, Robert H. Morrison Papers, Southern Historical Collection, University of North Carolina, Chapel Hill,; Kathleen Christine Berkeley, "'Like a Plague of Locusts': Immigration and Social Change in Memphis, Tennessee, 1850-1880" (PhD diss., University of California, Los Angeles, 1980), 14-19.

20. In basic outlook and worldview, antebellum Tennessee yeomen probably had values and potential opportunities similar to those of artisans. In effect, both played a reciprocal role in assisting the other with various degrees of self-sufficiency. Fred A. Bailey, *Class and Tennessee's Confederate Generation* (Chapel Hill: University of North Carolina Press, 1987), 30.

21. A. J. Derryberry, James Dickinson, Tennessee Civil War Veterans Questionnaires, TSLA; Seventh U.S. Census, Population, Agriculture, and Slave Schedules, Madison County, Tennessee, 1850.

22. Michele Gillespie's study established the concept of "planters in the making." See Gillespie, *Free Labor in an Unfree World: White Artisans in Slaveholding Georgia, 1789-1860* (Athens: University of Georgia Press, 2000), 1-36.

23. *The Goodspeed History of Madison County Tennessee* (Nashville, TN: Woodward and Stinson Printing, 1887), 850.

24. Frank Owsley, "The Pattern of Migration and Settlement on the Southern Frontier," *Journal of Southern History* 11 (May 1945): 147-76; Forrest McDonald and Grady McWhiney, "The Antebellum Southern Herdsman: A Reinterpretation," *Journal of Southern History* 41 (May 1975): 147-66. Two works that emphasize the use of herds as a source of income are Solomon Otto, "The Migration of the Southern Plain Folk: An Interdisciplinary Synthesis," *Journal of Southern History* 51 (May 1985): 183-200, and Bradley G. Bond, "Herders, Farmers, and Markets on the Inner Frontier: The Mississippi Piney Woods, 1850-1860," in *Plain Folk of the South Revisited*, ed. Samuel C. Hyde (Baton Rouge: Louisiana State University Press, 1997), 73-99.

25. Solon Robinson quoted in Winters, *Tennessee Farming*, 121. On the feeding of supplemental grain to hogs, see John Houston Bills Diary, December 5, 1843, Southern Historical Collection, University of North Carolina, Chapel Hill.

26. Cartmell Papers, July 1, August 31, 1859, TSLA.

27. For cotton prices and trends see Gray, *History of Agriculture in the Southern United States*, 2:699-700. Two works that generally uphold the view that herding represented a kind of "cash crop" as a transitional means toward established farming are Bond, "Herders, Farmers, and Markets," and Otto, "Migration of the Southern Plain Folk." Other studies also discovered that between 1850 and 1860 the number of swine declined even in the face of rising rural population. See Hahn, *Roots of Southern Populism*, 299, and McCurry, *Masters of Small Worlds*, 308-9.

It is worth noting that the cotton harvests for 1850 and 1860 could illuminate the agricultural choices of yeomen and planters alike. A larger harvest in 1860 would suggest greater emphasis on land improvement, perhaps even at the expense of livestock. Regional cotton harvests increased substantially; however, scholars have been reluctant to draw bold conclusions about the dramatic growth. Both of these years were anomalies with regard to the national cotton crop: the 1850 crop was unusually low because of a late frost across much of the South, while the 1860 yield was widely considered to be a bumper crop. Madison County planter Robert Cartmell confirmed that an April 1849 frost damaged southwestern Tennessee's crop. Cartmell Papers, January 1, 1853, TSLA. Nevertheless, the sum of the evidence suggests farmers and planters tended to allocate more resources toward cotton over time. The growing price and demand for cotton reinforces this. See Wright, *Political Economy of the Cotton South,* 104.

28. Gavin Wright observed that Owsley's assertion cannot be proven based solely on the available evidence. Instead, we might be better served by looking to agency and causation in order to uncover some plausible motivation behind the actions of the yeomanry. See Wright, *Political Economy of the Cotton South,* 69; and Owsley, *Plain Folk of the Old South,* 134.

29. Donald Winters' eight-county sample agrees with this trend and corroborates a wealth decile chart that identifies yeomen in the third down to the mid-eighth decile. Dickson D. Bruce Jr. found that yeomen produced a smaller percentage of cotton (7 percent of Mississippi's, for instance). See Winters, "'Plain Folk' of the Old South Reexamined: Economic Democracy in Tennessee," *Journal of Southern History* 53 (Nov. 1987): 565-86; Bruce, *And They All Sang Hallelujah: Plain Folk Camp-Meeting Religion, 1800-1845* (Knoxville: University of Tennessee Press, 1974).

30. Lorenzo Lea to Father, November 24, 1853, Lea Family Papers, Southern Historical Collection, University of North Carolina, Chapel Hill.

31. Profitability should not be confused with the calculated rationality of profit maximization. As individuals with the power to choose what was both utilitarian and economically sensible, yeomen considered a range of personal variables based on the intimate nature of their familial/labor relations. Profitability had to be compatible with family harmony. See Naomi R. Lamoreaux, "Rethinking the Transition to Capitalism in the Early American Northeast," *Journal of American History* 90, no. 2 (2003): 449-51, and Stanley Engerman and Robert Gallman, "The Emergence of a Market Economy before 1860," in *A Companion to Nineteenth Century America,* ed, William L. Barney (Oxford, UK: Blackwell Publishing, 2006), 121-38.

32. For regional cotton yields, see Cartmell Papers, January 1, 1853, TSLA, and Cottle, comp., "With Pen in Hand," 56. Cotton prices can be found in Gray, *History of Agriculture in the Southern United States,* 2:699-700.

33. The annual amount of cotton for a family was fifty pounds per adult and twenty-five per child. A four-hundred-pound bale might suffice for a large family with admittedly simple taste. This is an estimate based on county government charity annually distributed to widows and orphans. See County Clerk Minutes, March 7, 1842, Fayette County, Tennessee; Westley Sheets, Tennessee Civil War Veterans Questionnaires, TSLA.

34. Yeomen cotton harvests varied across the Old South, but three bales per farm is a reasonable average for nonslaveholders. Some studies draw a correlation between acreage and harvest size; others explore labor and harvest size. In the Old South, enslaved labor may be the critical variable. Slavery dominated a farmer's indebtedness as well as the ability to cultivate and harvest a labor-intensive crop. See Winters, *Tennessee Farming,* 59; McCurry, *Masters of Small Worlds,* 65-69; Baptist, *Creating an Old South,* 239-40; Bolton, *Poor Whites of the Antebellum South,* 90; Harris, *Plain Folk and Gentry in a Slave Society,* 23-24. In the Georgia Upcountry yeomen-sized farms of 50 to 199 acres raised 1 to 2.4 bales in 1850 but increased to 7 to 13.4 bales by 1880. The reasons for this dramatic change are varied. However, for the purposes of this study, it suggests that

many antebellum yeomen who could have grown more cotton on the same land chose not to. See Hahn, *Roots of Southern Populism*, 29, 299-300.

35. Seventh and Eighth U.S. Census, Population, Agriculture, and Slave Schedules, Madison County, Tennessee, 1850, 1860.

36. Ibid.

37. Ibid.

38. Stephanie McCurry pointed out that in South Carolina no evidence backed the assumption that since yeomen did not own expensive cotton gins, planters simply ginned and shipped it with their own. See *Masters of Small Worlds*, 103-4. Johnston, "Addendum to Memoirs," TSLA.

39. The question of "southern distinctiveness" continues to interest historians of the antebellum era. See Edward Pessen, "How Different Were the Antebellum North and South?" *American Historical Review* 85 (Dec. 1980): 1119-49; James McPherson, *Drawn with the Sword: Reflections on the American Civil War* (New York: Oxford University Press, 1996), 3-23; and Peter Kolchin, *American Slavery, 1619-1877* (New York: Hill and Wang, 1993), 170-74.

40. Eugene Genovese stated that yeomen in the plantation belt knew of little else. Plantation slavery was the world in which they also lived, thus they subsequently made sense out of their place in it in relation to the cultural and economic dominance of planters. See "Yeomen Farmers in a Slaveholders' Democracy," *Agricultural History* 49, no. 2 (April 1975): 331-42.

41. The discussion on this question followed in a disagreement between Eugene Genovese and James Oakes. See Genovese, *The Political Economy of Slavery* (New York: Pantheon, 1965), *Roll, Jordan, Roll: The World the Slaves Made* (New York: Pantheon, 1974), *The Slaveholders' Dilemma: Freedom and Progress in Southern Conservative Thought, 1820-1860* (Columbia: University of South Carolina Press, 1992), and with Elizabeth Fox-Genovese, *Fruits of Merchant Capital: Slavery and Bourgeois Property in the Rise and Expansion of Capitalism* (New York: Pantheon, 1983); and with Oakes, *The Ruling Race: A History of American Slaveholders* (New York: Knopf, 1982) and *Slavery and Freedom: An Interpretation of the Old South* (New York: Knopf, 1990). Oakes and Genovese eventually moderated their positions and conceded slavery probably constituted some hybridized form of capitalistic behavior.

42. The overrepresentation of women and children slaves is well documented for the South Carolina low country. See McCurry, *Masters of Small Worlds*, 47-50.

43. Seventh and Eighth U.S. Census, Population and Slave Schedules, Madison County, Tennessee, 1850, 1860.

44. For another explanation of pushing the threshold of yeomen identity up to the ownership of nine slaves, see McCurry, *Masters of Small Worlds*, 48-49. For information on the labor expectations of enslaved women and children see, George P. Rawick, ed., *The American Slave: A Composite Autobiography* (Westport, CT: Greenwood, 1972), and Deborah Gray White, *Ar'n't I a Woman? Female Slaves in the Plantation South* (New York: W.W. Norton, 1985). On the risks of small slaveholding, see William L. Barney, *The Road to Secession: A New Perspective on the Old South* (New York: Praeger, 1972), 113-14.

45. Seventh and Eighth U.S. Census, Agriculture, Population, and Slave Schedules, Fayette County, Tennessee, 1850, 1860; James Polk Hogan, Tennessee Civil War Veterans Questionnaires, TSLA.

46. Daniel Thorner, "Peasant Economy as a Category in Economic History," in *Peasants and Peasant Societies: Selected Readings*, ed, Teodor Shanin (Middlesex, UK, 1971), 207, cited in Hahn, "A Response: Common Cents or Historical Sense?" *Journal of Southern History* 59, no. 2 (1993): 245.

Chapter 5

"Chased Out on the Slippery Ice"

Rural Wage Laborers in Baltimore's Hinterlands, 1815-1860

Max L. Grivno

In 1848, shoemaker Alexander Redman led one of his children to a thicket outside their home in rural Washington County, Maryland. There, Redman took a razor and slashed the child's throat "so effectually as almost to have severed the head from the body." After committing the murder, the dazed cobbler wandered to a neighbor's house and confessed to killing the child "because he was afraid it would come to want." He then returned to his own home and committed suicide, leaving behind his wife, four dependent children, and "some little property." In the aftermath of these tragic events, Redman's friends testified that he suffered from "temporary fits of madness" caused by "excessive dissipation" but insisted that he had been sober for several months. Echoing the shoemaker's confession, they affirmed that he had been languishing under a "depression of spirit, caused by fear of coming to poverty and want."[1]

It may be unwise to attach undue significance to the gruesome drama that unfolded at Redman's home; his periodic bouts with alcoholism and "fits of madness" suggest a disturbed individual, not a social critique. Still, the gnawing anxiety that gripped Redman—the "fear of coming to poverty and want"—haunted many working men and women in Baltimore's hinterlands. Swiss immigrant J. Jakob Rutlinger likened the plight of the region's rural laborers to that of "someone who can't skate and is chased out on the slippery ice." Those who were "careful and capable of much work . . . can make a living," Rutlinger observed, "but it must be sought ceaselessly and anxiously."

Although he conceded that workers might find steady employment during the summer, Rutlinger hastened to add that their livelihoods became "uncertain and subject to capricious change" in the slack seasons. Rutlinger knew of what he spoke. During his family's first winter in Maryland, they had survived by binding books, making hat boxes, weaving straw hats, operating a singing school, and peddling firewood.[2]

The struggles of Redman and Rutlinger offer a rare glimpse into the world of the Old South's wage laborers, a group that has, until very recently, been relegated to the shadows of a literature dominated by planters, yeoman farmers, and slaves. Despite a spate of painstaking works by historians like Charles Bolton, Wilma Dunaway, and Jeff Forret, our knowledge of southern farmhands and tenants remains incomplete.[3] Certain topics, like the experience of rural free blacks, have received scant attention.[4] Likewise, scholars have overlooked the strategies that impoverished families cobbled together to survive the often unforgiving southern economy.[5] This chapter contributes to literature on poor southerners by examining the wage laborers—men and women, free blacks and whites—who worked in Baltimore's hinterlands. In addition to reconstructing their varied occupations and households, it also considers how a shifting constellation of gender, race, and legal restrictions shaped the lives of the region's free laborers and, in the end, prevented them from developing any overarching sense of common identity.

The workforce in Baltimore's hinterlands was an unstable concoction. Like a whirling kaleidoscope, its contours and composition were constantly in motion, shifting with the seasons and with the varied fortunes of the regional economy. The ranks of this protean workforce were filled by landless rural residents, members of small-landowning families, canal and railroad workers, displaced factory operatives and dockworkers, and under- or unemployed craftsmen and apprentices. It was, moreover, a mobile workforce. When winter brought the agricultural economy to a grinding halt, many laborers tramped into crossroad villages, river towns, and seaport cities, where they subsisted on intermittent employment or poor relief. As winter yielded to spring, small troops of farmhands drifted back into the countryside. This trickle became a torrent during the wheat harvest, when thousands followed the ripening wheat northward from Virginia into Pennsylvania. Not surprisingly, the workforce created by these accretions was a motley assemblage, riven along overlapping lines of age, ethnicity, gender, and race.

The churning waters of the agricultural workforce crested during the wheat harvest, when, as one newspaper noted, "every sickle is busy . . . and every idler capable of handling one has been pressed into service."[6] It is, therefore, fitting that a discussion of agricultural workers should begin at the harvest, for the roaming gangs of harvesters embodied the diversity, mobility, and instability that were the hallmarks of the rural proletariat. Moreover, the harvest season provides a counterpoint to the remainder of the year, when unemployment thinned the ranks and sent desperate laborers scrambling for a living. Farmhands' prospects shone brightest at harvest, when work abounded, wages were comparatively generous, and otherwise powerless workers could wrest concessions from employers.

The wheat harvest spawned a massive labor mobilization that blurred distinctions between rural and urban workforces. From the countryside, newspapers trumpeted the "great demand and uncommonly high wages" being offered to harvesters, enticing townsfolk "who are laboring for low wages, or even high wages at ordinary work, to come on and assist our farmers. A rich reward awaits them."[7] Urban workingmen answered such calls with enthusiasm. Indeed, the exodus of Hagerstown's workers startled an editor, who lamented the "general dullness and desertion of our streets during harvest." Likewise, a Washington County farmboy recalled that the wheat harvest "caused such a demand for labor that it depopulated the towns of all-able bodied men and boys."[8]

Unskilled workers from the region's internal improvement projects were swept along in the stampede to the harvest fields. As early as 1805, the managers of the Frederick-Town Turnpike Company announced that they would schedule their work around the busiest times of the growing season to avoid "raising the price of labor and interfering with the ordinary occupations of the farms and manufacturies in the vicinity of the road."[9] This overlap of the agricultural and nonagricultural workforce seems to have persisted over the following decades. In 1829, Frederick tailor Jacob Englebrecht commented on the movement of canal workers into the harvest workforce, noting that "hands are very plenty owing, I suppose, to the Chesapeake and Ohio Canal's stopping during the harvest to give the farmers a chance to have the grain cut."[10]

Like common laborers, rural craftsmen abandoned their regular pursuits during harvest. Among the harvesters on Joseph M. Wolfe's farm in Washington County were several neighborhood artisans, including saddler Hezekiah Hurley, shoemakers Ezra Smith and Isaiah Reese, and wagonmaker John Springer.[11] Apprentices, too, joined in the movement from workshop to harvest field. Maryland law provided that all apprentices, "except those bound to tradesmen and mechanics residing in any town," could be compelled to perform "reasonable labor" during the harvest unless their contracts stipulated otherwise.[12] Foregoing harvest earnings or surrendering them to a master craftsman was, however, unpalatable to many apprentices and their parents, who negotiated indentures that preserved their freedom to labor independently during harvest. When apprenticing himself to a rough carpenter, Joel Stimmel demanded "four weeks in harvest for his own use," while Peter Powell stipulated that his son receive eight days' harvest wages if he was needed in his master's blacksmith shop during harvest.[13]

The surge of harvest workers spilled across state borders, creating a migrant force that spanned the Mason-Dixon Line. Among those toiling in the harvest fields were residents of the mountainous regions of western Maryland, southern Pennsylvania, and northwest Virginia, who poured into the fertile valleys and followed the harvest's northerly march. "The grain in our section ripened some weeks before the Pennsylvania fields," recalled one Marylander, "and many persons journeyed from that state to our valley to help harvest the crop. In squads, many came from the mountainous portions of Huntington and Bedford counties, and were called 'backwoodsmen.'"[14]

The eagerness with which workers followed the harvest bespoke the vital importance of harvest wages. Unable to find steady employment during the winter, farmhands deprived of their harvest earnings might face severe privation. Elias Kroft made this connection explicit when he demanded additional daily wages of between $0.75 and $1 during the harvest, as "the support of his wife and children during the winter chiefly depended on what he earned during harvest time."[15] Hagerstown attorney Thomas Kennedy echoed this argument when he petitioned Governor Samuel Sprigg to pardon Samuel Riley, a free black man who had been convicted of assisting fugitive slaves. Noting that the jury had been sharply divided and that Riley's family had suffered during his fourteen-month imprisonment, Kennedy urged the governor to release his client before the upcoming wheat harvest. "Harvest is now at hand," he wrote, "and if released [Riley] will be able to do something to help himself and wife."[16]

Because regular employment and steady wages were scarce, farmhands lived with a gnawing uncertainty. The seasonal fluctuations in the agricultural labor market may have borne heavily upon Harry Luckett, a free black farmhand employed on Richard Vansant's Baltimore County farm from 1855 to 1859. During his forty-month tenure with Vansant, Luckett was seldom fully employed. On average, he worked only 14.7 days per month. During the slowest seasons, Luckett was often entirely unemployed. He found steadier work during the summer, but even haymaking and harvesting could not guarantee full employment. Indeed, there were only thirteen months during which Luckett worked more than 20 days. The irregularity of employment was matched by seasonal fluctuations in wages. Luckett's monthly earnings during the winter were paltry, often hovering around $5; but sometimes he received no wages at all in the winter months. Luckett was forced to garner a disproportionate share of his annual earnings—between 20 and 25 percent—during the harvest.[17]

The same seasonality marked the incomes of other agricultural workers. In 1851 and 1852, white farmhand John Stockman's daily wages ranged from $1.25 during the wheat harvest to a mere $0.50 in the winter.[18]

How workers coped with these seasonal patterns of under- and unemployment remains unclear. Rural laborers are an elusive quarry. They emerge from the shadows, flit through account books and court records, and then vanish from the historical record, making it difficult to track them across extended periods or to uncover the full range of their economic activities. What evidence we have, however, suggests that they danced between farmwork and nonagricultural employment with the changing seasons. The confession of Amos Green, a free black executed in 1851 for raping a German woman, offers a glimpse into the transient careers of the rural workers. When he met his alleged victim, Green was employed in the flour mills near Ellicott City, Maryland. When the mills suspended operation, Green drifted into the countryside, where he found periodic employment on farms in Howard and Prince George's counties. With the onset of winter, Green turned to working at the copper deposits in the Little Patuxent River.[19]

Seasonal movement between industries was not uncommon. Indeed, necessity often compelled workers to cross the porous boundary between agricultural and industrial pursuits. "Whenever I found myself pushed," recalled African Methodist Episcopal minister Thomas W. Henry, "I would turn to anything that I could get to do. Sometimes I was called upon to go to quarry rock—sometimes to the harvest; and in this way I supported myself and family."[20] In 1846, a farmer in northern Virginia described a similar movement between agricultural and nonagricultural employments, noting that a farmhand he had previously hired "is at work for the present some twenty miles off at [the] Canal."[21] Even members of landowning families scrambled between industries. David Heim, who managed his father's farm in Frederick County, also labored on neighboring farms, collected produce for urban merchants, followed the wheat harvest into Pennsylvania, and spent several months working on a canal boat.[22]

The seasonality that characterized the farm-labor market may have been less pronounced in the nonagricultural sector, but these industries, too, experienced seasonal downturns. Rural mills suspended operations during the coldest months, victims of frozen creeks and millponds. Nor were internal improvement projects immune from the general tightening of the labor market. Although contractors on the Baltimore and Ohio (B & O) Railroad retained a "large number of workmen," the "excessive severity" of the winter of 1828-1829 forced them to winnow their workforce to about 1,000—approximately half the number employed during spring and summer.[23] Turnpike construction and repair also slowed during winter. Between 1821 and 1823, contractor John Piper employed a modest crew on the National Road near Cumberland, Maryland, during the warmer seasons, but he discharged the entire force with the onset of winter.[24] The seasonal constriction of the labor market could have dire consequences for manual laborers. In 1849, Susanna Warfield of Carroll County, Maryland, discovered that an Irish family had squatted in a dilapidated shanty on a neighboring plantation. Although the structure's door and floorboards had been stripped by previous occupants, the family—which included a pregnant woman—spent several weeks in the shack, subsisting on charity from local whites. "They are fresh immigrants," Warfield lamented, "and all work being suspended on the road the man cannot get work."[25]

While alternating between agricultural and nonagricultural employment, workers sometimes migrated between town and country. Many of the felons sentenced to the Maryland Penitentiary from Baltimore and other towns listed their occupation as farm laborers, suggesting that unemployed farmhands regularly found their way into urban centers.[26] Typical, perhaps, was William Fry, a young laborer who was convicted for stealing horses in 1822. Describing the events preceding his arrest, Fry stated that "about the middle of March I left the neighborhood of Harper's Ferry, where I had spent the winter and come to Fredericktown to look for work." During his travels, Fry met Harry Carin, who claimed to be a farmer from Harrisburg, Pennsylvania. "He offered me good wages and steady employment if I would go home with him, and being out of employment and destitute of a home I readily agreed." Unfortunately, Carin had been stealing horses in Virginia and Maryland, and he soon pressured Fry into joining his criminal enterprise.[27]

As winter brought the rural economy to a standstill, unemployed workers who remained in the country drifted into an underworld of shooting matches, gambling houses, and grogshops.[28] There, they filled their idle hours—and empty pockets—engaging in activities that roused magistrates' suspicions but were nevertheless thoroughly engrained in the rural economy. Indeed, for many poor whites, operating an unlicensed gambling house or selling whiskey was a necessary adjunct to seasonal labor. James Brightwell, a Frederick County farmhand and woodcutter, sold "a small quantity of liquor" at a backwoods shooting match that he had organized during the winter of 1820-1821. Arrested and fined, the illiterate Brightwell called upon his friends, who petitioned the governor on his behalf. The shooting match, they argued, had been held "according to the customary practice of his neighborhood." Moreover, Brightwell's motive for hosting the event was to provide for his "wife and four small children," who were "altogether dependent upon his labor, [as] he has no property whatsoever."[29] For the rural poor, the boundaries between legal business, sociability, and criminal activity were often muddled.

Tossed about in the tumultuous economy, many workers survived by clinging together in fragile households. Although most of the region's free laborers were single men, an examination of census returns reveals that a significant percentage were married with children. Of the 2,892 workingmen enumerated in the 1850 federal census of Washington County, 1,831 (63 percent) were not heads of households. Only 510 of these were the children of landowning farmers, artisans, or professionals who might expect to inherit property, receive an education or craft training, or assume control of their father's business. Thus, many workingmen reached adulthood without accumulating significant amounts of real property or becoming artisans or professionals. Indeed, Washington County contained 1,061 landless workers who were heads of households. Most of these men were married. Of the 870 whites, only 16 were single, while all but 6 of the African American laborers who headed households were married. The vast majority of married laborers had children. Indeed, only 103 (12 percent) of the white families and 24 (13 percent) of the black families were childless. Workers' families tended to be young. Among those considered, 551 (63 percent) of the white families and 115 (60 percent) of the black families consisted of married couples and children under the age of fifteen. An additional 149 white families and 27 black families included both dependent and adult children, raising the overall percentage of laboring families with dependent children to about three-quarters. For poor workingmen, the earnings of a wife or children often made the difference between want and survival.

The account of Washington County merchant Jacob Reichard and tenant farmer John McFerren illuminates the tangled skein of dependency that united rural households. Having fallen into Reichard's debt, McFarren mustered the labor of his entire family in an unsuccessful attempt to square their accounts. He contributed corn, firewood, and staves, while his wife and daughters added butter, eggs, and rags. The family dog even lent a hand, adding "two puppies" to their credits.[30] Jeremiah Harlan's accounts with his tenants in Harford County further underscore the importance of women's and children's labor to a household's survival. In 1823, Harlan leased a cottage and provision grounds to "Negro Anthony Smith" and his family. Harlan retained them as tenants for several years, despite their inability to settle debts accrued for housing, bacon, cider, cornmeal, and beef. Smith's entire family contributed to the struggle to extricate themselves from debt: his daughter worked in wheat harvests, his wife earned $2.24 by spinning and washing, and he sold a cow, valued at $12, which had probably been cared for by his wife or daughter. The family's efforts proved futile. On April 25, 1826, Harlan issued a distress against them for the recovery of their outstanding debts and evicted them from his property.

Thomas West Sr., the white tenant farmer who replaced Anthony Smith, was, like his predecessor, dependent upon his family's earnings. In 1827, West's family accrued debts totaling $61.48 for rent, foodstuffs, and orders at nearby stores. Of the $57.46 credited to the family's account, $33.40 came from Thomas West Jr., who labored for fourteen days during the harvest and an additional 131 days during the remainder of the year.[31]

Because the survival of a poor household hinged upon each member's contribution, the disability of a husband, wife, or working child might plunge the family into ruin. After having "the bones of his arm dreadfully shattered" in an accident, Baltimore County farmhand Solomon Osburn saw "the savings of some years of industry" evaporate. His family became dependent upon handouts and the earnings of his wife, whose health deteriorated from exposure and overwork. Within two years, the combined pressure of his "melancholy affliction," mounting medical bills, and the unpredictability of private charity forced Osburn to petition Baltimore County's overseers of the poor for outdoor relief.[32] Women's wages might have softened the impact of a husband's incapacitation, but their domestic responsibilities kept them tethered to their households, further limiting their employment opportunities and earning potential. When black farmhand Hilleary Hillman became "seriously afflicted with a cancer" that left him bedridden, his wife attempted to support the family's several children. Despite making a determined effort, Hillman's wife discovered that her wages were "greatly inadequate for their support."[33]

In a society structured around households and whose labor market was dominated by single men or male-headed families, few opportunities were available to single women, and fewer still to unwed mothers. The wages of employed women on the region's farms were, on average, between one-quarter and one-third of men's, making it difficult for single women to support themselves.[34] Unable to wield the heavy cradles and scythes used during harvest, women were often excluded from the remunerative branches of farmwork. This disparity is apparent in the wages earned by carpenter Peter Fogle and his wife, Sarah, during the 1852 harvest. Both toiled for nine days, but Peter earned $9.50 for cradling compared to the meager $0.50 Sarah received for "cuking."[35] Although paltry, these wages were important to women, who sometimes joined the roaming bands of harvesters. In 1842, Sevilla Moonshour left her home in Frederick County and traveled to Carroll County, where she found employment with a farmer near Taneytown. She continued with that farmer from June 30 through July 3, when another farmer, Henry Hess, hired her to rake. Moonshour remained with Hess through July 9. The following day, she "was engaged in carrying water for some hands cutting grain" on yet another farm. By July 12, Moonshour had again changed employers.[36]

To seek outside employment, women needed to be free of domestic obligations—housework, pregnancies, and raising children might all prevent women from finding work. Thus, the plight of single mothers was often desperate. If employers sometimes hired married men in part to gain access to the labor of their wives and children, they were unwilling to engage single women with dependent children. The marginal position of such women in the rural economy became painfully clear to Rachel R. Dell and her infant children after they were abandoned by their alcoholic husband and father. Dell's petition for outdoor relief underscored employers' prejudice against single mothers. "I have heard it has been communicated to you that I would not work, which is all false," Dell declared. "I would be very glad to get a situation but that is very [hard] to get as they [the children] are so small one of them is only five months old and the other 18 months."[37]

Women might brighten their employment prospects and ease the strain on their family's resources by apprenticing their adolescent children, but this option was not available to those with young children. In her petition for outdoor relief, widow Eliza Koon pleaded that she had "two small children entirely two [*sic*] young to bind out," which left her family "dependent upon the charitableness of the people in their neighborhood."[38] In 1844, Catherine Taylor, a widow with three children, found herself in similar straits, claiming that she "made some effort to put her children out, but in consequence of their being too small no person wanted them and they have to remain on her hands."[39]

Because the rural economy afforded single women few opportunities, many sought their livelihoods on its shadowy fringes; they turned to petty production or operating unlicensed boardinghouses, grogshops, and restaurants. The marginality—or downright illegality—of these operations is suggested by the small number of female proprietors who bothered to purchase licenses from the county courts. In 1850, Frederick County granted 66 tavern licenses to men, but only 9 to women. The gender imbalance was even more skewed among merchants. Only 15 women received merchant licenses, compared to 266 men. Moreover, the average value of their stock ($259) lagged far behind that of men ($930).[40] The constraints of the rural economy forced some women to combine their marketing with illegal activities, such as peddling alcohol. Proprietors of small groceries and taverns danced along—and across—the boundary separating legal and illegal. Consider, for example, the plight of widow Mary Ockes, who supported herself and her seven children by peddling baked goods, vegetables, and—on occasion—alcohol to support her family. Arrested and fined $16 for selling liquor without a license, Ockes begged Governor Joseph Kent for a pardon, claiming that she could not afford to pay the fee.[41]

Given their desperate plight, it is not surprising that many single mothers became objects of charity. Free black Betsey Reister became dependent upon a neighboring family after giving birth; but being "incapable of compensating them in any way," she soon became a burden upon her caretakers, who grumbled that they "are not in a condition to keep her free of charge."[42] When private charity failed, single mothers turned to public assistance, becoming a disproportionate share of the young women on relief rolls. Of the nine female paupers of childbearing age in the Frederick County almshouse in 1850, seven were mothers with infant children. A similar pattern prevailed in the Washington County almshouse, where all five of the female paupers of childbearing age had infant children. Single mothers also constituted a significant share of the women receiving outdoor relief. Of the twenty-two women of childbearing age listed as paupers in the 1850 census of Frederick County, sixteen (73 percent) were single mothers.[43]

Single women with adolescent or adult children fared better, as employers and landlords were willing to engage them in order to gain access to their children's labor. An employer, landlord, or merchant might extend credit to an unwed or widowed mother if he believed her children's services might offset the expense. We see this in the case of Elizabeth Ware, a woman in her sixties who rented a house from Franklin Osburn, a farmer and merchant in Jefferson County, Virginia. In 1860, Ware headed a household that included herself, her son Richard, who was twenty-one years old, a daughter or daughter-in-law, Susan, age twenty-four, and three children who were eight, two, and two months old, respectively.[44] Between 1855 and 1861, Ware's family accumulated debts totaling $187.97 for rent, food, firewood, and credit at their landlord's store. Ware managed to settle a small part of her family's debt by working as a farmhand, but her age and sex prevented her from working routinely. In 1856, for example, she worked four days in the wheat harvest. The following year, she spent thirteen days harvesting and another four days hoeing and cutting corn. Her wages for this work were but $8.74, a mere fraction of her family's total debt. Elizabeth and Susan further contributed to the family's income by sewing clothing for Osburn's household and for sale in his store. Still, their income from seamstress work was meager, amounting to only $22 over the course of six years. It was Richard who earned the bulk of the family's income by working as a field hand. During his family's tenure at Osburn's farm, Richard earned $80.98, the vast majority of which—some $61.12—was earned harvesting wheat. Although the Wares never settled their accounts, Richard's agricultural work during critical periods of the growing season seems to have been crucial to the household's remaining on Osburn's property.[45] Heavily dependent upon their children's earnings, single mothers strove to secure the greatest possible return for their labor.

In 1840, the promise of higher wages impelled free black Fanny Baptist to remove her son, Tom, from Robert Archer's farm, where he had been working for food, clothing, and an annual wage of $40. "I kept this boy all winter and clothed him for twelve months," the angry farmer scrawled in his account book, "how he went off with his mother who said she could hire him for $6 pr. month."[46]

The survival of working families hinged upon women's contributions, but the codependency that characterized laboring families did not alter fundamental gendered inequalities within the rural labor market. A childless woman might muddle through without male support, but those with dependent children faced a dire situation. When abandonment, death, or divorce stripped a woman of her husband's support, she had little recourse but to seek public assistance or scrape out a living on the margins of the economy through petty marketing, operating an unlicensed grocery or grogshop, or prostitution.

Navigating the tempestuous rural economy was a difficult task. Under the best circumstances, working families had to harness the labor of men, women, and children while drawing upon reserves of ingenuity, perseverance, and luck. The burden shouldered by free blacks was, however, even more onerous. Living in slavery's long shadow, they were forced to support dependent relatives who remained in bondage while being denied the fruits of their enslaved kinsfolk's labor. The constraints that slavery imposed on free blacks' inter- and intrastate movements added to their woes. Free blacks lacked the mobility, the nimbleness, that laborers needed to survive in the unstable rural economy because they were often shackled to a neighborhood and dependent upon white protectors.

For many free black laborers, the most pressing need was to ransom their enslaved kinfolk. Because many black families straddled the line between slavery and freedom, free black families were often denied the labor of their husbands, wives, and children—a potential disaster when a family's success or failure hinged upon the wages of every working person. Yet liberating enslaved relatives was a formidable challenge. Indeed, few blacks managed to ransom their kinsfolk outright. An examination of fifty years of transactions recorded by the Court of Frederick County, Maryland, uncovered only 114 slaves who were purchased by their relatives. Their average cost was $139, which amounted to more than a year's wages for an adult male farmhand.[47] For those who owned little and whose principal possessions were their liberty and their labor, purchasing a family member's freedom sometimes meant mortgaging their own freedom. In 1846, free black Elias James attempted to secure his wife's freedom. Because the $125 demanded by slaveholder Joseph Christ was beyond his limited means, James was forced into peonage until the debt was retired. If James defaulted on the debt, or if he refused to work, the contract specified that he would forfeit his wages and that his wife "would again become the property of Jos. Christ."[48]

Those African Americans who succeeded in ransoming their children from bondage may have found that their victory was pyrrhic. Over the course of the antebellum decades, Maryland's General Assembly enacted a series of increasingly harsh apprenticeship laws that undermined black parents' authority over their free children. The emerging legal regime vested control of black children in the hands of county authorities, who exercised great latitude in wrenching young African Americans from their families and binding them to white masters. Although Maryland's original apprenticeship law had been race neutral, in 1808 the legislature authorized county courts to bind out "the child or children of any pauper or vagrant, or the child of lazy, indolent and worthless free negroes."[49] In 1819, that authority was broadened to include black children "not at service or learning a trade, or employed in the service of their parents." Thus, a parent's perceived turpitude or a child's unemployment became causes for removing African American children from their families. Worse, the legislation extended black women's term of service from sixteen to eighteen years and allowed masters to forego educating a black apprentice in exchange for a small cash payment.[50]

The grounds for binding out black children became even more nebulous in 1840, when the assembly enacted the state's most draconian apprenticeship code. Under the new statute, county officials could apprentice young blacks "to some white person" if they believed that such an arrangement "would be better for the habits and comfort" of the children. In a significant departure from previous laws, which required local officials to "gratify the inclinations" of the child's parents respecting the choice of a master or mistress, the 1840 statute contained no such provisions. To guarantee that its provisions would be aggressively enforced, the law provided cash incentives to county officials for pursuing black children. Moreover, "any negro or other person" who abducted or enticed a black apprentice would face a prison sentence ranging from one to four years.[51] The legislature further diminished black parents' authority in 1845, when it authorized the masters of black apprentices to sell the children's unexpired terms to persons within the same county.[52]

Despite the legal apparatus arrayed against African American families, relatively few black children were apprenticed. Between 1837 and 1860, only 465 blacks were apprenticed in Carroll, Frederick, Howard, and Washington counties. Blacks did, however, constitute a disproportionate percentage of those bound out. Most black apprenticeships were compulsory, triggered by a child's being impoverished, orphaned, or judged to be the offspring of "lazy and worthless negroes." The masters of these children were concerned with securing laborers for their farms, a fact reflected in the large number of adolescent male apprentices. Some 221 (48 percent) of the black apprentices were males between the ages of ten and twenty-one, the majority of whom were to learn farming, labor, or "usefulness." Black children bound under these circumstances had few opportunities to acquire skills; only 10 of the 363 African Americans bound out by county authorities were placed with tradesmen. Black parents fared little better in securing craft training for their children; of the ninety black children who were voluntarily apprenticed by their parents, only four were bound to craftsmen.[53]

The fierce resistance mounted by African American families might explain the small number of black apprentices. Abduction was the most direct strategy used by parents for thwarting their children's indenture. In 1829, for example, free black Adam Shorter was indicted for "stealing and carrying away three indented Negro children."[54] The struggle to free black children from the clutches of a white master sometimes mobilized entire families. When free black Priscilla Dorsey died and left behind five dependent children, her brothers and sisters "agreed to divide the children amongst them, as nearest of kin." As the children's father, a slave, had been sold outside Maryland, Samuel Dorsey took possession of his eight-year-old niece, Lucy Powell. Dorsey supported her by hiring her to different families for her clothing and food and for small cash payments. He continued this arrangement until one of his niece's employers claimed that he was "better able to care for her" and had Powell bound to him for three years. Samuel Dorsey and his siblings appealed the indenture and succeeded in having it annulled because it was made without their consent.[55]

The preponderance of economic and legal authority confronting African American families forced some to concede the battle over their children. Instead of resisting county authorities, they sought to negotiate the most advantageous contracts for their offspring and to guarantee that their households would continue to benefit from the children's labor. In some cases, black parents arranged contracts that protected their sons and daughters from the apprenticeship system's worst abuses. Thus, when free black William Riggs apprenticed his daughter Lucretia to learn housekeeping, he specified that her master must "enter into a recognizance with security to be forfeited in case he should remove or carry [her] out of the state." After his daughter's master refused to post the required security, Riggs successfully petitioned to have the apprenticeship agreement voided.[56] Others challenged the legitimacy of their children's indentures and demanded that they be bound to different masters. Free black Sophia Johnson conceded that she could not support her son, John Hammond, but insisted that his current master, Amos Welsh, held him "against his will and without authority." Citing irregularities in her son's indenture, she asked that John be bound to a master of her choosing.[57]

Another strategy employed by black parents to avoid the involuntary—and uncompensated—apprenticing of their children was to bind them to a white master in exchange for cash payments. Of the ninety black children apprenticed by their parents, thirty-two (36 percent) were bound for a monetary consideration. Such transactions reflected the changing legal climate, which was reducing black apprentices to chattel. Changes in Maryland's apprenticeship laws allowed masters to sell the unexpired terms of their black apprentices, an opportunity that many of them seized.[58] Recognizing that their hold on children was tenuous—and that their children were a valuable financial resource—some black parents preempted whites and sold their offspring into temporary servitude.

Black parents who decided to apprentice their children found numerous ways to leverage their labor. In some cases, they bound out their children as collateral. In 1841, for example, Absalom Reed apprenticed his son to Frederick County farmer James Nickum to secure a $100 loan.[59] More commonly, blacks bound out their children for a single payment or for annual wages. When Jane Dunn bound her teenage children, John and Mary Bryan, to a Washington County farmer, their indentures stipulated that Dunn was to receive annual payments of $35 and $25 for their labor.[60] The indentures that Dunn negotiated were quite advantageous, for the wages her children garnered would have matched her earnings as a domestic servant or dairymaid. Most agreements were not as remunerative. In 1853, for example, Nelly Fisher bound her son, Robert Stewart, age eleven, to farmer Martin Emmett, in return for which she received annual payments of $4.[61]

In apprenticing their children to white masters, some black parents were simply adding another component to their multifaceted relationships with employers or landlords. Consider, for example, the case of Nat Cooper, a black tenant on Robert Archer's farm in Harford County. Between 1829 and 1833, Cooper's family earned $220.98, the vast majority of which—some $164.64—was garnered by his children, Nat, Jane, and Jim. The younger Nat collected $34.25 by laboring in wheat harvests, while his sister Jane earned $8.75 by working as a domestic servant and seamstress during the winter. It was Jim, however, who made the largest contributions to the family's coffers, first by earning $40.46 through an annual contract and then by apprenticing himself until the age of twenty-one, for which he received $80.[62]

The legal strictures upon their families were but one of the impediments hobbling African Americans. Slaveholders had crafted the state's legal apparatus, which guaranteed that blacks seldom received a fair shake in the county courts. Indeed, free blacks may have been more vulnerable to the frauds landowners perpetrated on all their workers. Lewis Charlton remembered that a Harford County farmer once refused to pay his wages of $235 "but said he would compromise by giving me three cents and calling it square." Charlton fought a protracted, and ultimately futile, legal battle to recover his wages. The "court was a mockery," he later fumed. "[T]here was no such thing as justice . . . the law protected the white man and trampled upon black men."[63]

The freedom to roam throughout the countryside and to tramp across state boarders in search of employment was fundamental to workers' economic strategies. Farmhands followed the summer harvests northward from Virginia, through Maryland and into Pennsylvania, while boatmen, drovers, and wagoners crossed and recrossed state borders en route to commercial entrepôts. During the early nineteenth century, political boundaries were not insurmountable obstacles to black workers. In 1819, for example, merchant James Sheehan of Gettysburg, Pennsylvania, employed Lewis Johnson—whom he described as "one of the best colored men I ever knew"—to transport wares into Frederick County, Maryland.[64] As the antebellum decades progressed, however, free blacks found their movements increasingly circumscribed.

Fearful that free blacks would smuggle slaves into Pennsylvania or that outsiders would spread the contagion of abolitionism among their bondspeople, slaveowners in Maryland began clamoring for restrictions on blacks' interstate movements. In 1832, the Maryland General Assembly prohibited nonresident free blacks from entering the state and remaining ten successive days. Violations were punishable by a $50 fine for each week they remained in the state, and free blacks unable to pay their court expenses, fines, and prison fees were to be sold at public auction. The law also limited the ability of resident free blacks to travel outside the state. It stipulated that blacks leaving Maryland for an extended period (longer than thirty days) must file papers with their county court, lest they be considered nonresidents upon their return. In 1840, the General Assembly strengthened this statute by prohibiting free blacks from coming into Maryland at all.[65]

The statutes had a chilling effect on free blacks' mobility. John McClintock Jr., whose farm was four miles north of the Mason-Dixon Line, recalled that "the colored men employed as farmhands could not be sent across the line, even with a team, least they would be claimed as slaves."[66] McClintock's workers had reason for concern. Maryland's courts vigorously enforced the statutes prohibiting free blacks from entering the state. In April 1844, for example, the Carroll County court convicted Pennsylvanian James Allen of entering Maryland and imposed $41.73 in fines, prison fees, and court costs. Unable to discharge the penalties, Allen was sold into slavery for an unspecified term.[67]

The threat of being arrested and imprisoned as suspected fugitives further tightened the shackles on blacks' mobility. African Americans might navigate a particular neighborhood in relative safety, but those venturing farther away faced additional perils. Despite having lost his freedom papers in an "unaccountable accident," free black Damon Brown remained undisturbed until he moved outside his rural neighborhood, when he was beset by "frequent and every unpleasant interruptions."[68] Likewise, farmhand Sam Walker never bothered to obtain his freedom papers while laboring near the plantation of his deceased master. It was only upon discovering that "farmers in our part had . . . slaves or hands of their own" and concluding to "try some other parts" that he secured his papers.[69]

In addition to being anchored to certain neighborhoods by legal restraints, free blacks were also tethered by the presence of enslaved or apprenticed relatives. In 1820s, freewoman Monica Walker accompanied her husband, William Walker, "a bright mulatto slave," from his home in southern Frederick County to the plantation of his new master, John Gleason, near Libertytown, Maryland. Although her husband died soon after he was sold, Monica remained on the plantation for about eleven years, possibly because her freeborn son, Perry, had been apprenticed to Gleason.[70]

Dovetailing with the legal and social constraints upon free blacks' mobility was a series of ordinances and statutes that circumscribed their economic activities. Driven by fears that free blacks would fence property stolen by slaves, authorities erected legal barriers to prevent blacks from engaging in the petty production and proprietorship that was often essential to the working poor's economic survival. In 1827, authorities in Hagerstown directed constables to "disperse and prevent idle and disorderly persons, rude and noisy boys and persons of colour from frequenting the market-house."[71] In 1832, the Maryland General Assembly prohibited blacks from selling "bacon, pork, beef, mutton, corn, wheat, tobacco, rye, or oats" without first obtaining written permission from their employer, a justice of the peace, or "three respectable persons." The legislation also made it difficult for free blacks to obtain liquor licenses by stipulating that they must undergo additional examinations by a county court before receiving a license.[72]

The Maryland legislature also limited blacks' freedom to contract and change employers. Responding to concerns from farmers and planters on the Eastern Shore, who perceived a growing assertiveness among free blacks, in 1854 the General Assembly imposed penalties on blacks who abandoned their employers before the completion of their contracts. Those convicted under this statute could be arrested, returned to their employers, and held financially responsible for lost time and court expenses. Repeat offenders faced arrest, brief prison sentences, financial penalties, and being reduced to the status of a "free negro apprentice." The legislature also limited blacks' ability to entertain offers from competing employers. Any white person who knowingly contracted with a black man or woman who had already hired him- or herself to another employer could be fined an amount equivalent to two-fifths of the worker's wages and be compelled to return the employee to the original hirer.[73]

In many respects, the volatile labor market in Baltimore's hinterlands narrowed the distance between black and white farmhands. The lives of all farmworkers were defined by uncertainty: a catastrophic crop failure, a misstep near a threshing machine, or the mundane pattern of seasonal unemployment offered little quarter. Possessed of few skills and little property, white farmhands could neither drive their black counterparts from the fields nor demand special treatment from employers. Black and white laborers received identical wages, and landowners seemed indifferent to the racial composition of their workforces. In addition to working together, farmhands mingled during the holidays that punctuated the growing season. In 1856, "drunken rowdies, black and white, principally from the country," marked Whitsunday by swarming into Rockville, Maryland, and shattering "the quiet of our usually peaceable town."[74]

The rough equality imposed upon farmhands neither obscured nor undermined racial distinctions within the rural workforce. The racial distinctions in this group snapped into sharp relief in July 1861, when a white farmhand—identified only as Grimes—and several free black harvesters left the Carroll County store of C. S. Snouffer, where they had spent the evening drinking. As they milled around the store, "talking about the nearest road to the place they were at work," a Mr. Drum "took the idea that it was a squad of Negroes" and accosted the farmworkers. A local newspaper reported that "the darkies left (being afraid)" but that Grimes, who carried a pistol, took umbrage and challenged Drum. Outraged at the "black" man's impudence, Drum sprinted across the road and "struck him over the head two or three times with a cane, and tore his clothing very much, and also took [the] pistol out of Grimes's pocket." Grimes sought refuge inside the store, where he begged a young clerk for assistance. The clerk confronted Drum, who promptly threatened to "put the contents of his own pistol into him, which he immediately did." Having worked himself into a frenzy, Drum barged into the building and shot Grimes, inflicting a severe wound in his thigh.[75]

This violent encounter was, to a large extent, fueled by mistaken identities. In the dark, Drum had assumed that the farmhands assembled outside Snouffer's store were all African Americans, which made Grimes's resistance an unbearable insult and a challenge to the racial order. Grimes was not, however, confused about his racial identity. Poverty might have compelled him to work alongside African Americans, but he must have felt it unnecessary, even degrading, to suffer abuse from a white man. The black harvesters, for their part, had no illusions about their position in the racial hierarchy. Aware of their vulnerability and possessed of good sense, they scattered before the armed, besotted, and belligerent whites. Thus, amid the gunshots we snatch glimpses of how class and race operated in northern Maryland. Blacks and whites might find themselves in the same economic straits, working together in harvest fields, or mingling in grogshops, but these encounters occurred within the context of a slaveholding state, which guaranteed that racial boundaries would retain their terrible vigor.

Race reared its head whenever white laborers mustered the strength to impose racial hierarchies within their workplaces. Racial tensions flared at rural factories and internal improvement projects, where white workers flexed their collective muscle to prevent competition from blacks. In 1831, "an altercation of a very serious nature" transpired between black and white workmen on the B & O Railroad near New Market, Maryland. Although the causes of the riot remain unclear, it may have been triggered by the introduction of black workers or by whites attempting to defend skilled or supervisory positions.[76] Evidence from other industries suggests that white workers expected blacks to occupy the least desirable, lowest paying positions. When a manager at the Antietam Woolen Manufacturing Company complained that "it is hard to get white [workers] . . . in attending the carding machines on account of the dirtiness of the work and the wages [being] so low," he proposed to solve the problem by hiring "some little Negro Boys."[77]

Blacks who overstepped the boundaries of their white coworkers at industrial sites risked intimidation or violence. The Reverend Thomas W. Henry, who ministered to the enslaved workers at the Antietam Iron Works, recalled that "the white help had a spirit of animosity against [the] servants because of their being so well treated." The foundry's owner not only allowed the slaves to gather refuse fuel and earn overtime wages (privileges denied the white workers), he also appointed them as foremen and managers. The white ironworkers' resentment simmered until 1835 or 1836, when, during the owner's absence, they attempted to flog several of the slave workers. The slaves mounted a spirited resistance, forcing the whites to retreat to nearby Sharpsburg, where they summoned the militia. Upon their arrival at the furnace, the soldiers found that the slaves had scattered into the hills and woods, where they remained hidden for several days.[78]

While whites struggled to distance themselves socially from slaves and free blacks, they could never escape the gravitational pull of slavery. Poor whites may have insisted upon their racial prerogatives, but the uncertainty that characterized the rural economy drove them into an underground economy of cookhouses, grogshops, and tippling houses that underscored the similarities—and mutual dependency—among the different segments of the region's workforce. To the extent that public authorities scrutinized poor whites' non–wage labor activities, it was to prevent them from sapping slaveholders' authority. Many of the indictments filed against the operators of unlicensed businesses included charges that bespoke slave-owners' priorities. In 1819, for example, planter John Thomson Mason accused John Duncan of selling liquor without a license, dealing in stolen merchandise with a slave, and "keeping a disorderly house and permitting negro slaves and others to gamble."[79] Poor whites who operated on the shadowy borders of the region's economy found allies among free blacks and slaves, who may have preferred to conduct some of their business away from slaveholders' glare; at the same time, their underground economy was constrained by the dictates of preserving slavery.[80]

The rural economy simultaneously pushed together poor blacks and whites while maintaining the legal and social controls necessary for upholding slavery. Race guaranteed that whites would have fewer impediments placed in their paths than free blacks did, but it offered them few economic guarantees. Conversely, the exigencies of maintaining slavery left free blacks with a stunted, truncated form of freedom. The unskilled and unstable nature of agricultural labor may have prevented white farmhands from viewing themselves as a class, but the looming presence of slavery meant that they could not see their black neighbors, coworkers, and lovers as participants in the same struggle for survival.

NOTES

1. *Herald of Freedom and Torchlight* (Hagerstown, MD), June 21, 1848.

2. J. Jakob Rutlinger, "Day Book on a Journey to North America in the Year 1823," in *The Old Land and the New: The Journals of Two Swiss Families in America in the 1820s*, ed. and trans. Robert H. Billigmeier and Fred A. Picard (Minneapolis: University of Minnesota, 1965), 222-27.

3. The literature on poor rural southerners has begun blossoming over the past decade. See Charles C. Bolton, *Poor Whites of the Antebellum South: Tenants and Laborers in Central North Carolina and Northeast Mississippi* (Durham, NC: Duke University Press, 1994), Wilma A. Dunaway, *Women, Work, and Family in the Antebellum Mountain South* (Cambridge, UK: Cambridge University Press, 2008), Jeff Forret, *Race Relations at the Margins: Slaves and Poor Whites in the Antebellum Southern Countryside* (Baton Rouge: Louisiana State University Press, 2006), and Timothy J. Lockley, *Lines in the Sand: Race and Class in Lowcountry Georgia, 1750-1860* (Athens: University of Georgia Press, 2001).

4. There are but a handful of studies on rural free blacks. See, for example, Dunaway, *Women, Work, and Family*, Melvin Patrick Ely, *Israel on the Appomattox: A Southern Experiment in Black Freedom from the 1790s through the Civil War* (New York: Alfred A. Knopf, 2004), and Brenda E. Stevenson, *Life in Black and White: Family and Community in the Slave South* (New York: Oxford University Press, 1996), 258-319.

5. The same critique is not applicable to studies of the urban poor. For example, Seth Rockman's groundbreaking work on early national Baltimore has demonstrated the importance of the household to the laboring poor. "The centerpiece of working-class survival," he notes, "was the creation of collective economic enterprises, otherwise known as households." *Scraping By: Wage Labor, Slavery, and Survival in Early Baltimore*

(Baltimore: Johns Hopkins University Press, 2009), 160.

6. *Farmers' Register and Maryland Herald* (Hagerstown, MD), July 6, 1830.

7. *Hagerstown (MD) Courier,* July 4, 1838, quoted in *(Charles Town) Virginia Free Press,* July 12, 1838.

8. *Herald of Freedom and Torchlight* (Hagerstown, MD), July 24, 1856; Joseph R. Stonebraker, *A Rebel of '61* (New York: Wynook Hallenback Crawford, 1899), 31. The movement of urban workers to the country during the wheat harvest persisted after the Civil War. In 1866, the Freedmen's Bureau assistant superintendent at Harper's Ferry, Virginia, reported that "the time for Harvest being near at hand, those who have heretofore been laying about the Towns preferring a small ten cent job to going into the country at steady work, have left, unable to resist the offers of big wages tendered them. So soon however as the season is over they will return picking up a miserable existence here & there, rather than come down to daily labor." 1st Lt. A. F. Higgs to Sir, June 30, 1866, Reports Received from the Shenandoah Division, ser. 1977, Maryland and Delaware Assistant Commissioner, Records of the Bureau of Refugees, Freedmen, and Abandoned Lands, Record Group 95, NARA.

9. *Maryland Herald and Hagerstown Weekly Advertiser,* October 18, 1805.

10. William R. Quynn, ed., and James Lowry, trans., *The Diary of Jacob Englebrecht, 1818-82,* 2 vols. (Frederick, MD: Historical Society of Frederick County, 2002), 1:469.

11. Joseph M. Wolfe Ledgers, 1839-48 and 1848-59, Washington County Historical Society, Hagerstown, MD; 1850 U.S. Census, Schedule 1 (Population), Washington County, MD, NARA.

12. This provision was included in the state's first law concerning apprentices and remained in effect through at least 1860. "An Act for the Better Regulation of Apprentices," December 28, 1793, in *The Laws of Maryland,* comp. W[illia]m Kilty (Annapolis, MD: Frederick Green, 1800); Otho Scott and Hiram McCullogh, comp., *The Maryland Code: Public General Laws* (Baltimore, MD: John Murphy and Co., 1860).

13. Frederick County Register Of Wills (Indentures), Indenture of Joel Stimmel, April 24, 1816, Liber HS 1, ff. 95-97, MSA C799-4, MdHR 14,355; Washington County Register of Wills (Indentures), Indenture of William Powell, March 23, 1846, (no vol. number), ff. 34-36, MSA C1953-6, Maryland Hall of Records, Annapolis, MD (hereafter MdHR), 16, 361.

14. Stonebraker, *A Rebel of '61,* 31.

15. "Agricultural Transactions and Expenses of Elm Grove Farm" owned by Philip R. J. Friese, 1833-1834, in William P. Preston Collection, MS 978, Maryland Historical Society, Baltimore (hereafter MdHS).

16. Governor and Council (Pardon Papers), Thomas Kennedy to Governor Samuel Sprigg [n.d.], MSA 1061-20, MdHR 5401-20.

17. Richard Vansant Account Book, 1854-1874, 1896, MS 1054, MdHS.

18. Charles H. Lighter Account Book, 1851-1852, Middletown Valley Historical Society, Middletown, MD.

19. Secretary of State (Pardon Papers), Confession of Amos Green [n.d.], enclosed in Papers in the Case of Amos Green, 1851, MSA 1031-10, MdHR 5401-48.

20. Jean Libby, ed., *From Slavery to Salvation: The Autobiography of Rev. Thomas W. Henry of the A.M.E. Church* (Jackson: University Press of Mississippi, 1994), 43-44.

21. Arthur W. Machen to Lewis H. Machen, January 23, 1846, Lewis H. Machen Papers, Library of Congress, Washington, DC.

22. Frederick County Court (Land Records), Testimony in the case of *David Heim v. Elias Heim,* July 1844, Liber HS 23, ff. 587-96, MSA C814-151, MdHR 40,341-113-1.

23. *Third Annual Report of the President and Directors to the Stockholders of the Baltimore and Ohio Railroad Company* (Baltimore, MD: Wm. Woody, 1829), 22.

24. The size of Piper's crew varied from three to nineteen workers. John Piper Account Book, 1820-1826, Special Collections, University of Maryland, College Park.

25. Susannah Warfield Diary, January 8, 1849, in Warfield Family Diaries, 1845-1885, MS 760, MdHS.

26. Barbara Jeanne Fields, *Slavery and Freedom on the Middle Ground: Maryland during the Nineteenth Century* (New Haven, CT: Yale University Press, 1985), 85-89.

27. Governor and Council (Pardon Papers), Petition of William Fry, October 5, 1822, MSA S1061-22, MdHR 5401-21.

28. On the importance of such enterprises to poor whites, see Forret, *Race Relations on the Margins*, 74-114.

29. Governor and Council (Pardon Papers), Petition of James Brightwell, December 12, 1821, MSA S1061-21, MdHR 5401-21.

30. Jacob Reichard Ledger, 1833-1906, MS 2614, MdHS.

31. Jeremiah Harlan Papers, 1777-1885, MS 1008, MdHS.

32. Unsigned letter to William Fell Johnson, June 11, 1840, Johnson Papers [unprocessed collection], MdHS.

33. Carroll County Board of County Commissioners (Pension Papers), Petition of Hilleary Hillman, n.d. [1844], MSA C2131-1, MdHR.

34. A survey conducted by an agricultural journal in 1850 revealed that farmers in Frederick and Washington counties paid men between $8 and $10 per month, while women received between $2 and $4. A similar discrepancy characterized annual wages, which varied from $80 to $100 for men and from $30 to $40 for women. "Table of the Products of Maryland," *The Plough, the Loom, and the Anvil* 3 (January 1851): 432-33. The account book of Frederick County farmer Charles A. Lighter confirms these findings. In 1854, his male farmhand received $120 and board for nine months' labor, while the woman he employed as a dairymaid and house servant received a mere $42 for the entire year. Charles A. Lighter Account Book and Loose Papers, 1851-1897, Middletown Valley Historical Society, Middletown, MD.

35. Frederick County Circuit Court (Court Papers), Papers in the case of *Peter Fogle v. Fred Birely*, n.d. [1852], box 166, MSA T176-133, MdHR.

36. Frederick County Circuit Court (Court Papers), Affidavit of Samuel Fair, February 24, 1844, enclosed in *State of Maryland v. John Patterson*, box 89, MSA 176-121, MdHR.

37. Carroll County Board of County Commissioners (Pension Papers), Petition of Rachel R. Dell, August 6, 1860, MSA C2131-1, MdHR.

38. Carroll County Board of County Commissioners (Pension Papers), Petition of Eliza Koon, March 25, 1841, MSA C2131-1, MdHR.

39. Carroll County Board of County Commissioners (Pension Papers), Petition of Catherine Taylor, n.d. [1844], MSA C2131-1, MdHR.

40. Frederick County Circuit Court (License Record) 1845-1863, MSA T181-1, MdHR.

41. Governor and Council (Pardon Papers), Petition of Mary Ockes, April 12, 1827, MSA S1061-28, MdHR 5401-28.

42. Carroll County Board of County Commissioners (Pension Papers), Petition on behalf of Betsey Reister [n.d.], MSA C2131-1, MdHR.

43. "Childbearing age" is here defined as fifteen to fifty years old. Women who were described as idiotic, insane, blind, deaf, or dumb were excluded from this sample. 1850 U.S. Census, Schedule 1 (Population), Frederick and Washington Counties, MD, NARA.

44. 1860 U.S. Census, Schedule 1 (Population), Jefferson County, VA, NARA.

45. Franklin Osburn Account Book, Thornton Tayloe Perry Collection, Virginia Historical Society.

46. Special Collections (J. Alexis Shriver Collection), Robert Archer Ledger, 1826-1854, MSA SC 162-4-954, MdHR.

47. The data cover 1800-1832, 1840-1848, and 1853-1860. Frederick County Court (Land Records) and Frederick County Circuit Court (Land Records), MdHR.

48. Frederick County Court (Land Records), Purchase Agreement between Joseph Christ and Elias James, December 26, 1846, Liber WBT 3, ff. 507-08, MSA C814-154, MdHR 40,341-116-1.

49. The original statute made no reference to a child's race, stating simply that "such children as are suffering through the extreme indigence or poverty of their parents, the children of beggars, and also illegitimate children" could be bound out by county authorities. "An Act for the Better Regulation of Apprentices," December 28, 1793, *Laws of Maryland, Made and Passed at a Session of Assembly, Begun and Held at the City of Annapolis on Monday the Fourth of November, In the Year of Our Lord One Thousand Seven Hundred and Ninety-Three* (Annapolis: Frederick Green, 1794); "A Further Supplement to an Act, Entitled, An Act for the Better Regulation of Apprentices," December 23, 1808, William Killty, et al., comps., *The Laws of Maryland* (Annapolis: J. Green, 1815).

50. "An Act Authorizing the Judges of the Orphans Courts to Bind Out the Children of Free Negroes and Mulattoes," February 17, 1819, *Laws Made and Passed by the General Assembly of the State of Maryland, At a Session Begun and Held at the City of Annapolis, On Monday the Seventh Day of December, Eighteen Hundred and Eighteen* (Annapolis: J. Green, 1819).

51. "An Act to Provide for the Better Regulation of Free Negro and Mulatto Children within this State," March 20, 1840, *Laws Made and Passed by the General Assembly of the State of Maryland, At a Session Begun and Held at Annapolis, On Monday, the 30th Day of December, 1839, and Ended on Saturday, the 21st Day of March, 1840* (Annapolis: William McNeir, 1840).

52. "An Act Supplementary to an Act Entitled, An Act to Provide for the Better Regulation of Free Negroes and Mulatto Children within this State," March 8, 1845, *Laws Made and Passed by the General Assembly of the State of Maryland, At a Session Begun and Held at Annapolis, on Monday, the 30th Day of December, 1844, and Ended on Monday, the 10th Day of March, 1845* (Annapolis: William McNeir, 1845).

53. Carroll County Indentures, 1840-1860, Office of the Register of Wills, Westminster, MD; Frederick County Register of Wills (Indentures) 1837-1860, MdHR; Howard County Register of Wills (Indentures) 1840-1860, MdHR; and Washington County Register of Wills (Indentures) 1837-1860, MdHR.

54. Shorter was eventually acquitted of the crime. Washington County Circuit Court (Docket and Minutes) November 1829, MSA T3063-57, MdHR; and Washington County Circuit Court (Dockets and Minutes) November 1830, MSA T3063-59, MdHR.

55. Howard County Register of Wills (Petitions), Petition of Samuel Dorsey, [n.d.], MSA T1307, MdHR.

56. Frederick County Register of Wills (Indentures), Indenture of Lucretia Riggs, June 13, 1849, Liber GME 3, n.p., MSA C799-7, MdHR 14,358.

57. It is unclear how the court responded to Johnson's request. Howard County Register of Wills (Petitions), Petition of Sophia Johnson, n.d. [1847], MSA T1307, MdHR.

58. In 1856, for example, Howard County farmer Nicholas Ridgely sold the unexpired twelve years of apprentice James Matthews' term for $120. Three years later, William Lawrence sold the remaining term of his bound farmhand James Crabb for $150. Howard County Register of Wills (Indentures), Liber WG 1, ff. 130 and 182-84, MSA T2740-1, MdHR.

59. Frederick County Register of Wills (Indentures, Original), Indenture of John Francis Reed, March 1, 1841, MSA C800-2, MdHR 9602-2.

60. Washington County Register of Wills (Indentures), Indentures of John Bryan and Mary Bryan, March 2, 1855, (no volume number), ff. 208-10, MSA C1953-6, MdHR 16,361.

61. Washington County Register of Wills (Indentures), Indenture of Robert Emory Stewart, June 30, 1853 (no volume number), ff. 176-77, MSA C1953-6, MdHR 16,361.

62. Special Collections (J. Alexis Shriver Collection), Robert Archer Ledger, 1826-1854, MSA SC 162-4-954, MdHR.

63. Edward Everett Brown, *Sketch of the Life of Mr. Lewis Charlton, and Reminiscences of Slavery* (Portland, ME: Daily Press, n.d.), 6-7.

64. Special Collections (Annan Collection of Clotworthy Birnie Papers), James Sheehan to Clotworthy Birnie, July 13, 1819, MSA SC 725, MdHR.

65. "An Act Relating to Free Negroes and Slaves," March 14, 1832, *Laws Made and Passed by the General Assembly of the State of Maryland, at a Session Begun and Held at Annapolis, on Monday the 26th Day of December, 1831, and Ended on Wednesday the 14th Day of March 1832* (Annapolis: J. Hughes, 1832); "An Additional Supplement to . . . An Act Relating to Free Negroes and Slaves," March 18, 1840.

66. John McClintock, Jr., to Mrs. Zeamer, September 25, 1901, Zeamer Family Collection, Cumberland County Historical Society, Chambersburg, PA.

67. Carroll County Circuit Court (Criminal Docket) 1837-1852, MSA T3781-1, MdHR. For similar examples, see *Hagerstown (MD) Mail,* June 17, 1842 and August 12, 1842.

68. Frederick County Circuit Court (Court Papers), Affidavit of John P. [Dowlan], October 5, 1848, box 91, MSA T176-111, MdHR.

69. Richard W. Gil and John Johnson, eds., *Reports of Cases Argued and Determined in the Court of Appeals* (Baltimore, MD: F. Lucas Jr., 1832), 219-33.

70. Affidavit of John Gleason, December 9, 1840, Maryland Manuscripts Collection, University of Maryland, College Park.

71. *Torchlight and Public Advertiser* (Hagerstown, MD), May 24, 1827.

72. "An Act Relating to Free Negroes and Slaves," March 14, 1832.

73. "An Act to Provide a Remedy against Free Negroes Who May Hire for a Stipulated Period to Any Person, and Quit the Service of Such Person after Entering on the Same, and to Provide a Remedy against Persons Who May Employ such Free Negroes, with the Knowledge that They Had Previously Hired to Another, or Engage in Another's Service," March 10, 1854, *Laws Made and Passed by the General Assembly of the State of Maryland, At a Session Begun and Held at Annapolis on Wednesday, the 4th Day of January, 1853, and Ended on Friday, the 10th of March, 1854* (Annapolis: E. S. Riley, 1854).

74. *Montgomery County Sentinel* (Rockville, MD), May 17, 1856.

75. *Carroll County Democrat* (Westminster, MD), July 25, 1861.

76. *Republican Banner* (Williamsport, MD), August 27, 1831.

77. Unsigned letter to Board of Directors, July 17, 1815, Antietam Woolen Manufacturing Company Records, 1814-1843, Hagley Museum and Library, Wilmington, DE.

78. Libby, ed., *From Slavery to Salvation,* 27-28.

79. Washington County Circuit Court (Docket and Minutes) November 1819, MSA T3063-37, MdHR. For similar examples, see Indictment of Godley Bodreiner, October 1841, Indictment of Joseph Runkles, October 1841, and Indictment of Wm. Lloyd, October 1841, all in Frederick County Circuit Court (Court Papers), box 92, MSA T176-119, MdHR; Indictment of Julian Edwards, September 22, 1841, and Indictment of Mary Brown, n.d. [1842], both in Howard County Court Papers, Howard County Historical Society, Ellicott City, MD.

80. Other historians have documented a flourishing underground economy among poor whites, free blacks, and slaves. See, for example, Forret, *Race Relations at the Margins,* and Wayne K. Durrill, "Routine of Seasons: Labour Regimes and Social Ritual in an Antebellum Plantation Community," *Slavery and Abolition* 16 (Aug. 1995): 161-87.

Part III

The Rise of the Middle Classes

Chapter 6

Professionalization and the Southern Middle Class

Jonathan Daniel Wells

Recent studies of the Old South have emphasized the rapidly changing nature of the slave economy and southern culture, particularly in the 1850s.[1] While previous scholars saw the region as generally static, clinging to a system of bondage that promised wealth for the planters but little ability to modernize or diversify its economy and society, historians have altered this view by pointing to significant modernization in the region. Increasing investment on the part of southern states in manufacturing, internal improvements, education, and commerce occurred simultaneously with an increasing commitment to slavery. Although northern free-labor advocates considered slavery and capitalism antagonistic, white southerners saw no inherent contradiction between urbanization and industrialization and a continuance of slavery. They believed they could obtain all the positive aspects of modern society that they admired in the North, including large cities, cultural assets like schools, libraries, and exhibits, and a diversified manufacturing economy, with slavery not only merely continuing to function but indeed helping to make this modern new South become a reality. It was this vision that non-elite whites sought to create in the years before the Civil War.

Despite a number of significant obstacles, middling southerners managed to make substantial strides in creating this new South by 1861. The region was a far different place in 1861 than it had been in 1821 or 1841. What David Moltke-Hansen has called "the expansion of intellectual life" can be applied to other aspects of the Old South, for the growth of manufacturing, advances in internal improvements, the establishment of institutions like public schools and banks, and many other indicators show that the South was in fact undergoing a transformation well before New South boosters like Henry Grady became prominent.[2]

While economic changes were notable, especially after the Mexican War, the cultural shifts experienced in the antebellum South were perhaps more significant. By the 1850s, nearly every southern town and village presented opportunities for its residents to attend festivals, hear a lecture, peruse an exhibit, or witness school exercises. Yet one of the chief forms of engagement and entertainment in the Old South has gone largely unnoticed. Before the Civil War, white southerners invested a great deal of energy in associations and societies of all kinds, organizations that flourished in large urban areas like New Orleans as well as in the backcountry. Library societies, debating clubs, reading circles, professional groups, labor organizations, temperance and other reform groups, and many other kinds of associations were found in every southern community. These groups were often advertised in the newspapers and magazines that proliferated throughout the region.

With such economic and cultural change, it is not surprising that the region should also experience an increasingly complex and diversified social structure. Scholars are reexamining the nature of class in the nineteenth-century South and finding new ways to study work and class consciousness among the white middle class as well as among white and black laborers. Historians have found that a language of class, animosity between members of different elements of the social structure, and even an incipient class consciousness existed in a region previously considered lacking in class divisions. The middle class of professional and commercial interests, including doctors, teachers, dentists, editors, lawyers, and merchants, combined in the late antebellum era to battle secessionists, denounce planter dominance, and support slavery as the vehicle through which the region could expand manufacturing and create a new economy based upon the coexistence of capitalism and bondage.

One underexplored aspect of southern middle-class life is the extent to which doctors, dentists, teachers, and others sought to differentiate themselves in society by creating professional societies that would exclude amateurs, fight for political and economic advantages, and establish guidelines for specialized training and practice. Generally assumed to be a product of the Progressive Era, professional organizations like the American Medical Association were in place well before the Civil War. Southerners were active in these national associations but also formed societies of their own. As one Georgia doctor put it, medical societies "should exist in every State, they are an impetus to talent, and will eventually root out quackery, and put down knavery."[3]

As early as the 1820s, a few medical associations operated in the slave states, but by the 1850s there were dozens of such groups for the southern middle class, from state organizations with hundreds of members to county and even town societies with only a handful of participants. Much to the consternation of southern partisans, thousands of young doctors, lawyers, and teachers had been educated in northern colleges and schools, and calls rang out beginning in the 1830s for the erection of southern institutions. Until recently, historians have assumed that such professionalization among the middle class took root only in the later nineteenth century, and even then primarily in the northern states.

This essay will serve as a corrective to such assumptions by analyzing efforts to institute professional standards well before the outbreak of the Civil War and by arguing that studying professionalization helps us understand the broader ideological development of the antebellum southern middle class. When physicians, lawyers, teachers, or merchants joined together to form societies or to publish periodicals, they were expressing a sense of distinctiveness from the rest of southern society; when they formed chambers of commerce, they were engaging in collective activity to shape public discourse and political economy; when they set forth the particular standards of their professions, they were articulating methods for differentiating themselves from amateurs and uneducated pretenders to the field. Thus the professionalization of the southern middle class is a heretofore unexamined path for understanding the nature of class ideology as well as the transformation of southern society more broadly.

Though far behind the antebellum North in industrialization and urbanization by most measures, the South experienced notable economic progress in the 1850s. Investment in cotton and tobacco processing, growing numbers of factories, expansion of internal improvements like banks and railroads, and many other indicators of industrialization demonstrate that white southerners lived in a rapidly changing economy and society. This shift toward manufacturing occurred alongside the region's continuing commitment to agriculture and slavery. In fact, as historians have shown, many of the gains in southern industrialization and economic modernization were the consequence of slave labor. Table 1 shows the growth in the number of men and women employed in manufacturing establishments between 1850 and 1860. While numbers in a few states fell slightly or remained roughly the same, several southern states experienced noticeable increases in numbers in the span of just ten years.

Advances in manufacturing coincided with similar advances in other aspects of southern life. The banking industry, for example, expanded significantly in the antebellum era. From 1850 to 1860, the number of banks in Alabama rose from two to eight, in North Carolina from eighteen to fifty, in Tennessee from twenty-three to thirty-four, and in Virginia from

Table 1. Number of People Employed in Manufacturing Establishments

State	1850	1860
Alabama	4938	7889
Arkansas	903	1877
Florida	984	2454
Georgia	8378	11575
Kentucky	24376	21258
Louisiana	6437	8789
Maryland	30124	28403
Mississippi	3113	4775
North Carolina	12444	14217
South Carolina	7009	6994
Tennessee	12032	12528
Texas	1066	3449
Virginia	29109	36174

SOURCE: Seventh Census of the United States, 1850, and *Population of the United States in 1860* (Washington, 1864).

thirty-seven to sixty-five.[4] As table 2 indicates, southern banks benefitted from increased capital between 1850 and 1860. Table 3 similarly demonstrates the increase in circulation and deposits in just ten years, despite the severe financial panic that struck the nation in 1857.

Significant economic and societal changes in the region were pushed by an increasingly self-conscious southern middle class of professional and commercial interests. From 1850 to 1860, the number of physicians nationally rose from 40,755 to 55,055 and the number of dentists from 2,923 to 5,606. Over the same ten-year period, the number of teachers nationally increased from about 80,000 to 115,000.[5] Physicians, teachers, merchants, and other professionals made common cause on a wide range of issues, helping to shape a middle-class ideology but also fundamentally shaping the course of the South. Middling southerners attempted to convince the region to abandon what they viewed as vestiges of a barbaric past, such as dueling and obsession with honor. To this end, anti-dueling associations were formed in leading towns such as Savannah, and newspaper editors throughout the region repeatedly denounced the resort to violence to defend honor. They came together to push for advances in public education, which they consciously and openly wanted to model after schools like those encouraged by Horace Mann in Massachusetts. Middle-class southerners freely admitted that they wanted the urban growth of cities like New York, technological progress, and a broad manufacturing base of the kind they saw in the North.[6]

Table 2. Capital of Southern Banks, 1850 and 1860

State	Capital 1850	Capital 1860
Alabama	$1,800,589	$4,901,000
Georgia	13,482,198	16,689,560
Kentucky	7,536,927	12,835,670
Louisiana	12,370,390	24,496,866
Maryland	8,128,881	12,568,962
North Carolina	3,789,250	6,626,478
South Carolina	13,213,031	14,962,062
Tennessee	6,881,568	8,067,037
Virginia	9,824,545	16,005,156

SOURCE: Joseph C. G. Kennedy, *Preliminary Report on the Eighth Census, 1860* (Washington, 1862), 192-93.

Table 3. Circulation and Deposits in Southern Banks, 1850 and 1860

State	Circulation 1850	Circulation 1860	Deposits 1850	Deposits, 1860
AL	$3,568,285	$7,477,976	$1,474,963	$4,851,153
GA	9,898,827	8,798,100	2,580,826	4,738,289
KY	7,643,075	13,520,207	2,323,657	5,662,892
LA	5,059,229	11,579,313	8,464,389	19,777,812
MD	3,532,869	4,106,869	5,838,766	8,874,180
NC	4,249,883	5,594,047	942,098	1,487,273
SC	11,771,270	11,475,634	3,065,686	4,165,615
TN	6,814,376	5,538,378	1,917,757	4,324,799
VA	10,256,997	9,182,197	4,717,732	7,729,652

SOURCE: Joseph C. G. Kennedy, *Preliminary Report on the Eighth Census, 1860* (Washington, 1862), 192-93.

Although southerners in 1860 still relied heavily on northern publishers for printing books and pamphlets, the expansion of intellectual life was evident in every southern town in the 1850s. Printing presses in the South enhanced publishing opportunities; the value of printing jobs between 1850 and 1860 rose from $45,895 to $491,220 in Tennessee and from $131,200 to $304,600 in Kentucky.[7] An increase in the number of periodicals, read by a growing middle class, offers further evidence of the transformation of the region before the Civil War. Between 1800 and 1829, 121 magazines were started in the southern states. During the 1830s alone, 120 magazines began publication; and during the 1840s, 174 made their debut.

In the 1850s, however, 214 periodicals were launched, by far the most of any previous decade.[8]

Even with such cultural and economic advances, the southern middle class did not reject or really even question the legitimacy of slavery. In fact, by the 1850s middling southerners were as committed to preserving and expanding the system as were the most ardent planters. This ideological coherence between the planter class and the middle class came not from planter hegemony or because the middle class did not wish to upset wealthy rural fellow southerners. Rather, in its desire to achieve significant economic gains in manufacturing, the southern middle class concluded independently that the use of slave labor would help the region make gains in manufacturing as quickly as possible. Slavery promised to accomplish these modernizing goals without the labor disturbances and strikes that southerners read about in the North. Many middle-class merchants and capitalists, therefore, could be found at the forefront of the movement in the late 1850s to reopen the transatlantic slave trade, so that there would be a sufficient supply of bondspeople to farm the region's plantations and to toil in the factories and new businesses of the future South.

Thus, the picture now emerging from recent historical examinations emphasizes the complexity of a region that defended slavery and embraced modernization, that elevated the virtues of the independent farmer while championing capitalist enterprise and energy, that resisted the federal government even as calls rang out for more public investment in schools and internal improvements. However difficult it is for modern observers to make sense of the coexistence of all these seemingly contradictory ideologies, the southern middle class believed that within them lay the future of the region.

To further their vision of the region's future, the southern middle class formed a remarkable range of societies, clubs, associations, and organizations. By the start of the Civil War, for example, Mobile, Alabama, counted twenty-one associations of all kinds, including a Hebrew Benevolent Association, the Franklin Society, a Mechanic's Association, and fraternal organizations like the Odd Fellows and Masons.[9] The rich and diverse nature of these organizations, and the ways in which they both shaped and reflected life in the region, is a poorly understood but important aspect of the region's history. Southerners regarded these associations and clubs very seriously, taking pains to draft constitutions, elect officers, write by-laws, attend meetings, and publicize their activities. Such groups were particularly important to the South's middle class; and as professional and commercial men grew in number and visibility in the region, they formed specialized associations and published journals to promote their endeavors.

Professional colleges and societies left behind a rich record of their activities and self-awareness in the journals that dotted the southern landscape. One of the earliest, the *Southern Medical and Surgical Journal*, was published in Augusta in the late 1830s by two professors of the Georgia Medical College. These publications, and several others like them, offer considerable insight into the attempts by the southern middle class to draw clear boundaries between itself and others through the erection of professional standards and rules. Within the journals, the southern middle class excoriated amateur practitioners who lacked college training and used professional degrees to elevate their status and provide access to wealth, protected earning potential by limiting access to clients, and established means to discipline those who failed to uphold standards. State, county, and town societies created ethics codes and licensing boards to draw distinctions between themselves and laypeople and to establish rules that only group members knew and followed. They lobbied political bodies to support their interests, especially on tax policy, and they gathered frequently in state conventions and regional meetings to promote their distinct interests. Through careful analysis of the extensive professional journals, all these activities can be traced, lending further power to the notion that in the Old South an energetic middle class viewed itself as a distinct group within southern society and viewed professionalization as a way to codify such distinctions.

Physicians operated in the South from the early colonial period, but only in the early nineteenth century did doctors begin to form associations to define their profession, marginalize the "quack" purveyors of cure-alls, establish educational standards, and erect a code of ethics. In *Doctoring the South*, historian Steven M. Stowe found that in the early 1800s, the field of medicine was rooted in traditional practices, tied closely to the community, inchoate, and often dangerously unregulated. "Democratic in one sense," Stowe argues, "entrepreneurial in another, it was a world of laissez-faire improvisation and *caveat emptor* results, with healers coming forward in every community with roots, pills, powders, and various mixtures in generous solutions of sugar or alcohol."[10] Southern doctors quickly realized that their profession lacked respect within the community, and patients had little faith in the knowledge, training, or abilities of their physicians. By creating professional standards, including the medical degree, doctors hoped to assuage doubters and establish guidelines that would earn them respect and justify fees. Although physicians in modern Western society possess both significant prestige and income potential, nineteenth-century doctors constantly complained about low or unpaid fees or competition from poorly trained hacks. As Stowe argues, these southerners should be viewed as middle class, not as members of the elite: "mid-nineteenth-century medical practice was nowhere near the authoritative profession it would become[;] neither was it financially lucrative for the great majority of practitioners, many of whom practiced part time."[11]

Efforts to raise educational standards, and thus justify higher fees, can be appreciated by examining the increasing number of southern medical colleges as well as by considering the fact that many antebellum southern students attended northern schools. The Medical College of Georgia, for example, attempted to elevate the profession through rigorous training and coursework. "To those who are content with the stamp of mediocrity on their front," a professor of obstetrics claimed, "we have no reflections to offer; but to the honest, zealous, progressive physician, we would confidently appeal."[12] By the late antebellum era, medical colleges had emerged in the South's major cities and most of its states to offer professional degrees. The normal course of study included a dozen or so classes on anatomy, chemistry, physics, pathology, surgery, obstetrics, and other subjects so that the general practitioner would be familiar with a range of diseases and possible remedies.

Despite growth in the number of medical colleges, doctors themselves often lamented the faulty training even the college-educated received. As Dr. Joseph A. Eve argued in 1836, "The present defectiveness of medical instruction in the United States is acknowledged and deplored, by the most enlightened and distinguished physicians of our country."[13] Chief among the complaints was that medical schools taught largely in the abstract, with little practical application. Even schools that used cadavers did not truly provide practical understanding, critics argued, because medicine could only be learned by treating real patients under everyday conditions. Medical colleges in the South failed to elevate the profession, many doctors argued, because of faulty lectures, interest only in turning out graduates regardless of whether diplomas were deserved or not, and other deficiencies in medical education. The *New Orleans Medical News* complained in an 1854 editorial that "their limited materials, their modes of teaching, are of serious disadvantage to students inducing them to spend time and means in acquiring, not what would be called a proper preliminary medical education, but a certificate to practice medicine."[14] The chief problem with medical schools, the editorial declared, was the lack of hands-on training. "The practice of medicine can only be acquired in hospitals, in dissecting rooms, in being near the body."[15] As a result of such criticisms, medical schools began to advertise their ability to conduct dissections and other practical examinations, but protests continued throughout the South in the 1850s. Veteran physicians lamented that in addition to facing competition from quacks, the profession itself was turning out graduates who passed college exams but who were scarcely more prepared to practice than were the quack doctors who had no formal training at all.

Partly because of the poor reputation of southern colleges, students from wealthier families often elected to attend medical school in northern cities, especially Philadelphia. Historian Daniel Kilbride has studied the matriculation of southern young men in two colleges, the University of Pennsylvania Medical School and nearby Jefferson Medical College. Kilbride found that between 1835 and 1845, southerners comprised more than 40 percent of the students at Jefferson Medical College and that by the late 1840s southerners made up more than half the school's graduates.[16] The percentage of southern graduates of the University of Pennsylvania was even larger, with nearly 70 percent of the graduating class in the 1830s and 1840s hailing from the slave states.[17] These numbers declined only in the late 1850s, when sectional hostility mounted and southerners left the Pennsylvania schools to attend native institutions. Still, by the 1850s, thousands of southerners had earned their medical credentials in northern schools, adding significantly to the growing number of alumni from southern campuses.

Many southern medical colleges, like their northern sister institutions, published monthly journals for physicians. These professional publications were an important marker for the increasing commitment to raising professional standards among southern physicians. By the 1850s, more than a dozen specialized journals for doctors offered detailed information on the latest diagnoses and treatments, news on local and national meetings and associations, and reviews of the latest medical books. In the introduction to the *Southern Medical and Surgical Journal*, published monthly in Augusta, Georgia, beginning in the 1830s, the editors claimed that "medical periodicals" were vitally important as a "means of collecting and communicating useful information in a condensed form." Subscription prices were low, often one or two dollars per year, and the increasingly sophisticated postal system ensured that specialized journals could be distributed to country doctors as well as urban practitioners. Such publications were especially valuable to southern doctors, as the *Medical and Surgical Journal* pointed out: "scattered over a thinly populated . . . country, in which the labours of the physicians are most arduous and their remuneration inadequate, few individuals can command money to purchase or leisure to read a sufficient number of books to enable them to keep pace with the improvements that are constantly made in medicine."[18] Professional journals filled this gap. A Georgia physician and editor claimed that his publication was "an organ for the Country Physician, the city practitioner and all honorable men."[19]

Physicians' journals followed a well-established pattern. For example, the *Western and Southern Medical Recorder*, affiliated with Transylvania University, published original essays, reviews of books and professional periodicals, editorials on the state of the profession, reprints of lectures, and detailed case studies of problems, diagnoses, and treatments. These journals were remarkably open in their discussions of sex, male and female genitalia, and sexual problems such as impotence.[20] Although specialized journals were often associated with a medical college and published in the South's larger towns and cities, they were also important focal points for rural physicians who might not attend state or national meetings but who could nevertheless benefit from discussions found in the journals; the *Nashville Journal of Medicine and Surgery* printed correspondence from country doctors throughout Tennessee and the southwest.[21] Like its sister publications, the *Nashville Journa*l covered the meetings of the American Medical Association and the Convention of the Connecticut Medical Society, providing valuable information to subscribers about the most recent trends in the field and also linking doctors across the country.[22]

An important function of state medical societies and the journals they published was to serve as a focal point for physicians throughout the state. Doctors in rural areas, far removed from the daily interaction that often existed among doctors in larger towns and cities, could obtain valuable lessons on the latest treatments and medicines. The *Stethoscope and Virginia Medical Gazette* printed speeches from county and town meetings, further aiding collegiality. The journal reported on a meeting of the Medical Society of Clarke County, which consisted of eight physicians who discussed typhoid fever, drafted by-laws and a constitution, and elected officers.[23] Physicians established associations at the local level as well as the state and national levels to serve as an advocate for their professional interests. These organizations provided fellowship for their members and allowed them to exchange information and elect delegates to state and national meetings. Equally important, such specialized groups helped members establish a code of ethics to help differentiate them from nonmembers. Such codes of ethics were largely uniform across the country. Doctor-patient confidentiality, opposition to abortion, and other ethical matters consumed numerous pages in physicians' journals. The *Atlanta Medical and Surgical Journal* editorialized against "immoral advertisements" for abortion pills and called on doctors to shun such practices.[24] Since the goal of these organizations was to elevate the status of the profession, ethical standards became central to attempts to marginalize those outside professional medical associations.

Southern medical periodicals dedicated many issues to denunciations of "quackery," a term doctors employed to discredit what they perceived to be medicine practiced by uneducated conmen. The *Atlanta Medical and Surgical Journal*, associated with Atlanta Medical College, was particularly active on this score. In its inaugural volume, published in 1855, Dr. Joseph P. Logan admitted that the public held little regard for physicians and had even less faith in medicine as a science. He acknowledged that the "pretension and actual ignorance, which has so often been found in the ranks of the medical profession," has led to "the world's judgment, that stupidity and confidence are the prominent requisites for the position of

Doctor."[25] Physicians, painfully aware of their reputation, responded to such views by drawing sharp distinctions between trained professionals and quacks. Advertisements for patented medicines earned scorn, and the *Atlanta Medical and Surgical Journal* chastised newspapers for printing scurrilous claims. "The enormous amount of medicine indiscriminately swallowed by the public is a well-know cause of ill-health," the journal argued in an editorial reprinted from a Boston periodical. In addition to possible physical harm from these medicines, quack medicine also cost doctors money, as the journal readily acknowledged: "It is as much for the pecuniary interest of the physician that the community should take quack-medicine, as it is for the lawyer that popular directions for making a will should be extensively circulated."[26] Still, amateurs persisted in offering all manner of cure-alls, much to the displeasure of southerners who advocated more stringent regulation of the field. "Rampant quackery," one southerner complained, "lays so many victims in the grave, that it becomes a duty of every man to stay its progress."[27]

Southern doctors often took issue with those peddling patented medicine. In his unusually outspoken medical journal, the *Georgia Blister and Critic*, editor and physician H. A. Ramsay of Atlanta even railed against established doctors or medical college professors who patented their medicines. "By our Code of Ethics, no vender of Patent Medicine can occupy a seat in any medical college, and maintain the character of the school as a reputable institution. No Patent Medicine *certifier* or *abettor* is a fit subject for a Professor, because he is not a regular and accredited member of our order."[28]

Doctors often blamed the public at large for its faith in untrained practitioners, and medical societies and their journals worked vigorously to convince ordinary citizens that callowness pervaded the field. "It is . . . a humiliating circumstance," the *New Orleans Medical News and Hospital Gazette* announced in an editorial, "to the true and honorable physician, to witness the extent to which arrant quackery is patronized by our people . . . [D]uring a few winter months there comes flocking in a horde of lung doctors, pile doctors, corn doctors, biologists, phrenologists, electricians, etc., etc., etc., who fill their pockets through the miserable credulity of mankind."[29]

Other physicians believed that the general public had every interest in ensuring a high skill level for their doctors and that patients could be enlisted to help thwart quackery. As one southerner wrote in 1849, there were too many quacks inhabiting southern towns and villages "who promise to cure corns, cancers and consumption with blue-pill or lobelia. The public are interested in maintaining the dignity of the medical profession."[30] One way for the citizenry to aid the profession was by supporting medical colleges. Southerners were often invited to graduation ceremonies even though they had no direct connection to the schools. Communities took pride in their medical colleges, much as they did in the general colleges and universities in their midst. Lectures, graduations, and other events became community affairs, engaging the public and providing a broader base of community support.

A crucial path to gaining the public's trust and to thwarting untrained practitioners, medical journals suggested, was the establishment of medical licenses and state-sanctioned boards to certify a certain level of expertise. The *Stethoscope* devoted considerable effort to advocating the establishment of state medical licensing throughout the 1850s. In an 1852 editorial, for example, the journal complained that while lawyers had to undergo an extensive series of examinations, the state's citizens had no guarantee that their doctors were "skilled" or "well-educated."[31] The journal urged that the state legislature be enjoined to ensure that all doctors were prepared "to exercise the high, noble and responsible calling of practitioners of medicine and surgery."[32] Virginia doctors, for example, advocated the establishment of such a body. "Let us put aside all jealousies and party animosities," a Virginia physician argued, ". . . and let us unceasingly strive to obtain . . . a board of medical examiners for the state."[33] In journals and before medical society meetings, physicians devoted considerable energy to blasting amateur practitioners, proclaiming the science and experimentation behind "real" medicine, and devising ways to distinguish the trained and the untrained.

Physicians tried to elevate their profession by censuring amateurs, but they also sought to reassure the public of medicine's legitimacy by establishing professional organizations and societies that shared information with their northern counterparts. In 1856, the *Atlanta Medical and Surgical Journal* printed the lengthy proceedings of the recently formed American Medical Association, to which numerous southern physicians belonged.[34] The journal also published communications from and information on the Massachusetts South District Medical Society, the British Association for the Advancement of Medical Science, and the Illinois State Medical Society.[35] The *Stethoscope and Virginia Medical Gazette*, originating in Richmond, printed a lengthy report on the AMA, correspondence from the Medical Society of Fredericksburg, and reports from the *Canada Medical Journal*.[36]

Southern doctors used these connections to exchange medical information, but they also employed them to advance their professional and class interests. The *Stethoscope and Virginia Medical Gazette*, for example, fought vigorously against a proposed tax on physicians' services. Virginians were especially alarmed in the spring of 1855 when both the Richmond city council and the state legislature threatened to tax doctors' earnings, amounting to "a double tax for the exercise of a profession, the laborious duties of which are too often rendered without fee or reward."[37]

In opposing specific taxes and denouncing quackery, doctors created ways to lobby for their class and professional interests. But physicians engaged in other activities to limit competition, including collusion in pricing. The *Stethoscope* went so far as to publish a lengthy fee schedule agreed upon by the one hundred or so doctors who worked in Richmond. The schedule, which ran for four pages in the journal, established fees for office visits, surgeries, obstetrics, and other services. The prices ranged from one dollar for each visit within the city during the day, to as much as one hundred dollars for "attendance on complicated, protracted or instrumental labors, including visits for eight days," to two dollars for vaccinating a slave.[38] Such collusion resulted from a widespread sentiment among doctors that they were unappreciated by patients, a feeling they felt was reflected in low pay. "There is no class of men," a New Orleans editor moaned, "who, in pursuit of a livelihood, suffer the same anxiety, the same responsibility, the same fatigue, and whose services are so poorly appreciated as physicians. There are none who are so badly remunerated, or whose fees are so rarely paid cheerfully."[39] Scholars have discovered that southern doctors were not as poorly paid as their lamentations would suggest.[40] Still, from their perspective, continued vigilance was necessary. An 1859 editorial in the *Medical Journal of North Carolina* agreed that "professional huckstering" generated price competition that lowered wages for all physicians. Explicitly comparing medicine to practices in the commercial world, the editorial argued "that the success which results from underbidding is [necessarily] ephemeral, that the practice thus secured [is] usually lost in the end, that such Physicians are employed as a matter of speculation alone." Older doctors often blamed younger ones for this practice, and recent medical college graduates responded in turn that they had to pay debts for tuition or compensate for the initial expenses of setting up a practice. Veterans attempted to thwart underbidding among their younger colleagues. "Professional honor is like female chastity," the North Carolina journal declared: "the slightest blot is an indelible stain, a single lapse an irretrievable error."[41] A Georgia physician concurred. In a letter to an editor, he maintained that practitioners should not "depend upon putting down his professional brethren by low and underhanded means, going from house to house begging practice for the pitiful sum of *one dollar per visit, no mileage fees, and throw in the medicine in the bargain.*"[42]

Although doctors targeted newspapers for publishing graphic and sizable advertisements for patented medicine and "quack" remedies, the medical profession relied on the same papers to publicize medical schools and societies. Charleston's *Southern Patriot*, for example, devoted considerable space to printing the proceedings of the state medical convention in 1848.[43] Georgia's *Macon Telegraph* published a list of graduates from the

Medical College of Georgia, as well as a lengthy account of the graduation exercises.[44]

The increasing self-awareness and desire for specialized identity extended far beyond the medical profession. In the early nineteenth century, practitioners in other fields were also coming to consider themselves as part of distinct groups within southern society; and like doctors, these groups sought ways to draw distinctions between professionals and amateurs. Lawyers, for example, established the *Carolina Law Journal* in 1830 and the *Louisiana Law Journal* in 1840. The *Carolina Law Journal*, a monthly published in Columbia, South Carolina, was edited by prominent attorney David J. McCord (husband of essayist Louisa McCord) and published court decisions, biographies of judges, and reviews of books. By subscribing to this specialized publication, lawyers could learn about important new precedents and decisions, such as an 1831 case involving the liability of husbands for their wives' debts.[45] In the decades before the Civil War, attorneys could choose from dozens of professional journals published in New York, Boston, Philadelphia, and the South.

Like physicians and lawyers, dentists in the late antebellum period developed a self-conscious identity expressed in organizations and periodicals. The North Carolina Dental Society was formed in Raleigh in 1856—the only such group in the nation. Although the dental association did not publish a journal, it actively promoted the professionalization of dentistry in the Old South, and its members made raising the standards of their profession paramount. The by-laws limited membership to those who had graduated from dental colleges, such as the Baltimore College of Dental Surgery.[46] In the 1830s and 1840s, leading North Carolina dentists such as W. R. Scott, John W. Howlett, Francis Lee, Joshua King, and E. R. Hubbard had graduated from the Baltimore school and wanted to separate themselves from practitioners who had no formal training.[47]

Much like the physicians who formed specialized groups to marginalize amateurs, dentists were concerned that patients failed to distinguish between skilled and unskilled dentists. Middle-class professionals of all fields referred to their chosen fields as a "calling," and associations helped to give meaning to this term by emphasizing ethical and moral behavior among members. One observer remarked at the dental society's founding that the members should be praised for raising "the dignity of their profession and the advancement of their calling."[48] Members came to the annual conventions from throughout the state to discuss "the collective experience and professional knowledge accumulated during the year."[49] Papers were read on topics such as artificial dentures, surgical techniques, and medicine. Most important, the North Carolina Dental Society established a code of ethics that from its founding guided professional standards: "It is unprofessional to resort to public advertisements, cards, hand-bills, posters or signs, calling attention to 'peculiar styles of work,' lowness of price, special modes of operating, or to claim superiority over neighboring practitioners, . . . to go from house to house to solicit or to perform operations, [or] to circulate or recommend nostrums."[50] Like doctors, dentists devised a set of ethical standards to limit competition from those who sought patients using the same techniques that one might use to sell other products and services.

Southern dentists, in fact, were responsible for the legal definition of dentistry as a subset of medicine. During the Civil War, dentists sought and secured legal status on par with doctors. North Carolina dentist J. W. Hunter was conscripted by the state during the early years of the war, but he claimed that the state law exempting practicing doctors should apply to dentists as well. The state Supreme Court agreed in a precedent that remains in effect.[51]

Southern teachers formed their own specialized associations and published journals to promote their professional status. Although few public schools in the modern sense of the term existed in the antebellum era, education for white southern boys and girls was a topic of great concern. State-sponsored schools were almost nonexistent except for poor, blind, or hearing-impaired children. Southern communities, however, invested significant resources into building schools, aiding them financially by supporting building costs. Graduation ceremonies and special events attracted large numbers of families from the surrounding region. Thus, the schools of the antebellum South really were "public" in that they received financial support and benefited from significant community involvement.

The importance of education in the antebellum South can be seen in the emergence of teaching as a respected profession. Most teachers in the early nineteenth century were men, though northern and southern women entered the field in increasing numbers as well. Whether in large towns or rural areas, teachers sought intellectual and professional engagement with colleagues within the region and across the country. Indeed, in the 1840s and 1850s, many teachers and advocates of common school systems wrote to Massachusetts educational reformer Horace Mann, requesting subscriptions to his school journal, seeking advice on mustering public support, and asking questions about teaching methods. Clearly, southern teachers were conscious of their need for specialized knowledge, and journals played a central role key in raising the status of the profession.

One such professional publication for teachers was the *North Carolina Journal* of Education, published in Greensboro and Raleigh beginning in 1858. Like doctors and dentists, teachers sought in their periodicals to elevate the status and reputation of their field. Calvin Wiley, the journal's editor and a state school official, constantly cajoled teachers into engaging each other more. As he observed in the journal, "Our teachers must be aroused to a spirit of self-improvement, and of *mutual* improvement. They stand too much aloof from each other, seemingly possessing little or no community of feeling."[52] Wiley might have been overly pessimistic here, for even he acknowledged that many counties in the state had formed their own teachers' societies. Like the specialized periodicals published for doctors, teaching journals lobbied for reforms, provided news of meetings, published essays of interest to the field, and provided a forum through which teachers living in rural and urban areas could connect. As state superintendent, Wiley was able to secure funding for each school to receive a subscription to the *North Carolina Journal of Education*, underscoring the importance of these professional journals in the eyes of practitioners.[53] While Wiley's *North Carolina Journal* is perhaps the most prominent southern education magazine of the antebellum South, others dotted the landscape. The *North Carolina Common School Journal* (1856-1857) was openly modeled after Horace Mann's northern magazine, the *Common School Journal*. The *Alabama Educational Journal* (1858-1859), the *Tennessee Journal of Education* (1859-1860), and others helped link southern teachers in common endeavors to advance public schools.

The rich culture of associations and their periodicals demonstrate that the Old South was indeed undergoing a significant transformation in the decades before the Civil War. Instead of letting the rural and sparsely settled nature of the region inhibit interaction and engagement among southern professionals, those men and women actively sought opportunities to connect with colleagues through clubs and organizations. Associations for physicians, lawyers, teachers, and dentists also suggest that by the 1850s, occupations in the region were becoming more diverse and specialized. At the heart of all these activities was a new and important southern middle class, whose energy and ambition shaped the region's economy, culture, and society.

This energy and ambition is amply evident in the yellowed pages of professional journals. Scholars have only begun to tap the rich historical resources that these teaching, medical, dental, and legal publications offer. In part this neglect is the consequence of the broader historical passing-over of the southern social structure. Long regarded as a region primarily of planters and slaves, scholars have ignored classes and groups within the antebellum South that complicated this bifurcated class structure. Yet, as recent scholarship has suggested, understanding the nuances of the region's social system does not diminish the importance of slavery or of the plantation economy. Rather, by examining the commercial and professional middle class, and particularly the active role the class played in the South's urban and industrial transformation, we understand better the complex interaction between slavery and capitalism. After all, white southerners themselves believed strongly that slavery could exist comfortably with progress, and that in fact the two could bring to fruition their dreams of a new South. Professionalization went hand-in-hand with this philosophy.

By raising professional standards and by fostering licensing programs, the southern middle class sought to elevate its class status above ordinary laborers and above amateurs. At the same time, professionalization fit comfortably into the southern middle-class's ideology of progress for itself and the region. Advancement in professional standards and training brought the middle-class vision of a modernizing South closer to reality. If the North could have large cities, public schools and libraries, professional associations, and other elements of progress, then so too could the South. In the eyes of the southern middle class, slavery was not an impediment but a boon to their modernizing aspirations. Together with slavery, southern industrialization, and urbanization, professionalization promised a prosperous and modern future, a new South that would one day compete favorably with the North.

NOTES

1. Jennifer R. Green, *Military Education and the Emerging Middle Class in the Old South* (Cambridge, UK: Cambridge University Press, 2008); Bruce W. Eelman, *Entrepreneurs in the Southern Upcountry: Commercial Culture in Spartanburg, South Carolina, 1845-1880* (Athens: University of Georgia Press, 2008); Jonathan Daniel Wells, *The Origins of the Southern Middle Class, 1800-1861* (Chapel Hill: University of North Carolina Press, 2004).

2. David Moltke-Hansen, "The Expansion of Intellectual Life: A Prospectus," in *Intellectual Life in Antebellum Charleston,* ed. Michael O'Brien and David Moltke-Hansen (Knoxville: University of Tennessee Press, 1986), 3-44.

3. H. A. Ramsay, "Medical Society of North Carolina, 1853," *Georgia Blister and Critic* 1 (July 1854): 124.

4. Joseph C. G. Kennedy, *Preliminary Report on the Eighth Census, 1860* (Washington, DC, 1862), 192-93.

5. U.S. Census Bureau, *Historical Statistics of the United States* (Washington, DC: U.S. Government Printing Office, 1949).

6. For a fuller discussion of these points, see Wells, *Origins of the Southern Middle Class.*

7. Kennedy, *Preliminary Report on the Eighth Census, 1860,* 174.

8. Gertrude C. Gilmer, *Checklist of Southern Periodicals to 1861* (Boston: F.W. Faxon, 1934), sect. 3.

9. Ibid., 90.

10. Steven M. Stowe, *Doctoring the South: Southern Physicians and Everyday Medicine in the Mid-Nineteenth Century* (Chapel Hill: University of North Carolina Press, 2004), 7.

11. Ibid., 10. See also Ronald L. Numbers and Todd L. Savitt, eds., *Science and Medicine in the Old South* (Baton Rouge: Louisiana State University Press, 1989).

12. Milton Anthony, "Reviews and Extracts," *Southern Medical and Surgical Journal* 1 (June 1836): 29.

13. Joseph A. Eve, "Medical Education," *Southern Medical and Surgical Journal* 1 (Sept. 1836): 216.

14. "Editorial," *New Orleans Medical News and Hospital Gazette* 1 (May 15, 1854): 122.

15. Ibid., 123.

16. Daniel Kilbride, "Southern Medical Students in Philadelphia, 1800–1861: Science and Sociability in the 'Republic of Medicine,'" *Journal of Southern History* 65 (Nov. 1999): 701.

17. Ibid., 703-4.

18. "Introduction," *Southern Medical and Surgical Journal* 1 (June 1836): 1.

19. H. A. Ramsay, "Editorial Life," *Georgia Blister and Critic* 1 (July 1854): 115.

20. For example, see the discussion of impotence in *Western and Southern Medical Recorder* 1 (June 1842): 380.

21. See correspondence from physicians in Flat Rock and Greenville, Tennessee, and Bluffton, Arkansas, in *Nashville Journal of Medicine and Surgery* 18 (March 1860): 195-200.

22. "Transactions of the American Medical Association," ibid., 236-39.

23. "The Medical Society of Clarke County, Virginia," *Stethoscope and Virginia Medical Gazette* 1 (April 1851): 240.

24. "Immoral Advertisements," *Atlanta Medical and Surgical Journal* 3 (Feb. 1858): 379.

25. Joseph P. Logan, "Medicine as it is," *Atlanta Medical and Surgical Journal* 1 (Sept. 1855): 5.

26. "Newspaper Recommendations of Quack Medicine," *Atlanta Medical and Surgical Journal* 1 (Jan. 1856): 319.

27. "Communicated," *Georgia Telegraph*, Jan. 30, 1849, 3.

28. H. A. Ramsay, "Patent Medicine—Professors," *Georgia Blister and Critic* 1 (Aug. 1854): 151.

29. "Quackery," *New Orleans Medical News and Hospital Gazette* 5 (Feb. 1859): 841.

30. "Communicated," *Georgia Telegraph*, 3.

31. "The Licensing of Physicians," *Stethoscope and Virginia Medical Gazette* 2 (April 1852): 202.

32. Ibid., 206.

33. "Tax on Physicians," *Stethoscope and Virginia Medical Gazette* 5 (March 1855): 135.

34. "Proceedings," *Atlanta Medical and Surgical Journal* 1 (June 1856): 636-40.

35. See, for example, "Address by the President of the Illinois State Medical Society," *Atlanta Medical and Surgical Journal* 2 (Dec. 1856): 205-15.

36. *Stethoscope and Virginia Medical Gazette* 1 (Jan. 1851): 29-37; 1 (June 1851): 329-45; 2 (Dec. 1852): 701-2.

37. "Tax on Physicians," 133. See also "Opinion of John M. Patton, Esq. on the Constitutionality of Taxing Physicians," ibid., 5 (April 1855): 197-202.

38. "Tariff of Fees," ibid., 1 (March 1851): 177-80.

39. "Editorial," *New Orleans Medical News and Hospital Gazette* 1 (Aug. 15, 1854): 266.

40. E. Brooks Holifield, "The Wealth of Nineteenth-Century American Physicians," *Bulletin of the History of Medicine* 64 (Spring 1990): 79-85.

41. "Underbidding," *Medical Journal of North Carolina* 2 (June 1859): 606-7.

42. Medicus, "Ethical Question," *Georgia Blister and Critic* 1 (July 1854): 105.

43. "Proceedings of the Medical Convention," *(Charleston, SC) Southern Patriot*, Feb. 15, 1848, 2.

44. "Medical College of Georgia," *Macon Weekly Telegraph*, March 11, 1846, 3.

45. "Liability of the Husband for the Debts of the Wife," *Carolina Law Journal* 1 (Jan. 1, 1831): 363.

46. J. Martin Fleming, *The History of the North Carolina Dental Society* (Raleigh, 1939), 15.

47. Ibid., 13.

48. Ibid., 17.

49. Ibid.

50. Ibid.

51. Ibid., 33-34.

52. Calvin Wiley, "The Teacher and His Calling," *North Carolina Journal of Education* 2 (Jan. 1859): 32. See the notice for the Lenoir County Educational Association, ibid. (June 1859): 181, and news of the formation of a similar group in Forsyth County, ibid. (Oct. 1859): 326.

53. Ibid., 2 (Sept. 1859), 285.

Chapter 7

Education and Professionals in the Old South

Schooling's Impact on Career and Social Class

Jennifer R. Green

The number and proportion of professionals in the southern population, especially attorneys and physicians, increased throughout the 1840s and 1850s. The significance of southern professionals lay not only in their contribution to the formation of the southern middle class but also in the social and ideological support they provided for industrial and commercial development in the region. Although the South remained primarily agricultural, young southern men increasingly trained in the antebellum decades to become professionals—defined for the purposes of this study as the knowledge-based occupations of lawyers, doctors, clergy, judges, engineers, and teachers. The number of southern physicians, for instance, increased in the 1840 and 1850s, with an especially large spike in the 1850s, when physicians came to make up 49 percent of southern professionals, according to the 1860 census. The law became almost equally popular as an occupation. By that year, approximately 1.6 percent of the U.S. workforce was in the learned professions of minister, lawyer, and doctor. In addition, just over 0.5 percent worked in some type of scientific occupation.[1]

Some planters' sons, especially younger ones, as well as kin who could not enter planting, sought their livelihoods in these professions. So did the members of an emerging southern middle class, which was forming in the 1840s and 1850s and using schooling (in addition to other institutions and processes, of course) to develop its professional occupations, social stability, and what have been identified as bourgeois values.

One way to identify the social rank of antebellum professionals is to look at the type of institutions from which they tended to graduate. Although one study of 103 Virginians born between 1830 and 1843 does not differentiate between types of schools, the majority of these southerners worked outside of agriculture and were divided almost equally as lawyers, students, and teachers, and less than 3 percent of the remaining men worked in professional occupations.[2] This and other studies that document the rise in professionals encourage further research into the connection between social class, secondary education, and the professions; such a connection is borne out by a detailed examination of southern education and alumni employment.

One difficulty in pursuing a study of antebellum southern education is the dearth of scholarship, commonly lamented by historians of education, and of resources. Indeed, the lack of bureaucratization and records in the southern educational system makes certain types of studies all but impossible. Many schools left few or no records, and the information that does exist rarely records details of student backgrounds or post-graduation careers. Southern state university histories focus on the institutions and their administrations rather than on the social position of students or graduates except when praising an individual alumnus or the high standing of their students generally.[3] Two large datasets do, in fact, exist that allow for analysis of the relationship between education and the status of southern professionals. Colin B. Burke's *American Collegiate Populations* (1982) provides a massive source base for national university and liberal arts college students; it presents occupational data on 1,107 southern state university graduates and 1,558 southern small college graduates of the 1840s and 1850s. Forming a picture of the majority of educated southerners who attended schools of lower status proves more difficult. Records of military school alumni, however, provide career data for 855 antebellum men and a solid basis for comparison.[4] This essay uses these datasets to compare the occupations of elite university graduates to those of college and academy alumni. It examines, in turn, employment in agriculture, professions, and business to identify how the different types of schooling influenced the matriculants' career trajectories and how those careers and institutions contributed to ongoing class and occupational transformations in the Old South.

The small minority of white southern young men who advanced to secondary education found a range of institutions available to them. They could enter large state universities, smaller denominational or independent colleges, or academies, which were mid-range institutions that represented the final stage of a youth's education, referred to as "higher schooling." State universities were supported by legislative funding and maintained a classical curriculum that required knowledge of Latin and Greek for entrance and focused on these languages throughout their degree programs.

State universities represented the pinnacle of the antebellum educational hierarchy in the South and included the University of North Carolina (UNC), opened in 1795; the University of Georgia (UGA), 1801; South Carolina College (SCC), 1805; and the Universities of Virginia (1825), Alabama (1831), and Mississippi (1848). They were (usually) well funded, and the size of their student bodies often rivaled those of Yale, Harvard, and other established northeastern universities. Because of their price, curriculum, housing, and ideology, they primarily attracted the sons of elite families.[5]

Given the elite nature of the southern state universities, with curriculum and costs that opened the doors to mostly the wealthy, it is unsurprising that planters' sons dominated as attendees. The planter was the pinnacle of status in the Old South. Schooling, never necessary for planting, reflected elite gentility. For example, it allowed elite southerners to demonstrate their honor and mastery in classics and oratory.[6] More than 25 percent of southern state university alumni became "planters or large farmers," and still more must have possessed small farms. Because the majority of men labored on the land in the antebellum United States, especially so in the South, many educated southerners joined the majority of the people living around them in agriculture. Burke finds that the percentage of state university graduates who entered agriculture ranged from 18 to 54, depending on the school, between 1830 and 1860. UNC graduated agriculturalists with the lowest frequency, but this rate increased over the period to 22 percent in the 1850s. The other state universities produced planters at a higher rate, although that rate declined over the years: at the University of Virginia (UVA) the planter rate dropped from 41 to 26 percent and at the University of Alabama (UAL) it decreased from 54 to 36 percent between 1850 and 1860. An institutional history of UGA students from 1804 to 1860 calculated that 17.8 percent became planters and another 5.4 percent were farmers; these findings fall within Burke's range of approximately one-quarter of the students becoming planters. An additional 15.6 percent of the total UGA graduates, moreover, worked dual careers in agriculture and law, medicine, or education, so that as many as 40 percent may have been connected to agriculture.[7]

Below the elite university level, the number of alumni entering agriculture decreased. More significant, however, is that the ratio of planters to farmers reversed: state universities reproduced the master class, and smaller, less prestigious schools maintained the agricultural focus of antebellum society but produced farmers rather than planters. Small colleges blossomed in the antebellum years partly because of the founding of denominational colleges but also because of the expansion of education across the nation that was catching up in the South and West. In Georgia, for example, Emory, Oglethorpe, and Mercer colleges (in addition to Wesleyan Female College) coexisted, and Alabama housed seventeen colleges by

1860. Colleges offered bachelor's degrees but were more heterogeneous than state universities in their curricula. Burke contends that the southern lack of public education and low social mobility caused liberal arts colleges and state universities to resemble each other more closely in the region than elsewhere. Indeed, Robert F. Pace's 2004 *Halls of Honor* asserts that state universities and small colleges both educated the southern elite.[8] Colleges that duplicated the classical curriculum of their larger state models surely found their clientele among the higher social echelons. One such school, Transylvania University in Kentucky, produced many successful graduates. As Jefferson Davis, class of 1824, recalled, he was "one of six graduates of Transylvania" to hold a seat in the U.S. Senate; a total of seventeen congressmen attended Transylvania over the three years of 1822 through 1824. Davis became a cotton planter at age 27 (through marriage). The elite rank of the student body of Transylvania and similar colleges is apparent in an antebellum newspaper clipping that estimates student yearly expenditures at $500, an amount equal to half of one of their professors' annual salaries or all of a clerk's.[9]

In contrast to these classical programs, colleges could also introduce curricula with English and French at their core, which obviated the need for students to have spent years studying with Latin and Greek tutors to gain entry, or they could focus more on science. In 1828, Transylvania implemented two degree tracks: in addition to the classical course, a track in English literature was offered for the first time in an attempt to democratize the school. At the same time, the college introduced a dress code in order to erase physical markers of social differences (much as military academy uniforms served to do).[10] Emory and Henry College opened in southwest Virginia as a manual labor school, requiring that students work at least eighteen hours per month toward their tuition and board.[11] Thus, colleges attracted students from a range of social positions on the basis of their curricula, costs, and structure.

The agricultural fathers of students who attended small colleges were below the planter rank, as were fathers who sent their sons for higher schooling at academies. Less than one-quarter of the graduates of both liberal arts colleges and military schools were agricultural. Burke observes that southern liberal arts colleges were four times more likely to produce agriculturalists than northern schools, whose rate remained constant at 8 percent or below (southern colleges never reached 30 percent, however, as did the universities). Statistics for southern colleges were similar to those of their larger state counterparts: between 16 and 25 percent of their graduates entered agriculture. Whereas men in classical programs probably had similar rates of running plantations, those who enrolled in practical programs and entered agriculture were surely farmers. Planters would have been infrequently attracted to smaller colleges that lacked classical studies or high status. In each decade, overall, the percentage of agriculturalists who graduated from colleges was lower than the percentage graduating from the state universities.[12]

Families attracted to the final educational option—higher schooling—seemed even less likely to become planters or agriculturalists in general. Non-elite young men had difficulty entering state universities because of the high tuition and classical training required. State universities in the South tended to make fewer concessions to non-elites than did large universities in the northeast. Small private colleges and academies in both regions were the institutions that more often implemented nonclassical curricula and housing arrangements to encourage non-elite enrollment.[13] Higher schools—those schools above the common-school level and below the institutions that offered bachelor's degrees—made schooling available for the social ranks above African Americans and the lowest white classes. Those southerners who completed higher schooling, probably the majority of youth in the Old South who pursued secondary education, received certificates of completion or diplomas rather than B.A.s. As access to schooling increased, southerners of the emerging middle class promoted educational reform in part to provide opportunities for its members. One offshoot of their lobbying for public education and practical curricula was the creation of specialized academies, such as manual labor schools, and more than eighty military academies, including the Virginia Military Institute (VMI) and the Citadel. Southern higher schools included twelve state-funded military institutes and more than seventy additional military academies run as private enterprises. These schools operated with a military routine grafted onto a scientific curriculum and with schedules almost identical to that at West Point, the U.S. service academy. Private and state military school graduates were *not* assured entry into the army and found civilian occupations approximately 95 percent of the time.

Parents might choose to send a younger son to a military school if they could not afford to send him to a college or a university. One father wrote of his decision to send his son to the state military institute, "I had intended if I was able to give him a year or two at the University, but my resources have been so crippled by the failure of my Judge to do business in my court, for a year or two."[14] His son taught for two years after graduation at his alma mater and then became a civil engineer and railroad man. Cadets mostly came from nonagricultural households in a lower social stratum than the plantation elite of the Old South and even outside the dominant occupation of farming; only 30 percent of their fathers were in agriculture.

Less than one-quarter of military school alumni pursued solely agricultural careers, and rarely could those men be classified as planters. Only 21.2 percent of men with one occupation before the Civil War remained in agriculture; among all military school alumni, the figure was slightly higher at 23.4 percent. This nonagricultural focus, again, in part reflects the status and situation of graduates' fathers. The difference in fathers' occupations suggests different classes' interests in different institutions: planters tended to make use of state universities when they placed their sons in formal institutions of secondary education and lent those institutions their stature, whereas non-elites selected smaller colleges and higher schooling for their sons. Thus, one-quarter or more of state university alumni became planters, whereas other graduates joined the majority occupation of agriculture below the elite rank.

Becoming a farmer (or planter) in the 1850s would have been the most common career in the region, but an increasing number of young men selected professional occupations after completing their education. Because antebellum southerners did not require schooling for most careers, especially farming, the small percentage of men who were educated shared some characteristics. Family preference played into the choice, as it did in the selection of type of school and specific institution. Resources—both money and social status—created more options (as they always have). Wealth would allow a young man to travel to a school and pay its costs. One trait that encouraged fathers to educate their sons was their own occupation and standing. Children of professional fathers often dominated student bodies at all levels of schooling, as the professions required and supported education in ways that other potential occupations did not. Professionals in two Tennessee counties enrolled their children in primary schools more often than did fathers from other occupations, despite only 10 to 11 percent of schoolchildren coming from nonagricultural homes.[15]

Burke discovers that the older southern schools served elite and urban professionals: almost 30 percent of the student bodies of UNC and UVA were the sons of professionals or businessmen, and small colleges "consistently showed a higher percentage of ministers, businessmen, and professionals than did the state institutions." As the social status of institutions and their clientele decreased, the number of fathers in planting correspondingly declined and the number of fathers in the professions rose. This relationship is borne out in military academies, for example, where 53 percent of fathers were professionals, 20 percent greater than Burke's findings for elite state university fathers. That professionals made up a large share of those who sent their sons for secondary education makes it unsurprising that their sons frequently followed in their fathers' footsteps and entered the professions.[16]

Focusing on the educational origins of professionals in the 1830s through the 1850s, state university graduates often reflected their fathers' elite positions. Descriptions of elite graduates from the state universities highlight them as leaders of their states. Graduates of SCC or UVA played prominent roles in their states and are often showcased in social and political histories. SCC produced a series of successful graduates. Three representative (although somewhat notorious) graduates demonstrate the college's dominance: Preston Brooks, class of 1839 (expelled just prior to graduation), and planter Laurence M. Keitt, class of 1843, were both fire-eaters from well-established families and entered the legal profession and eventually the U.S. Congress; and James Henry Hammond, a contemporary of Jefferson Davis, started with lower-than-elite status but, after his graduation from SCC, replicated traditional values and used teaching and editing to secure a plantation (through marriage) and governorship.[17] These alumni demonstrated their elite standing by combining a profession and planting or using a profession to move into planting.

As these men illustrate, graduates of southern state universities entered agriculture in large percentages but also found their way into the professions. Just as law appealed to Brooks and Keitt, it was the most chosen profession of similarly educated young men, attracting approximately 20 percent (and up to 30 percent) of southern university graduates. The rates remained constant across the antebellum decades (slightly higher in the 1830s) and similar to those of doctors. The number of doctors coming out of the universities waned in the 1840s and 1850s, dropping from a range of 21 to 36 percent in the 1840s (with UGA at the particularly low figure of 11 percent) to 18 to 29 percent in the 1850s. This drop is interesting given the increase in southern doctors overall. It should also be noted that doctors in the late antebellum years were more likely than their predecessors to have attended one of the South's six antebellum medical schools. Because professional education was not necessary before the war, as apprenticeships worked just as well for a young man wishing to enter a medical or law career, attendance at these medical schools suggests elite status. Daniel Kilbride identifies this elite standing among southerners who went to the University of Pennsylvania for medical school.[18]

Burke also records that, especially after the 1830s, the rate at which university graduates became ministers fell off. By the 1840s and 1850s, less than 10 percent of university graduates selected the ministry for their career. (UVA was the only outlier, at 12 percent.) Judgeships remained consistently low across the board, at less than 5 percent for both university and college graduates; the absence of this occupation could represent the alumni's youth before the outbreak of the war.[19]

A few of the institutional histories of southern universities detail their most successful graduates. A 1956 history of the University of Georgia, for example, lists the 39 most influential graduates from 1821 through 1844, who include 12 congressmen, 6 governors, and 13 U.S. or state Supreme Court justices. On the less notable side, it also records 6 college presidents, 2 professors, 2 authors, and 2 doctors. A more recent UGA institutional history concluded that among the 474 people who matriculated between 1804 and 1860 for whom occupational information was available, 39 percent became lawyers, 13.2 percent doctors, 12.2 percent clergy, and 2.5 percent teachers.[20] UGA graduates further exhibited a high proportion of public service in the government and judgeships: one-sixth of all students for whom occupational information was available entered the state legislature, and they were more likely to enter public service and judgeships than their non–university educated peers. Almost everyone included on a short list of successful UNC graduates, likewise, became a lawyer and legislator (mostly in the North Carolina legislature or the U.S. House of Representatives).[21] State university graduates most often selected the law as a high-status profession that would keep them connected to their family's elite rank, but they also entered other professions.

Among liberal arts college graduates, those included in the Burke dataset entered professions at a substantial rate, with 17 to 38 percent selecting law or medicine in the last three decades before the Civil War. These figures were routinely lower than the figures from state universities: graduates of colleges in the South Atlantic states entered professions at rates of 17 and 16 percent, respectively, as compared with 27 and 29 percent for UVA graduates, 36 and 18 percent for UNC graduates, and 22 percent for both careers for UGA graduates in the 1850s. The rate of college alumni becoming clergy, however, was considerably higher than that of university graduates. While less than 13 percent of graduates of the state universities entered the ministry, this figure was greater than 25 percent for the colleges. In the 1850s, when 5 percent of the 285 UVA graduates and 8 percent of the 157 UNC graduates became clergy, 25 to 29 percent of small college alumni selected that career. The prevalence of denominational colleges must have encouraged this tendency.[22]

The professions attracted graduates of higher schools in even larger proportions than they did matriculants of the other types of institutions. Among military alumni, 64.4 percent found their way into professional occupations between 1840 and 1860. They primarily entered the same professions as their college- and university-educated peers: law and medicine. Alumni who pursued multiple jobs entered teaching, law, and medicine, in that order. More men who pursued only one career became physicians than attorneys, but when men with multiple careers (either sequential or dual) are considered, more of them worked in the law. Nearly 20 percent became lawyers, and just over 15 percent worked as doctors. The number of clergy is interestingly low at only 2 percent of the total.[23] Nearly 200 of the 294 alumni for whom father/son data are available maintained the professional status of their fathers. Edmund Pendleton, for example, a member of VMI's first graduating class and the son of a doctor, moved to Ohio and Louisiana to practice law.

Also apparent at the lower-status end of the educational spectrum is a greater proportion of students entering teaching and engineering, neglected fields among the graduates at the opposite end of the southern higher education spectrum. Whereas less than 3 percent of southern college students entered science or engineering professions (5 percent in the Mid-Atlantic and Midwest states), a full 12 percent of military school alumni worked as engineers or for the railroads. "I think it probable that the Virginia Military Institute has turned out more civil Engineers than any ten of our Southern Colleges united," calculated D. H. Hill, college professor and founder of the North Carolina Military Institute; "in fact, the Colleges both North and South have done but little in this respect."[24]

Within the antebellum educational environment, military schools were the institutions most successful at producing engineers in the nation. The number of schools with science or engineering curricula increased as the antebellum years proceeded. Southern and western state universities and colleges began to offer one or two engineering courses as part of the regular curriculum, commonly requiring that seniors take a surveying or drafting course. However, low graduation rates at all antebellum schools (commonly below 50 percent) kept most college and university students out of those courses. As part of this trend, UAL and UVA both instituted civil engineering programs, but with little success. A historian of engineering at Alabama could only locate two graduates working in the antebellum railroad industry as engineers. The school of engineering at Alabama closed in 1846, but individual courses resumed in 1851, the same decade that the state of Alabama chartered forty-nine railroads and laid more than 500 miles of track. Clearly, that educational development was connected to industrial development in the South; at least four board members and a president of UAL held positions with railroads in the same period. To take a non–state university example, the College of William and Mary, a Virginia institution stressing classical education, started a school of engineering that survived for only three years, between 1836 and 1839. At the same time that universities and most colleges chose not to foreground engineering programs, West Point and Rensselaer Polytechnic Institute (RPI)—both New York institutions—were the top engineering schools in the antebellum years. West Point attracted southerners and graduated 150 engineers before 1840 (30 percent of whom became chief engineers on railroads, canals, or public works); RPI enrolled only 6 engineering students of 35 total students in 1845, just when the Virginia and Alabama programs were failing in the difficult times following the Panic of 1837.[25]

In this same period, state military schools enjoyed public financing that kept their enrollments high. VMI admitted thirty new cadets in 1845. Military school matriculants studied mathematics for more years and at higher levels in addition to taking engineering courses (also in the senior year, however). As a historian of engineering at the University of Virginia stated, "VMI educated career engineers."[26] West Point graduate P. G. T. Beauregard worked as an army engineer and enrolled his sons in the Louisiana State Seminary and Military Academy when it opened in 1859, selecting for the boys a scientific education that mirrored his own, but without the government service requirement. These differences indicate the vocational nature of the schools that produced engineers; higher schools used non-classical curriculum to produce engineers and often did so even in cases where alumni were younger planters' sons, such as Beauregard's. Thus, it was non-elite schools that primarily fulfilled the new need for technical professionals. Although many young southerners promoted "progress," the non-elite, vocational men engaged in those professions connected most closely to that theme.[27]

An examination of teachers also sheds light on the ranks of professionals in the South. Schools with a non-elite clientele trained an increasing number of teachers and significantly more than the state universities in the period under study. Burke records that among state universities, UVA and UAL had the highest percentage of teachers graduating in the 1840s, and UVA and UGA in the 1850s: between 10 and 12 percent for those twenty years.[28] College graduates in the South Atlantic states were more likely to enter teaching, at 15 and 22 percent in the same decades. These figures suggest that education was a less desirable career than law or medicine.

The approximately 10 percent of southern university and 20 percent of college graduates who became teachers in 1850 compares to 25 percent of military school matriculants (and a much higher 39 percent of graduates) who entered the teaching profession. Scholarships at the twelve state military schools, especially VMI and South Carolina's Citadel, required their recipients to teach in their respective states for two years after graduation. Teachers graduated from colleges and academies more often than from universities. The numbers rose over the decades, increasing above 20 percent at South Atlantic colleges, and also increased as higher schools trained more men. The lower number of teachers coming out of universities indicates the universities' elite status, with their graduates selecting more prestigious occupations.

Part of the reason for the increasing number of teachers from among higher schooling alumni was the occupation's ability to facilitate better careers. Men with fewer resources than those of the elites could teach prior to entering higher-status professions, using the money they earned to finance additional study. Men without sufficient resources would teach to earn money for tuition and board. Lancelot Blackford, for example, taught to earn the more than $400 yearly needed to attend UVA, and many young men reported doing so at academies. (The year-round schedule at military schools often precluded that option.)[29] Nearly 50 percent of military alumni who were teachers used that career as a steppingstone to something better. Augustus Powell, for example, taught from his VMI graduation until 1847, when he began preaching, although his career was cut short by his death in Alabama at the age of twenty-six. Southern academies appear to have facilitated occupational mobility in the same way New York academies represented non-elite education and upward mobility.[30]

Another reason for the increasing number of teachers from higher schooling was the professionalization of the career and its rise in status in the late antebellum years. The 50 percent of military alumni who became teachers remained in the occupation, apparently judging it worthy of status. The choice of a teaching career after graduation implied that money was necessary for launching a youth into a career or that a youth had an individual proclivity for that field. Young men with connections could enter apprenticeships; those with wealth, professional schools; and a young man with a landed estate could manage his own or his father's plantation. Teaching conveyed moderate status in the early nineteenth century, but the occupation increased in status throughout the antebellum period as it professionalized. A school principal described the happy circumstances of William A. Forbes, who remained in the occupation in 1851: "The result to him, was a beautiful wife with $10,000 in cash, and the Presidency of a Southern College at $1200 per an. and prerequisites."[31] Forbes, the son and grandson of lawyers, must have felt that a college presidency was a comparable achievement to a career in law. Just as they graduated more teachers, colleges produced more principals, professors, and college presidents than did state universities; but graduates from all three types of institutions never totaled more than 9 percent in those occupations.[32]

Given the concentration of graduates of all types of southern institutions of higher education in agriculture and the professions, it makes sense that most state university, college, and academy graduates did not find themselves in business or in other white-collar jobs. Young men selected the learned professions more than they did business, whether they graduated from a university, college, or military school. Burke's figures show that university graduates, similar to college graduates, sought out business careers in low numbers. Less than 20 percent of them entered the fields of business, commerce, manufacturing, and banking and finance; the numbers specifically for manufacturers and bankers/financiers were lower than even teaching, below 4 percent from 1840 through1860 for both universities and colleges. Burke's figures do not include lower-status white-collar workers, such as clerks, so it is difficult to track such men, who were perhaps starting out in their careers. Thomas Dyer's 1985 UGA survey includes 2.7 percent merchants and no other businessmen.[33] Burke specifically notes that "business did not offer a great opportunity of mobility to liberal arts students," finding that families with elite backgrounds, established business connections, and urban residences best succeeded in the field. Despite the volatility of business careers, however, the rate of college graduates entering business slightly increased from the 1840s to the 1850s.[34]

A similar pattern emerged from military academy alumni, few of whom found their sole careers in proprietorships or white-collar positions. Eleven percent entered occupations such as business, banking, building, accounting, clerking, or selling merchandise as sole careers. Not surprisingly, these occupations were more likely to provide additional income or launching pads as one part of an alumnus's overall career than to be sole pursuits. Thus, 16.7 percent of men with single and multiple careers had some portion of them in a proprietorship or white-collar job. Whereas elites neglected business because it was lower-status than planting and the professions, non-elites selected it infrequently because it was difficult for their class to succeed in. As one father told his cadet son, "I fear too it is a bad time for a young man to set out in business, he must however be diligent and industrious for some time before he can establish himself in any business."[35]

That so few young men of the Old South pursued a secondary education encouraged those who did to consider professional occupation; thus, some professions attracted university, college, and military academy graduates at similar rates. All schools produced similar percentages of lawyers, for example. Upward of 75 percent of the graduates of state universities became agriculturalists or professionals or both, so it is unsurprising that those schools produced only a minority of students who pursued other careers. This pattern is similar for small colleges and military academies, although the agricultural rate was lower, and the professional rate often greater, than the rates at state universities. In fact, the comprehensive University of Georgia data and the military academy data show an almost identical percentage of alumni becoming professionals (64 percent). UGA graduates, however, became planters more than three times more often than they became farmers, and virtually none of them pursued business, teaching, or scientific occupations. Middle-class cadets used the specific qualities of military education to enter professional and nonagricultural careers, especially ones for which their schooling most qualified them. The data indicate that planters tended to come out of the state universities, less frequently out of colleges, and rarely out of higher schools.

Antebellum higher schooling proved to be the most common form of secondary education in the antebellum South, meaning that it put more alumni into southern society than elite universities or even small colleges. Southern state universities were large in size for antebellum schools (most with student bodies over 100), but with one institution per state, the number of their graduates was miniscule next to the tens or hundred thousands of higher schooling alumni across the Old South. UGA had an estimated

1,500 antebellum matriculants; Emory and Henry enrolled up to nearly 200 students at a time in its twenty-three years before the war, suggesting a similar count; and VMI had slightly under 1,000 matriculants in its twenty-two years of antebellum operation.[36] In comparison, a conservative estimate put the number of academies at 6,185 in the United States in 1850, including 97 in Texas, with 12,712 students in Kentucky academies (the most in the southern states).[37]

Thus, non-elite higher schools, including military academies, supplied the most southern professionals in the period. Elite universities produced more planters alongside a solid number of professionals. Nonclassical education, while certainly viewed by antebellum southerners as less prestigious than classical studies, nonetheless provided the necessary vocational training for non-elite men to enter the professions. Surely higher school graduates account for the spike in southern doctors at the same time as the number of physicians decreased among southern university alumni. Engineering and teaching even better demonstrate the prominent role nonclassical and non-elite education played in the development of the professions, as well as their contribution to southern middle-class formation. Members of the emerging middle class, whether north or south of the Mason-Dixon Line, valued and entered education, and its members sought schooling as their ranks grew, promoting those non-elite colleges and higher schools.

Considering their educational backgrounds, the majority of new professionals in the 1840s and 1850s appear to have reflected an emerging southern middle class that was propagating itself. Given the development of the market economy and of the group in the North, it is not entirely surprising to find it a national trend. In 2004, Jonathan Daniel Wells defined the southern middle class as urban men in commercial and professional occupations, who made up 10 percent of the southern white population. Yet rural white-collar men, too, should be included as part of the southern middle class. Part of that group found work in management in the expanding manufacturing enterprises, although apparently largely without first receiving a secondary education. Despite moderate rates of businessmen from alumni of all three types of schooling, successful commercial men also formed a portion of the developing class. Another segment of the middle class entered the professions via higher schooling. Together, this small but growing constituency of lawyers, industrialists, teachers, and other non-manual workers fit into the social structure of white southerners alongside other groups and occupations that have been examined by scholars.[38] Thus the emerging southern middle class constituted men in the professions—many with some form of secondary education—and in industry, commerce, and business.

The significance of this development extends beyond the change in the class and the occupational structures of the Old South, although it did encourage middle-class formation and the shift in the occupational structure away from agriculture. The number of professionals, industrialists, technical positions, and managers increased and these men began to coalesce into a middle class. Professions occupied a lower status than planting, but the number of professionals exiting state universities grew as the antebellum years passed, apparently mirroring decreasing percentages of agriculturalists. Given the difficulty of obtaining land, especially in the established states, this shift in occupations is unsurprising. The growth in the professions and the values that the work encouraged—especially their valuation of the status of professional occupations—continued the transformation of the surrounding society.

Of particular significance in the emergence of large numbers of professionals from non-elite schools and less-than-elite southern families was their movement to professionalize their occupations and, centrally, to increase the status of professions in general. Whereas planters' sons might dabble in the professions—and the data on state universities suggest that was the case—many of them sought to become planters themselves. That drive was consistent with southern ideology: planters dominated the social hierarchy, displaying their success with land, slaves, homes, families, possessions, and behavior (including gentility, mastery, and honor). Young men within southern society often emulated that ideal. For example, Micah Jenkins, youngest son of a South Carolina planter, graduated from the Citadel (his older brothers had attended the more prestigious SCC) and ran a military school for five years before he spoke of purchasing a plantation (although his finances led him to buy a smaller farm instead).[39]

Rather than being dedicated to becoming planters (like Jenkins), southern middle-class youths sought professional success, thus redefining the southern understanding of social mobility. In contrast to planters' sons and likeminded young men, by the end of the 1840s and 1850s, non-elites, especially those young men in the emerging southern middle class, were becoming professionals with no intention of eventually becoming planters. They sought instead to solidify their status as professionals, joining American Medical Association chapters in Memphis after 1849, for example. Young men with these goals appear to have been the majority of those who filled the professional ranks, based on their schools' abundance and graduation rates. Professional careers gained in status in comparison to planting, although they never surpassed it. This large mass of men was redefining social mobility and status in the late antebellum years, though their views did not dominate in the Old South.

Educated southerners who selected professional careers also engaged in another trend that reinforced the emerging middle class and reshaped the environment: urbanization. Across the nation, professional men moved to cities. Southerners remained rural at greater rates than their northern peers—the plantation elite encouraged this trend—and less than 6 percent of 1850s students left the South.[40] Higher school attendees in the North most often came from small towns rather than cities or rural communities, whereas academy attendees may have been more rural. As no study has examined the southern academy student body, precise student origins remain unclear. Once out of school, however, these middle-class professionals often congregated in larger towns; one study found that the populations of southern cities grew 3.5 times faster than the non-urban southern population (and more rapidly than northern cities in the same 1800-1850 period).[41] Young men entering professions often moved to cities; nearly twenty years apart, VMI graduates John Strange of rural Fluvanna County and Charles Steptoe of rural Bedford County accepted positions at the same academy in the growing Virginia town of Norfolk. Burke considers the home and career residences of ministers, lawyers, physicians, agriculturalists, and businessmen and finds no significant difference between college and university alumni, as both groups remained more rural than those men living outside the South. Around one-quarter of college and university students entered professional occupations in "larger cities," but businessmen were most likely to live in urban areas (up to 41 percent); agriculturalists, on the other hand, lived outside of cities more than 90 percent of the time.[42] Thus education in the South could have encouraged men to become more urban than their peers and continue the growth of the southern middle class.

Even the promotion of education changed southern society, so that more schools opened in the South and Southwest than in other regions. Young southern men and women were increasingly educated, and even public schools received increased funding. Schooling across the nation fostered the formation of the middle class in a variety of ways, including the association of its members in one location during their formative years, the values learned at schools and in careers, and occupational similarities.[43]

The growth in these values not only represents some concurrence of middle-class values across the nation but also indicates changes in southern society. Across the board, there were many similarities in the career paths of educated southerners, and given their small percentage in the Old South, the similarity is unsurprising. The differences, however, suggest the transformation in the occupational structure created and reflected social changes in behavior and values (including an honor system different from that among the elite described by Bertram Wyatt Brown, as well as a different vision of manhood). Less elite schools were more likely to graduate teachers and engineers than were more elite universities and less likely to graduate agriculturalists, particularly planters. Educated men increasingly chose business careers in which upward mobility may have been difficult, but as southern society grew and changed, those positions were more needed, better paid, and held in higher esteem.

Investigating the schooling of professionals helps to redress gaps in the history of education in the antebellum South and improves our understanding of its connection to the emerging middle class in that region. Secondary education became more common in the Old South and was part of larger trends influencing the region and nation as a whole. It demonstrates that education played a fundamental role in the development of the southern middle class and in changing perceptions about occupation and professionalization; such changes both resulted from and facilitated larger shifts in the antebellum society and economy. Nonclassical and non-elite education was thus important to the creation of the emerging middle class and to historians' ability to examine antebellum social structure.

NOTES

1. Steven M. Stowe, *Doctoring the South: Southern Physicians and Everyday Medicine in the Mid-Nineteenth Century* (Chapel Hill: University of North Carolina Press, 2004), 8-9; Colin B. Burke, *American Collegiate Populations: A Test of the Traditional View* (New York: New York University Press, 1982), 143, 186. Teaching is often omitted in the consideration of the professions; however, in the Old South, it was a career increasingly professionalized by men in the late antebellum years and could rely on specific knowledge (science, for example) and was increasingly degree-oriented; see Jennifer R. Green, "Networks of Military Educators: Middle-Class Stability and Professionalization in the Late Antebellum South," *Journal of Southern History* 73 (Feb. 2007). Other white-collar occupations will be considered with business.

2. Peter S. Carmichael, *The Last Generation: Young Virginians in Peace, War, and Reunion* (Chapel Hill: University of North Carolina Press, 2005), appendix, tables 4 and 10.

3. John Hardin Best, "Education in the Forming of the American South," *History of Education Quarterly* 36 (Spring 1996), esp. 44, 48; Wayne Urban, "History of Education: A Southern Exposure," *History of Education Quarterly* 21 (Summer 1981): 133-36. In the only recent anthology on academies, only two of fifteen essays examined southern education, and they focused on white women and African Americans. See Nancy Beadie and Kim Tolley, eds., *Chartered Schools: Two Hundred Years of Independent Academies in the United States, 1727-1925* (New York: RoutledgeFalmer, 2002). Nancy Beadie's essay "Internal Improvement," in *Chartered Schools*, 99, points out the lack of scholarship on southern academies. James Allen Cabaniss, *The University of Mississippi: Its First Hundred Years*, 2nd ed. (Hattiesburg: University and College Press of Mississippi, 1971), xi, specifically states his is an *"institutional history,"* which does not consider graduates or students.

4. Burke, *American Collegiate Populations*. All military school data come from the author's archival research; see Jennifer R. Green, *Military Education and the Emerging Middle Class in the Old South* (Cambridge, UK: Cambridge University Press, 2008). A broader study of southern academies is still needed to confirm the similarities between military academies and other higher schools. My research identifies matriculants, but Burke is unclear if he includes only graduates or also matriculants; this essay uses the terms *graduate, alumnus*, and *matriculant* interchangeably.

5. Beadie and Tolley, eds., *Chartered Schools*, 3, 21; the term *higher schooling* indicates the lack of definitional boundaries in nineteenth-century educational terminology. Robert F. Pace, *Halls of Honor: College Men in the Old South* (Baton Rouge: Louisiana State University Press, 2004); Michael Sugrue, "South Carolina College: The Education of an Antebellum Elite" (PhD diss., Columbia University, 1992); Frederick Rudolph, *The American College and University: A History* (New York: Alfred A. Knopf, 1962), and *Curriculum: A History of the American Undergraduate Course of Study Since 1636* (San Francisco: Jossey-Bass, 1977).

6. Neither schools nor Burke recorded slave ownership data. Scholars define planters by their slave and land ownership, usually more than twenty slaves and hundreds of acres.

7. Burke, *American Collegiate Populations*, 188, table 4.3; Thomas G. Dyer, *The University of Georgia: A Bicentennial History, 1785-1985* (Athens: University of Georgia Press, 1985), 47. Burke separates schools in the South Atlantic and Southwest regions, which I have combined, and specifically identifies data for UAL, UGA, UNC, and UVA. In a study of elite planters, approximately 20 percent had dual careers, although these were not always professional; William Kauffman Scarborough, *Masters of the Big House* (Baton Rouge: Louisiana State University Press, 2003), 219.

8. Burke, *American Collegiate Populations*, 193; Jonathan Daniel Wells, *The Origins of the Southern Middle Class, 1800-1861* (Chapel Hill: University of North Carolina Press, 2004), 175; Pace, *Halls of Honor*, 4; David Allmendinger, *Paupers and Scholars: The Transformation of Student Life in Nineteenth-Century New England* (New York: St. Martins, 1975).

9. Margaret Newnan Wagers, *The Education of a Gentleman: Jefferson Davis at Transylvania, 1821-1824* (Lexington, KY: Buckley & Reading, 1943), 11 (quotation), 25. Lawrence A. Cremin, *American Education: The National Experience, 1783-1876* (New York: Harper and Row, 1980), 400-406.

10. Wagers, *Education of a Gentleman*; John D. Wright Jr., *Transylvania: Tutor to the West* (Lexington: University Press of Kentucky, 1975), 122-23.

11. George J. Stevenson, *Increase in Excellence: A History of Emory and Henry College* (New York: Appleton-Century-Crofts, 1963), esp. 73-74.

12. Burke, *American Collegiate Populations*, 188, table 4.3. Burke states secular colleges were more likely than denominational ones to produce agriculturalists.

13. Ibid., esp. 119; Pace, *Halls of Honor*; Beadie and Tolley, eds., *Chartered Schools*.

14. David Rodes to Francis H. Smith, May 25, 1848, Robert E. Rodes Student File, Preston Library, Virginia Military Institute Archives (hereafter VMI Archives).

15. Keith Whitescarver, "Political Economy, Schooling, and Literacy in the South" (Ed D diss., Harvard University, 1995), 73-74.

16. Burke, *American Collegiate Populations*, 125.

17. Drew Gilpin Faust, *James Henry Hammond: A Design for Mastery* (Baton Rouge: Louisiana State University Press, 1982); Stephen W. Berry II, *All That Makes a Man* (New York: Oxford University Press, 2003), chap. 2.

18. Stowe, *Doctoring the South*; Burke, *American Collegiate Populations*, 186; Kilbride, "Southern Medical Students in Philadelphia, 1800-1860: Science and Sociability in the 'Republic of Medicine,'" *Journal of Southern History* 65 (Nov. 1999).

19. Burke, *American Collegiate Populations*, 184, tables 4.1 and 4.3.

20. Robert Preston Brooks, *The University of Georgia under Sixteen Administrations, 1785-1955* (Athens: University of Georgia Press, 1956), 33-35; Dyer, *University of Georgia*, 47.

21. William S. Powell, *The First State University: A Pictorial History of the University of North Carolina* (Chapel Hill: University of North Carolina Press, 1972), 50-77; Dyer, *University of Georgia*, 47; Sugrue, "South Carolina College," esp. 342-74.

22. Burke, *American Collegiate Populations*, tables 4.1 and 4.3. Burke, 183, notes that

some schools underreported dual or secondary careers, which means that denominational colleges may have inflated the number of alumni ministers.

23. An uncorroborated list in the Citadel Archives and Museum records more alumni ministers, but I did not include them in this data because the list did not separate pre- and postwar careers, and many military alumni became clergy after the war. Carmichael's data confirms this trend in Virginia.

24. Burke, *American Collegiate Populations*, 191, table 4.3. Hill, "Remarks of Major D. H. Hill, of the N. C. Military Institute at Charlotte, Before the Committee on Education of the North Carolina Legislature" (n.p., [1860]) (quotations).

25. Robert J. Norrell, *A Promising Field: Engineering at Alabama, 1837-1987* (Tuscaloosa: University of Alabama Press, 1990), 9-20, 28-29; O. Allan Giannin Jr., "The Overlooked Southern Approach to Engineering Education: One and a Half Centuries at the University of Virginia, 1836-1986," in *Proceedings of the 150th Anniversary Symposium on Technology and Society* (Tuscaloosa: University of Alabama Press, 1988), 154-56. Terry S. Reynolds, "The Education of Engineers in America before the Morrill Act of 1862," *History of Education Quarterly* 32 (Winter 1992): 479-80, records comparable figures: Yale graduated 30 engineers before 1866; Harvard, 41; Union College, 46; RPI, 124; and UVA, 80 by 1874 (without an antebellum breakdown). Terry Mark Aldrich, *Rates of Return on Investment in Technical Education in the Ante-Bellum American Economy* (New York: Arno Press, 1975), table 1, counts the number of West Point graduates annually working as civil engineers (1825-1840), and the highest number is 107 in 1837.

26. Norrell, *Promising Field*, 20; Giannini, "Overlooked Southern Approach to Engineering Education," 157 (quotation); James Gregory McGivern, *First Hundred Years of Engineering Education in the United States (1807-1907)* (Spokane, WA: Gonzaga University Press, 1960), 33, 83. Reynolds, "Education of Engineers in America," 459-82, acknowledges military schools' roles in engineering education.

27. See Carmichael, *Last Generation*, e.g., 26; Green, *Military Education and the Emerging Middle Class*, chap. 5. See Robert H. Simpson to Francis H. Smith, December 12, 1853, VMI Archives.

28. Burke, *American Collegiate Populations*, 148, 150. Southwest colleges matched the universities at 11 and 10 percent.

29. Carmichael, *Last Generation*, 47.

30. Beadie, "Internal Improvement," 103.

31. T. F. Johnson to Francis H. Smith, February 11, 1851, William A. Forbes Student File, VMI Archives.

32. Burke, *American Collegiate Populations*, tables 4.1 and 4.3

33. UAL graduates in the 1850s are an exception, with 43 percent in business. That is three times the number of other schools and twice the number of UAL 1840's graduates who went into business. It is not explainable unless the increase in industrial and manufacturing positions attracted men in that decade and region. Dyer, *University of Georgia*, 47.

34. Burke, *American Collegiate Populations*, 135 (quotation), 186, table 4.3.

35. John Winn to Philip Winn, December 25, 1840, John and Philip James Winn Papers, Rare Books, Manuscript, and Special Collections Library, Duke University.

36. Dyer, *University of Georgia*, 46; Stevenson, *Increase in Excellence*.

37. Kim Tolley, "Mapping the Landscape of Higher Schooling, 1727-1850," in *Chartered Schools*, ed. Beadie and Tolley, 31-34; Theodore R. Sizer, *The Age of Academies* (New York: Teachers College, 1964), 1, 12-13, 18. Higher schooling also educated young women at the greatest rates in the Old South.

38. Excellent scholarship has worked to flesh out our understanding of white southern society below the planter class. Over the last thirty years, the historical discussion of the

groups has followed a number of directions, including: 1. Identifying them, such as the work of James Oakes on middle-class planters; Steven Hahn and Stephanie McCurry, among others, on yeomen; Samuel C. Hyde Jr. on plain folk; and Charles Bolton and Jeff Forret on poor whites; 2. Studying occupational groups, such as Susanna Delfino on industrialists; Michele Gillespie and L. Diane Barnes on artisans; Steven Stowe on doctors; Beth Barton Schweiger on ministers; Frank Byrne on merchants; 3. Analyzing class culture(s), such as Ami Pflugrad-Jackisch on secret societies; and 4. Integrating the individual groups/careers or definitional work done by Hyde, Jonathan D. Wells, myself, and others.

39. John and Micah Jenkins Papers, South Caroliniana Library, University of South Carolina.

40. Burke, *American Collegiate Populations*, 193, 199, table 4.5.

41. Beadie, "Internal Improvement," 98; Wells, *Origins of the Southern Middle Class*, 163.

42. Burke, *American Collegiate Population*, 193, tables 4.5 and 4.6.

43. Beadie and Tolley, eds., *Chartered Schools*, 6, 102; Wells, *Origins of the Southern Middle Class*, e.g., 175. This promotion of education even extended, to a minor extent, to African Americans, including an attempt at an interracial school in Kentucky (later Berea College); on African American schooling in Baltimore, see Hilary J. Moss, *Schooling Citizens: The Struggle for African American Education in Antebellum America* (Chicago: University of Chicago Press, 2009).

Part IV

Entrepreneurial and Financial Aspects of the Transformations

Chapter 8

Corporate Entrepreneurship in the Antebellum South

Robert E. Wright

The antebellum South's economic backwardness was as palpable as slavery itself. British traveler Joseph John Gurney's description of the Mason-Dixon Line is one of numerous, similar indictments of Southern economic underdevelopment:

> The distance between the two cities [Annapolis, Maryland, and Philadelphia] is about 100 miles, and one circumstance on the journey is well calculated to interest a stranger. It is the conspicuousness of the line, though without any natural division, which separates the slave-wrought lands of Maryland from the free territory of Pennsylvania. The sudden transit from inferior to superior cultivation, and from impoverished soil to fertility, is extremely striking—especially at the more advanced seasons of the year—and certainly it speaks volumes for the instruction of statesmen, in proof of the utter impolicy of slavery. One can hardly imagine on what grounds this perpetual visible evidence can be long resisted.

The prewar South indeed lagged the North in many developmental indicators, including financial services (commercial banking; savings and mortgage banking; life, marine, and fire insurance; and securities markets), the number, size, and sophistication of high productivity industrial, transportation, and professional services enterprises, and degree of urbanization. Yet, the South was far from impoverished. Excluding slaves, its per-capita income in 1860 slightly exceeded that of the North. Including slaves (as most economists argue they should be), the South that year enjoyed one of the highest incomes in the world, ranking perhaps as high as fourth after Britain, Holland, and the North. The South's industrial sector could not match that of the North, but its industrial base was as large and advanced as that of what we today call the Midwest. In 1860, it ranked—in per-capita terms—eighth in the world in iron production and fifth or sixth in cotton manufacturing. Richmond and Louisville produced more industrial goods by value than Pittsburgh, Indianapolis, or Chicago. The South's 9,500 miles of railroad track constituted only one-third of the national total but exceeded the mileage of European economic powerhouses like Britain, France, and Germany.[1]

Reconciling the South's palpable backwardness with its relatively high income and industrial development nonplussed antebellum observers and later researchers alike. Some scholars insisted that slavery was a losing business proposition perpetuated only by cultural preferences like racism and a precapitalist ethos. Others retorted that in most cases it was quite profitable indeed. Some thought slavery economically inefficient (more output could have been produced from the same inputs), while others believed the gang-labor system employed on large plantations was more efficient than small-scale family farming, especially for crops like sugar, cotton, rice, hemp, and, to a lesser extent, tobacco. Heated scholarly discourse, coupled with additional empirical research, led to the refinement of initial arguments and summoned forth new perspectives. Gavin Wright, for example, argued persuasively that slaveholders should be thought of as "laborlords" capable of concentrating their efforts on commercial crops because they knew that they could command the labor necessary to harvest them, a decided advantage over nonslaveholders. Nevertheless, a clear explanation of how slavery enriched slaveholders while simultaneously stunting economic development long remained elusive.[2]

Today, scholars increasingly realize that, like large factories that gush noxious effluents into the air and water, the institution of slavery spewed "pollution" from every pore. In the parlance of economists, slavery created significant negative externalities, costs borne by all of society instead of only slaveholders. Those costs, which ranged from direct institutions of repression, like slave patrols and suppression of itinerant peddlers, to massive distortions of representative politics to psychological anguish over breaking up slave families and fear of rebellion, were pervasive and enormous. Slaveholders not only stole the labor of their slaves, they robbed the rest of the economy by imposing a large portion of the costs of their peculiar institution onto nonslaveholders, particularly in the South. Massive negative externalities explain unequivocally how slaveholders thrived while the southern economy struggled to keep up with that of the North.[3]

Freed from the slave efficiency/profitability debate and its many trappings, a new generation of scholars has turned afresh to the antebellum southern economy. What they have discovered below the old stereotypes about mint julep–sipping plantation patriarchs, happily uppity slaves, and an undifferentiated mass of poor whites is a dynamic capitalist entity that, were it not for the stifling pollution of slavery, could have matched the economies of the North or any European power. The goal of this chapter is more modest, to quantitatively document that many southern states enjoyed a level of corporate entrepreneurship, as measured by the per capita number and minimum authorized capitalizations (MINAC) of specially incorporated companies,[4] that dwarfed similar endeavors in Europe and that by the Civil War approached the level of activity found in the North.[5]

Most early businesses, North and South, were too small to need substantial long-term external sources of capital. Such enterprises—which included farms and plantations; retail grocers and dry goods stores; construction firms; flour, saw, grist, lumber and other mills; breweries; cooperages; millineries; publishing and mercantile houses; professional services providers like doctors and lawyers; and harness maker, cartwright, goldsmith, and blacksmith shops—almost always remained unincorporated sole proprietorships or partnerships. They were important components of the economy, but more in the aggregate than as individual entities. To help finance their activities, proprietorships and partnerships borrowed short-term from banks and longer-term from a few individuals. They rarely borrowed substantial sums from a large number of individuals for any length of time.[6]

Corporate entrepreneurs, by contrast, formed new, for-profit businesses large enough to require substantial long-term capital from relatively large numbers of investors. Incorporation served mainly to reduce the otherwise considerable costs of coordinating and protecting the property of those investors, including owners (stockholders) and creditors (banks and bondholders). Specifically, corporate charters provided companies with five major tools for attracting both equity (stock) and debt (loan, bond) investors: 1) the right of perpetual succession; 2) the right to sue and be sued in the corporate name; 3) limited liability; 4) negotiable shares; 5) formal governance procedures. Perpetual succession allowed companies to continue their existence regardless of changes in ownership. The right to use the courts as a single entity reduced borrowing, lending, and litigation costs. Limited liability and negotiable shares allowed investors to buy into or sell out of companies without risking their entire fortunes or tying up their resources for extended periods. Formal governance procedures, including limitations on what activities corporations could undertake, stockholder voting and information rights, and rules concerning the payment of dividends, sought to protect stockholders and creditors from opportunistic behavior on the part of managers or holders of large blocks of stock. Although not foolproof, early corporate governance mechanisms were at least as effective at protecting investors as today's laws are, and in some ways were superior.[7]

The term *corporate entrepreneurship* is almost an oxymoron today. Since about World War II, venture capitalists have financed the activities of entrepreneurial start-up companies. Most falter; but those that thrive, like Amazon and eBay, eventually become large corporations by selling shares in themselves to the public via investment bank–intermediated initial public offerings (IPOs). Before the Civil War, by contrast, entrepreneurs north and south of the Mason-Dixon Line sold shares in themselves at start-up via unintermediated direct public offerings (DPOs).[8]

Untested early U.S. corporations were able to sell shares in themselves, even without the aid of investment bankers, for four reasons. First, even the nation's largest cities were geographically and socially compact. Entrepreneurs and potential investors knew each other, often quite well, or at least knew of each other. So when J. R. Poinsett, Stephen Elliott, John Wilson, and John L. Sullivan advertised the establishment of the South Carolina Steam Navigation Company in 1820, most potential investors knew one or more of them personally, or knew somebody who did, facilitating analysis of the company's published business plan. If advertisements failed to stimulate sufficient sales, company stock commissioners and boosters, like James Cocke, could generate interest by actively pushing shares to men of known means, as they did in Richmond and Lynchburg in late 1834 when the James River and Kanawha Company's charter was threatened with repeal due to inactivity.[9]

Second, DPOs were largely unregulated, allowing entrepreneurs to engage in selective disclosure, as in private placements or private equity transactions today. Selective disclosure mitigated one of the major costs of public offerings, namely, full disclosure. Some investors could learn important details of the business plan while others, suspected competitors, were told little, perhaps only the names of the people who had already subscribed. In 1828, Virginian Littleton Tazewell explained to Christopher Tompkins how selective disclosure worked. "If you choose to hold" the stock in the James River Steam Boat Company that Tazewell planned on exchanging with Tompkins for a river schooner, "the agent of the Company will shew you their books, and can give you any information you may desire to have in relation to its value and situation."[10]

Third, minority stockholders had little to fear from outright fraud because their investments were well-protected by a culture of activist corporate governance. When business went awry, stockholders could and usually did step in, investigate, issue reports, and implement reforms. In 1851, for instance, a stockholder committee investigated the affairs of the Staunton and James River Turnpike Company in Virginia, chastised the former managers for the "extremely irregular and un-businesslike manner" in which they managed the company's affairs, and rallied other investors to come up with the funds necessary to complete the road.[11]

"Prudent mean" stockholder voting rules, which lay between the extremes of one vote per share and one vote per shareholder, also protected minority stockholders.[12] The charter of the Galveston and Brazos Navigation Company of Texas, for example, stipulated that in corporate elections shareholders would receive one vote for each share they owned up to twenty, but only one vote for every five shares they owned over that. Other prudent mean rules were more elaborate. Shareholders in the Planters' Bank of the State of Georgia received one vote for each of their first two shares but only one vote for every two shares owned between three and eight. For shares between nine and twenty, they received one vote for every four shares, which was generous compared to the one vote per eight shares they received for shares between twenty-one and sixty and the one vote per twelve shares for shares between sixty and one hundred, the maximum number of shares any one individual or company could lawfully own in the bank. Antebellum charters also protected stockholders by carefully circumscribing permissible corporate activities. When the Hampshire and Morgan Turnpike of Virginia wanted to build a branch road, for example, it had to receive legislative approval for the move as well as for the necessary increase in its capital stock.[13]

Fourth, early U.S. corporations in their DPOs technically sold call options on shares rather than the shares themselves. Subscribers initially put down a dollar or two per share. After the company organized, corporate officers called in the par value of the share in installments. Subscribers could walk away at any time by selling their options to other investors or by forfeiting their shares. The $10, $25, $50, $100, or $1,000 par value per share was usually not fully paid in until some weeks, months, or years after the corporation began business, giving investors some idea of its operations before they were "all in." The Pittsylvania, Franklin, and Botetourt Turnpike Company of Virginia, for example, called in 5 percent of its capital stock each month for twenty months.[14]

Some corporations, north and south, were able to raise enough capital very quickly, in just a few hours, in order to begin operations, Others took days or weeks to fill their subscription books. A few corporations struggled for months to raise sufficient capital and some of those were never able to start operating. That most early corporations raised enough equity to form belies the old canard that early Americans "lacked capital." Northerners, westerners, and southerners had resources at their disposal that they were eager to invest in a variety of potentially profitable ventures, including business corporations.

• • •

A close comparison of corporate entrepreneurship in Virginia and Pennsylvania supports the notion that the antebellum South was home to an impressive number and diversity of corporations. Virginia was "the most significant Southern state for corporate activity before the Civil War,"[15] an honor that Pennsylvania shared with New York and Massachusetts in the North. Although Pennsylvania and Virginia differed in many respects, scholars have found it useful to compare these two states because they were certainly more alike than, say, Vermont and South Carolina, or Illinois and Georgia. Both were original colonies that stretched from the seacoast across the mountains. They also enjoyed a similar climate and mix of crops and significant deposits of coal. Controlling for important variables like climate and crops, if only in a general way, allows the effects of slavery to be isolated to some extent, a fact not lost on scholars.[16]

In *A House Dividing*, for example, John Majewski blames slavery for slowing Virginia's economic development, emphasizing the role it played in stunting urbanization. At just 40,000 people in 1860, Richmond was but a country town compared to Philadelphia with its population that topped 565,000. The lack of a large urban market, Majewski argues, left Virginia "without the concentration of capital and traffic necessary to build an adequate interregional railroad network." That, in turn, dampened manufacturing by keeping transportation costs relatively high and markets relatively small. Instead of working together to develop an entire region, inconsequential Virginia towns, backed by a handful of planter-investors, competed with each other for government subsidies and preferment. As a result, Virginia belatedly built numerous small transportation improvements and factories instead of the major trunk lines, bridges, turnpikes, canals, and industries found in Pennsylvania, where numerous small investors capitalized large corporations relatively easily. As a result, government investment was less necessary in Pennsylvania, a good outcome given the economic distortions that government meddling usually caused.[17]

Sean Adams takes a different tack in *Old Dominion, Industrial Commonwealth*, arguing that differences in political economy allowed Pennsylvania's production of coal to outstrip that of antebellum Virginia, which had voluminous bituminous deposits in the east as well as extensive bituminous and anthracite fields in its west (now West Virginia). Pennsylvania's more democratically elected and representative state government fostered entrepreneurship and efficiency-inducing economic competition, while the legislature of the Old Dominion jealously guarded the interests of an entrenched planter elite. Well-fed with coal and foreign investment, Pennsylvania's industrial and transportation sectors grew, expanded, and developed while those of Virginia remained sclerotic, short of nonlocal investors and shackled to the limitations inherent in slave-labor agriculture.[18]

Although there is a good deal of truth in Adams's and Majewski's analyses, quantitative measures of corporate entrepreneurship, summarized in tables 1 and 2, cast Virginia's entrepreneurs and investors in a much more favorable light. After a slow start, Virginia's special chartering activity, as measured by the number of charters granted and the total minimum capitalization authorized, caught up to, and sometimes exceeded, that of Pennsylvania on a per-capita basis.[19] (General incorporation was not a major factor in either state before the Civil War, so table 1 does not include charters granted under general acts of incorporation or, in Virginia's case, those chartered by circuit courts, of which there were sixty-nine.[20])

Both before and after 1830, Pennsylvania generally dominated in the number and minimum authorized capitalization of banks and insurance companies, gas and water utilities, and bridges, railroads, and turnpikes. In the three decades before the Civil War, however, Virginia entrepreneurs incorporated more, and were authorized to invest more capital in, chartered hotels, resorts, and spas, manufacturing companies, and savings banks than Pennsylvania entrepreneurs were. In canal, mining, and transportation companies (steamship lines, tugboat companies, and the like), the two states were fairly evenly matched, with Virginia chartering more but smaller companies. Smaller average firm size was probably unimportant once a low minimum threshold had been passed, particularly in manufacturing, because increasing returns to scale were small to nonexistent in most early nineteenth-century industries. After a point, in other words, bigger was not necessarily better.[21]

As table 3 shows, Virginia may have been a leader, but it was no aberration. Other southern states, from Georgia to Texas and Alabama to Kentucky, also specially chartered significant numbers of businesses before 1861. After clearly lagging up to 1830, states like Georgia caught up to their northern counterparts by 1850 or so, though partly because some northern states like Ohio had by that time eschewed special incorporation in favor of broad general incorporation statutes. Southern MINAC per capita also reached high levels in the generally booming 1830s and 1850s but shrank dramatically in the 1840s, a decade of recession, suggesting perhaps that the southern corporate sector was more volatile than that of the North.[22]

Was the southern corporate sector qualitatively inferior to that of the North? Did southern corporations fail to begin operations at a more robust rate, perhaps because of a higher cost of capital? Did they go bankrupt more quickly than their northern counterparts? Were their profits lower, all else equal? Answers to those questions must await further research, but initial investigations indicate that corporate activity differed little in the states, free or slave, comprising the Ohio River Valley.[23]

Many contemporaries realized that corporate entrepreneurship was strong in the antebellum South. "*Every state in the union,*" remarked corporate scholars Joseph Angell and Samuel Ames in the early 1830s, "was an extensive manufacturer of home made corporations." "The increase of corporations, in aid of private industry and enterprise," famed New York jurist James Kent later observed, "has kept pace *in every part of our country* with the increase of wealth and improvement." Although the South lagged the North by some metrics, both sections far outstripped the limited corporate entrepreneurship found even in the most advanced European economies of the day. As Angell and Ames put it:

> In no country have corporations been multiplied to so great an extent, as in our own. If a native of Europe, who has never traversed the wide barrier which separates him from us should be informed, even with tolerable accuracy, of the number of Banking Companies, Insurance Companies, Canal Companies, Turnpike Companies, Manufacturing Companies &c. . . . that are diffused throughout these United States, and fully invested with corporate privileges, he could not be made to believe that he was told the truth.[24]

Hoary claims that southerners were by nature reluctant entrepreneurs and incompetent managers no longer make sense, except perhaps in comparison to their somewhat more advanced northern neighbors. The peripatetic nature of early Americans, most famously east to west but also north to south and south to north, also render claims of regional cultural differences difficult to believe. The question remains, though: Why did the South lag the North at all? It appears that the pollution that spewed forth from the slave system, much like its effect on the overall economy, stunted the growth of corporate entrepreneurship but did not completely stifle it.[25]

Barely visible in the 1790s, corporations were a ubiquitous force throughout the economy by the Civil War. As shown in table 3, new charter activity increased dramatically in the 1790s and then again in the 1830s. The rapid expansion of corporate activity generated angst that manifested itself in considerable anti-corporate rhetoric. In the 1790s, criticism of corporations tended to be generalized, rooted in vague concerns about potential political corruption and Adam Smith's biting critique of the corporate form, which was based on Britain's rather limited experience with that model. Smith considered most corporations evil monopolies plagued by the principal-agent problem, the radical divergence of the interests of owners (stockholders, maximization of profits) from control (management, maximization of managerial salaries and perks).[26]

By the 1830s, anti-corporate angst came in sectional varieties. In the North, concerns about corporate market power ("monopoly" in the parlance of the day) and corruption remained paramount but were ultimately, if somewhat ironically, allayed by more liberal rules for granting charters, including general incorporation statutes. In the South, a host of other issues also spawned anti-corporate sentiments from politically powerful planters. When it came to corporations, planters were of two minds. On the one hand, corporations were often lucrative investments, good customers for plantation produce, and the best available suppliers of important goods and services. On the other hand, corporations posed an increasingly potent threat to planter political hegemony, a key component of slaveholders' ability to displace the costs of slavery onto the rest of society. At the state level, only corporations had the political and economic clout to quash the subsidies upon which planters depended. As an editorialist noted in the *Richmond Enquirer* in 1837, if corporations took control of the legislature they would create "a splendid country checkered with rail-roads and canals, here and there ornamented with a palace, but with a poor, oppressed community of people, governed by combinations of privileged corporations, and pampered stock-holders and stock-jobbers."[27] Planters injured by the invasive tactics of railroads like the South Carolina Canal and Railroad Company learned firsthand that combating big business was a costly proposition. Moreover, planters feared that financiers, large-scale manufacturers, railroad magnates, and other corporate potentates could topple them from the top of the social heap and win the allegiance of the region's many poor whites.[28]

Some planters also feared that corporate entrepreneurship weakened slavery by crowding out investment in slaves. Funds diverted to corporations were no longer available, in journalist J. D. B. DeBow's famous words, to invest in "more cotton to buy more negroes, to raise more cotton to buy more negroes."[29] Although investment in corporations, especially manufacturing companies, may have yielded higher average returns than investment in slave agriculture did, most planters continued to favor land and slaves over stocks and bonds. Perceptions of higher risk (more variable returns) and harder work for industrial pursuits help to explain planters' preferences, but social pressure may also have played a role at a time when corporate stockholdings were community knowledge. Demand for land and slaves kept their prices up and the peculiar institution intact. Finally, planters also saw corporations as a threat when they actively competed with them for labor, especially when slave prices were high and supplies tight.[30]

Planters also had numerous reasons to support corporations. They benefited from becoming customers of banks, insurance companies, railroads, turnpikes, hotels, and the other forms of corporate entrepreneurship. For those with slaves to sell or lease, corporate demand for slave labor kept volumes and prices up. Many planters, especially retired ones, diversified their agricultural and small-scale mining and manufacturing interests by buying corporate equities and bonds. John Tayloe III of Virginia, for example, owned shares in the Washington Bridge Company, the Potomac Steam Boat Company, the Chesapeake and Ohio Canal Company, and at least four banks, two of which, the Bank of the Metropolis and the Bank of the United States, he served as director. Membership on corporate boards by large slaveholders was far from unusual; over one-third of the directors of South Carolina railroads during the 1850s, for example, were planters.[31]

Some planters also saw southern corporations as a way of decreasing their dependence on the North. "We have been tributary to the North long enough," one pro-railroad Virginian legislator declared in the House of Delegates in 1834, "and in order to divert the trade from that quarter we must construct roads to every portion of the interior." In 1852, the *Georgia Telegraph* called for "a connection of the rail-roads of Georgia with the Gulf" and the creation of Gulf steamship lines so that "the monopoly, by the North, of the commerce and travel to the Pacific will be broken up, and a large portion of it secured to our own cities on the Gulf and South Atlantic coast." About the same time, a convention urged the creation of a Southern transcontinental railroad for much the same reason.[32]

Southern nationalism also summoned forth a desire to diversify the region's economy into manufacturing in order to lessen its reliance on northern manufactured goods. "Why not spin as well as plant cotton?" one proponent of southern corporate entrepreneurship asked.[33] This was no pipe dream, as the appearance of corporations, particularly railroads but other types of businesses as well, often transformed entire districts, increasing property values, population densities, and the total volume of business transacted. Railroads economically enlivened vast swaths of Alabama and upland South Carolina in the 1840s and 1850s, for example. Railroads became so earnestly desired that when they could not attract sufficient equity investment, corporate entrepreneurs often managed to get banking privileges built into their charters to help spur investor demand.[34]

Finally, some planters saw in corporate entrepreneurship a way to keep poor whites in their place and complaisant. Railroads, factories, turnpikes, and other corporations meant employment for large numbers of unskilled workers. Their hands occupied during the day and their bellies full at night, poor whites were much less likely to consort with slaves, undertake criminal activities, or plot rebellion. The large mills of Lowell, Massachusetts, were extolled and to some degree emulated in part because they were believed to help the working classes morally and materially.[35]

Nonplanters, including merchants, professionals, small farmers, and others who owned fewer than twenty slaves, were also of two minds when it came to corporations. A typical attitude was that one's own corporation was necessary to keep the economy from collapsing but someone else's corporation threatened the very existence of the Republic. That is only a slight exaggeration. In 1835, salt producers in Virginia's Kanawha County claimed that any corporation allowed to enter its market would rule the entire valley. A dozen years later, the region's salt producers formed a cartel to try to stymie competition from New York and Ohio. By 1851, all but one of the Kanawha firms had merged into a single joint-stock company. In Charleston, mechanics complained about a bank but only after being shut out of its DPO. In upstate South Carolina, early railroad boosters like John Springs turned into wild-eyed critics of new roads, especially those like the Blue Ridge Railroad that sought extensive government investment. Such roads were potential competitors and major threats to the state government's fiscal probity.[36]

Nonplanters faced fewer social pressures regarding their investment decisions and apparently were more likely to invest in corporations than slaveholders were: Charleston merchants, for example, were avid investors in banks and other corporations. But nonplanters had less wealth to invest, because the wealthiest 1 percent of southerners, almost all large slaveholders, owned 25 percent of the region's wealth. In Georgia in the late 1850s, agricultural land and slaves accounted for just under 70 percent of taxable assets, with city and town real estate, money, banking capital, merchandise, shipping, manufacturing capital, household furniture, and miscellaneous personal property making up the balance.[37]

In some states, such as Alabama, South Carolina, and Virginia, nonplanters resisted corporation formation and other forms of economic development because they feared that the planter-elites in control of the government would use such projects to extract economic rents from them. State and local government investments in corporations, which were common in Virginia, Georgia, and elsewhere, were just one means by which elites could redistribute wealth from all taxpayers to themselves.[38] (Early corporations paid taxes, too, but generally at the same rate as individuals and on the same assets, like land, horses, slaves, and money at interest.[39])

For many southerners, planters and nonplanters alike, "Old Fogyism," or a general fear of change and the unknown, constituted another source of powerful, if unfocused and largely inarticulate, anti-corporate sentiment. Like Luddites and machinery, Old Fogies saw in corporations little to like and much to fear. Where they did not actively oppose corporations, they met them with a damning indifference that could stop the progress of an incorporation bill in committee or render a new corporation's DPO a slow, labored affair. Old Fogyism suffused the Lower South but was particularly strong in South Carolina, which after the Revolution gave up the cosmopolitan outlook of colonial Charleston for the isolationism inherent in the new, more open and liberal postwar mercantile environment.[40]

More vociferous and sometimes more effective opposition to the proliferation of corporations came from critics of specific business practices. Anti-bank sentiments, for example, often waxed strong after financial panics like those in 1819, 1837, 1839, and 1857. Some complaints were simply sour grapes, while others stemmed from deep misunderstandings of commercial practices. Other opponents, however, were right on the mark, including those who argued that banks often held too few specie reserves and that miscreants sometimes managed to get elected as bank directors.[41]

Despite resistance from both planters and nonplanters, would-be corporate entrepreneurs were far from powerless. Like their northern counterparts, southerners wanted public goods such as bridges, roads, canals, and, later, railroads, but they did not want to pay high taxes. Hamstrung politicians therefore had little alternative to chartering large numbers of private businesses to provide those and like goods. Thwarted incorporators of location-specific companies, like infrastructure and mining companies, could always bide time and try to obtain a charter from a subsequent legislature. More mobile concerns, including manufacturers and financial services firms, could move, or threaten to move, to another state. William Gregg, for example, claimed he would move his textile operations to Georgia if South Carolina denied his firm a charter. That was not an idle threat, because a liberal, pro-business, pro-corporation ethos usually waxed strong in Georgia, rendering it a useful haven for would-be corporate entrepreneurs disappointed by their home states.[42]

The antebellum South was not quite as rich or developed as the North. It was, however, easily one of the richest and most developed regions of the world, held back only by the negative externalities or polluting effects of its peculiar institution. In corporate entrepreneurship, as measured by the per capita number and MINAC of specially chartered financial services, hospitality, manufacturing, mining, transportation, and other companies, it was by the late antebellum period a close second behind the North. Here, too, slavery played a retarding role by multiplying and magnifying traditional criticisms of the corporate form inherited from Adam Smith's fears of corporate inefficiency, monopoly, and political power. As a result, the North's solution to the corporation conundrum, the incorporation of most (and eventually all) entrepreneurs who sought a charter, was adopted more slowly and less completely in the South. It was nonetheless eventually embraced there.

Table 1 Special Charters in Pennsylvania and Virginia before 1861

Pennsylvania	**Through 1830**	**1831-1860**
Number	449	1,890
MINAC $mill.	66.334	304.629
MINAC/pop. $	14.37	47.18
Virginia	**Through 1830**	**1831-1860**
Number	238	1,625
MINAC $mill.	30.998	239.727
MINAC/pop. $	5.94	56.45

SOURCES: State Session Laws; U.S. Census

Table 2. Pennsylvania and Virginia Special Charters by Business Type

Corporation Type	PA Through 1830	VA Through 1830	PA 1831-1860	VA 1831-1860
Banks (no.)	55	6	58	64
MINAC (mill. $)	25.330	4.850	15.350	8.675
Avg. MINAC ($)	460,545	808,333	269,298	139,919
Bridges (no.)	60	20	160	44
MINAC (mill. $)	2.863	.625	3.221	.842
Avg. MINAC ($)	55,063	36,375	22,526	18,716
Building and Loans (no.)	0	0	5	2
MINAC (mill. $)	0	0	.573	.015
Avg. MINAC ($)	0.00	0.00	114,600	7,500
Canals (no.)	38	67	32	49
MINAC (mill. $)	13.517	11.329	12.855	9.148
Avg. MINAC ($)	386,209	192,017	428,483	190,583
Cemeteries (no.)	0	0	7	0
MINAC (mill. $)	0	0	0	0
Avg. MINAC ($)	0.00	0.00	0.00	0.00
Gas Works (no.)	1	0	70	12
MINAC (mill. $)	.020	0	2.927	.485
Avg. MINAC ($)	20,000	0.00	41,807	40,417
Hotels (no.)	0	0	17	65
MINAC (mill. $)	0	0	3.070	9.069
Avg. MINAC ($)	0.00	0.00	191,875	139,517
Insurance Companies (no.)	16	9	234	57
MINAC (mill. $)	4.500	2.500	17.785	4.115
Avg. MINAC ($)	375,000	357,143	169,381	87,553
Manufacturing Companies (no.)	12	18	49	244
MINAC (mill. $)	1.209	.393	10.670	29.064
Avg. MINAC ($)	100,708	23,118	217,755	119,116
Market Companies (no.)	0	0	24	0
MINAC (mill. $)	0	0	4.493	0

Avg. MINAC ($)	0.00	0.00	187,208	0.00
Mining Companies (no.)	1	0	107	345
MINAC (mill. $)	.300	0	33.158	36.312
Avg. MINAC ($)	300,000.00	0.00	364,368	105,866
Miscellaneous (No.)	5	0	28	10
MINAC (mill. $)	.130	0	8.411	.167
Avg. MINAC ($)	43,333	0.00	400,505	18,556
Park Associations (No.)	0	0	6	0
MINAC (mill. $)	0	0	.445	0
Avg. MINAC ($)	0.00	0.00	74,125	0.00
Railroads (No.)	22	2	279	97
MINAC (mill. $)	6.850	.500	162.266	109.252
Avg. MINAC ($)	311,364	250,000	607,738	1,126,309
Savings Banks (No.)	1	0	48	170
MINAC (mill. $)	0	0	3.373	5.717
Avg. MINAC ($)	0.00	0.00	105,406	64,966
Telegraph Companies (No.)	0	0	11	7
MINAC (mill. $)	0	0	.581	.423
Avg. MINAC ($)	0.00	0.00	83,000	105,625
Transportation Companies (No.)	5	3	49	44
MINAC (mill. $)	.375	.070	9.268	9.117
Avg. MINAC ($)	75,000	70,000	205,956	227,925
Turnpikes (No.)	200	106	650	393
MINAC (mill. $)	8.334	7.437	14.967	8.494
Avg. MINAC ($)	47,624	70,825	23,422	21,948
Water Utilities (No.)	14	4	55	8
MINAC (mill. $)	.165	.052	1.329	.722
Avg. MINAC ($)	18,278	12,875	27,695	90,250

NOTE: Average minimum authorized capital (MINAC) figures are for those companies whose charters specified a minimum authorized capitalization.
SOURCE: State Session Laws

Table 3. Special Chartering Activity and MINAC by Section and Decade

Section/Decade	Number	Per 100K	MINAC mill.$	Per capita $
North through 1790	17	0.84	0.400	0.24
South through 1790	15	0.79	0.687	0.36
West through 1790	0	0.00	0.000	0.00
North, 1791-1800	239	10.00	7.855	4.08
South, 1791-1800	44	1.97	4.493	2.01
West, 1791-1800	0	0.00	0.000	0.00
North, 1801-1810	754	22.91	27.41	10.89
South, 1801-1810	113	3.79	21.812	7.31
West, 1801-1810	0	0.00	0.000	0.00
North, 1811-1820	1,096	24.20	86.339	25.67
South, 1811-1820	374	9.56	59.87	15.31
West, 1811-1820	0	0.00	0.000	0.00
North, 1821-1830	1,363	22.13	128.742	28.53
South, 1821-1830	296	5.81	66.751	13.11
West, 1821-1830	0	0.00	0.000	0.00
North, 1831-1840	3,493	41.45	433.428	69.32
South, 1831-1840	1,604	24.62	393.257	60.37
West, 1831-1840	9	41.75	1.383	64.16
North, 1841-1850	3,052	26.53	433.45	49.60
South, 1841-1850	1,400	16.64	212.531	25.26
West, 1841-1850	19	9.28	0.894	4.37
North, 1851-1860	4,197	27.19	777.575	65.08
South, 1851-1860	3,563	32.73	1,077.054	98.92
West, 1851-1860	450	47.70	521.041	552.25

NOTES:
North: CT, DE, IL, IN, ME, MA, MI, NH, NJ, OH, PA, RI, VT, WI (NY numbers only thru 1840).
South: AL, AR, DC, FL, GA, KY, LA, MD, MS, MO, NC, SC, TE, TX, VA
West: CA, CO, IA, KS, MN, NE, NM, OR, UT, WA
The average of the official U.S. Census population figures at each decade's endpoint (e.g., 1850 and 1860) were used to compute the per-capita figures, except for the pre-1790s period, which used only the 1790 Census numbers.

NOTES

This essay was written with the aid of research grants from the Berkley Center for Entrepreneurial Studies and the National Science Foundation (SES-0751577). All errors of omission and commission, however, remain the sole responsibility of the author.

1. John Majewski, *A House Dividing: Economic Development in Pennsylvania and Virginia before the Civil War* (Cambridge, UK: Cambridge University Press, 2000), 1-3; Joseph John Gurney, *A Journey in North America* (Norwich, 1841), 188-89; Robert Fogel, *Without Consent or Contract: The Rise and Fall of American Slavery* (New York: W.W. Norton, 1989), 67, 85-87, 103; Fred Bateman and Thomas Weiss, *A Deplorable Scarcity: The Failure of Industrialization in the Slave Economy* (Chapel Hill: University of North Carolina Press, 1981), 3-4, 19-21, 25, 42-43.

2. Fogel, *Without Consent or Contract*, 72-113; Gavin Wright, *Slavery and American Economic Development* (Baton Rouge: Louisiana State University Press, 2006); Douglas Egerton, "Markets without a Market Revolution: Southern Planters and Capitalism," *Journal of the Early Republic* 16 (Summer 1996): 207-21.

3. There were a few slaves in the North, but not enough to distort its economy. Even in Delaware, which is here treated as a Northern state because in 1860 had about 2,000 slaves out of a total population of about 110,000, slavery was but a minor drag, especially outside of Sussex County. According to the 1860 Census, no Delaware slaveholder owned more than 19 slaves, so technically speaking it was home to not even a single planter. Francis Corbin to Robert Beverely, November 26, 1806, August 5, 1810, Beverely Family Papers, Virginia Historical Society; Stanley Elkins, *Slavery: A Problem in American Institutional and Intellectual Life*, 3rd ed. (Chicago: University of Chicago Press, 1976); Tom Downey, *Planting a Capitalist South: Masters, Merchants, and Manufacturers in the Southern Interior, 1790-1860* (Baton Rouge: Louisiana State University Press, 2006), 162-63; Robert E. Wright, *Fubarnomics: A Lighthearted, Serious Look at America's Economic Ills* (Buffalo, NY: Prometheus, 2010).

4. There were two other types of joint-stock companies in existence, unchartered companies and chartered ones that incorporated under so-called general incorporation laws. Unchartered joint-stock companies typically incorporated eventually, were relatively few in number, and were not unusually prevalent in any one state, region, or section so they do not influence the conclusions reached here. General incorporation laws were more prevalent in the North than the South by the 1850s and may help to explain some of the convergence between the regions in that decade. Ohio's special chartering activity, for example, dropped almost to nil after passage of a general incorporation act in the early 1850s. For a variety of reasons, corporations chartered under general laws are much more difficult to study than specially incorporated ones, so scholars may never be able to assess their full impact on the North's chartering activity in the 1850s.

5. The apex of the traditional view of the Southern economy as pre-capitalist was Egerton, "Markets without a Market Revolution."" Nobody has yet compiled a complete list of joint-stock companies formed in Britain, Europe's leading economy and incorporator. Nevertheless, the overall level of incorporation and joint-stock company formation in Britain can be pieced together from studies covering major industries like banking, insurance, railways, canals, and water and gas utilities. See James Taylor, *Creating Capitalism: Joint-Stock Enterprise in British Politics and Culture, 1800-1870* (Woodbridge, UK: Boydell, 2006), tables 1-9; Ron Harris, *Industrializing English Law: Entrepreneurship and Business Organization, 1720-1844* (Cambridge, UK: Cambridge University Press, 2000), table 8.3; Robin Pearson, *Insuring the Industrial Revolution: Fire Insurance in Great Britain, 1700-1850* (London: Ashgate, 2004), table 1.1; "Returns

from Gas Companies Established by Act of Parliament in the UK," *British Parliamentary Papers* 44 (1847): 360-407; M. E. Falkus, "The British Gas Industry before 1850," *Economic History Review* 20 (1967): 494-508; J. A. Hassan, "The Growth and Impact of the British Water Industry in the Nineteenth Century," *Economic History Review* 38 (1985): 531-47; Chris Cook and John Stevenson, *British Historical Facts, 1760-1830* (London: Macmillan 1980). According to British economic historian Robin Pearson, Britain and Ireland established just over 1,400 joint stock companies of all kinds to 1844. Robin Pearson, e-mail message to author, June 12, 2008. See also "Manufacturing Corporations," *American Jurist* (July 1829): 94.

6. Robert Cull, Lance E. Davis, Naomi R. Lamoreaux, and Jean-Laurent Rosenthal, "Historical Financing of Small- and Medium-Size Enterprises," *Journal of Banking and Finance* 30 (Nov. 2006): 3017-46. Robert E. Wright, *Origins of Commercial Banking in America, 1750-1800* (New York: Rowman & Littlefield, 2001); Howard Bodenhorn, *A History of Banking in Antebellum America: Financial Markets and Economic Development in an Age of Nation Building* (Cambridge, UK: Cambridge University Press, 2000); Howard Bodenhorn, *State Banking in Early America: A New Economic History* (New York: Oxford University Press, 2003); J. Mills Thornton III, *Politics and Power in a Slave Society: Alabama, 1800-1860* (Baton Rouge: Louisiana State University Press, 1978), 280; Bateman and Weiss, *A Deplorable Scarcity*, 10; Milton Heath, *Constructive Liberalism: The Role of the State in Economic Development in Georgia to 1860* (Cambridge, MA: Harvard University Press, 1954), 295; Downey, *Planting a Capitalist South*, 56-63, 139, 157.

7. Robert E. Wright, Wray Barber, Matthew Crafton, and Anand Jain, eds., *History of Corporate Governance: The Importance of Stakeholder Activism*, 6 vols. (London: Pickering & Chatto, 2004); Heath, *Constructive Liberalism*, 314.

8. Robert E. Wright, *The Wealth of Nations Rediscovered: Integration and Expansion in American Financial Markets, 1780-1850* (Cambridge, UK: Cambridge University Press, 2002).

9. "On the Proposed Steam Navigation Company," *Charleston Courier*, January 5, 1820, 2; "Terms of Subscription and Plan of the S. Carolina Steam Navigation Company," *Camden (SC) Gazette*, February 3, 1820, 3; Majewski, *House Dividing*, 32-36; "Virginia Legislature. House of Delegates, Tuesday, December 30," *Richmond (VA) Enquirer*, January 1, 1835, 3; "James River and Kanawha Improvement, Friday, January 9," *Richmond (VA) Enquirer*, January 15, 1835, 4.

10. Littleton Waller Tazewell to Christopher Tompkins, September 25, 1828, Virginia Historical Society.

11. *Report of a Committee Appointed to Investigate the Affairs of the Staunton and James River Turnpike Company* (Scottsville, VA: December 6, 1851).

12. Robert E. Wright and Richard E. Sylla, "Corporate Governance and Stockholder Activism in the United States, 1790-1860," in *Origins of Shareholder Advocacy*, ed. Jonathan Koppell (New York: Palgrave McMillan, forthcoming).

13. William H. Pease and Jane H. Pease, *The Web of Progress: Private Values and Public Styles in Boston and Charleston, 1828-1843* (New York: Oxford University Press, 1985), 18; Heath, *Constructive Liberalism*, 333; Thornton, *Politics and Power*, 105-6; Robert L. Baker to Richard E. Byrd, May 12, 1851, Byrd Family Papers, Virginia Historical Society; *Virginia Session Laws* (1848): 125, (1849): 87, (1850): 102.

14. Receipts of J. Early, Early Family Papers, Virginia Historical Society.

15. Edwin Merrick Dodd, *American Business Corporations until 1860, with Special Reference to Massachusetts* (Cambridge, MA: Harvard University Press, 1954), 441.

16. Majewski, *House Dividing*, 3-7.

17. Ibid., 11, 12-140.

18. Sean Patrick Adams, *Old Dominion, Industrial Commonwealth: Coal, Politics, and Economy in Antebellum America* (Baltimore, MD: Johns Hopkins University Press, 2004).

19. The tables in this essay come from a database created by research assistants (RAs) under the direction of Richard Sylla and myself. The RAs have scoured the legislative records (primarily state session laws) of every state to enter the Union before the Civil War looking for and coding all specially incorporated for-profit businesses. Where possible, their work has been checked against extant primary and secondary sources and always found to closely correspond to them. Only New York remained incomplete at the time of writing.

20. Adams, *Old Dominion*, 184.

21. Bateman and Weiss, *A Deplorable Scarcity*, 55-64.

22. Heath, *Constructive Liberalism*, 310.

23. Robert E. Wright, "Corporations and the Economic Growth and Development of the Antebellum Ohio River Valley," *Ohio Valley History* (Winter 2009): 47-70.

24. Emphasis added. James Kent, *Commentaries on American Law*, 4 vols. (New York: Banks and Brothers, 1894), 2:272n. Joseph Angell and Samuel Ames, *A Treatise on the Law of Private Corporations Aggregate* (Boston: Hilliard, Gray, Little & Wilkins, 1832), v–vi, 35, 36.

25. Bateman and Weiss, *A Deplorable Scarcity*, 35-37; Heath, *Constructive Liberalism*, 294-95; Jennifer Goloboy, "'Success to Trade': Charleston's Merchants in the Revolutionary Era" (PhD diss., Harvard University, 2003), 66-67; Downey, *Planting a Capitalist South*, 85.

26. Adam Smith, *An Inquiry into the Nature and Causes of the Wealth of Nations* (New York: Modern Library, 1937), 699-716; Pauline Maier, "The Revolutionary Origins of the American Corporation," *William and Mary Quarterly* 50 (1993): 51-84; Heath, *Constructive Liberalism*, 294; Taylor, *Creating Capitalism*, 6, 22, 32, 51, 99.

27. As quoted in Adams, *Old Dominion*, 153.

28. Thornton, *Politics and Power*, 108-9, 310; Adams, *Old Dominion*, 152-188; Robert Wiebe, *The Search for Order, 1877-1920* (New York: Hill and Wang, 1967), 53; Downey, *Planting a Capitalist South*, 83-84, 133, 141, 177-81.

29. As quoted in Bateman and Weiss, *A Deplorable Scarcity*, 74.

30. Downey, *Planting a Capitalist South*, 127-28; Bateman and Weiss, *A Deplorable Scarcity*, 29, 117-27, 133-42; Pease and Pease, *Web of Progress*, 19-20; Fogel, *Without Consent or Contract*, 108-9.

31. Downey, *Planting a Capitalist South*, 97, 136; Laurie Kamoie, *Irons in the Fire: The Business History of the Tayloe Family and Virginia's Gentry, 1700-1860* (Charlottesville: University of Virginia Press, 2007), 135-39; Lacy K. Ford, Jr., *Origins of Southern Radicalism: The South Carolina Upcountry, 1800-1860* (New York: Oxford University Press, 1988), 233; Robert E. Wright, *One Nation under Debt: Hamilton, Jefferson, and the History of What We Owe* (New York: McGraw-Hill, 2008), 246-51, 315-22. For examples of corporate ownership of slaves, see Upper Appomattox Company (twenty-nine slaves on January 1, 1809) in their corporate Records, 1796-1935, and Richmond, Fredericksburg, and Potomac Railroad (fifteen slaves in 1843) in the Elias Hore Account Book, Stafford County tax collector, 1843, Virginia Historical Society.

32. *The Home Manufacturing Company of Winchester* (Winchester, VA, Sept. 17, 1860); Daniel H. London, "Commercial, Agricultural, and Intellectual Independence of the South," *DeBow's Review* (October 1860): 466-88; Pease and Pease, *Web of Progress*, 55; Downey, *Planting a Capitalist South*, 142; "House of Delegates, Wednesday, January 8," *Richmond (VA) Enquirer*, January 21, 1834, 1; "Internal Improvements," *DeBow's Review* (July 1852): 80; "The Great Southern Convention in Charleston," *DeBow's Review* (June 1854): 632-41.

33. As quoted in Downey, *Planting a Capitalist South*, 118.

34. Thornton, *Politics and Power*, 280-81; Ford, *Origins of Southern Radicalism*, 235-40; Downey, *Planting a Capitalist South*, 92-117, 122-23; Pease and Pease, *Web of Progress*, 175; Heath, *Constructive Liberalism*, 262-66.

35. "Cotton Manufactures, Part III," *DeBow's Review* (April 1855): 532-33; Downey, *Planting a Capitalist South*, 142-43.

36. Heath, *Constructive Liberalism*, 323; Adams, *Old Dominion*, 179; John Stealey, ed., *Kanawhan Prelude to Nineteenth-Century Monopoly in the United States* (Richmond: Virginia Historical Society, 2000); Pease and Pease, *Web of Progress*, 177-78; Ford, *Origins of Southern Radicalism*, 315-16.

37. Pease and Pease, *Web of Progress*, 17-20; Goloboy, "'Success to Trade,'" 24-25, 45-48; Downey, *Planting a Capitalist South*, 137; Fogel, *Without Consent or Contract*, 83; Thornton, *Politics and Power*, 105; Heath, *Constructive Liberalism*, 388.

38. Goloboy, "'Success to Trade,'" 148-55; Heath, *Constructive Liberalism*, 328-33; Thornton, *Politics and Power*, xix–xx, 105-9.

39. See, for example, the taxes laid on the Potomac Silk and Agricultural Company (391 acres of land) and the Richmond, Fredericksburg, and Potomac Railroad (fifteen slaves) in the Elias Hore Account Book, Stafford County tax collector, 1843, Virginia Historical Society.

40. Ford, *Origins of Southern Radicalism*, 318-19; Thornton, *Politics and Power*, 108-9, 431-32; Goloboy, "'Success to Trade,'" 1-9, 13.

41. George Clarke to Robert Beverely, October 3, 1815, Peter Randolph Beverely to Robert Beverely, May 8, 1826, Peter Randolph Beverely to Robert Beverely, March 16, December 14, 28, 1819, December 22, 1820, Beverley Family Papers, Virginia Historical Society; "Department of Internal Improvements," *DeBow's Review* (July 1851): 78; Ford, *Origins of Southern Radicalism*, 324-36.

42. Downey, *Planting a Capitalist South*, 36-38, 67-68; Bateman and Weiss, *A Deplorable Scarcity*, 11, 30; Heath, *Constructive Liberalism*, 295-335.

Chapter 9

"In Pursuit of Their Livelihood"

Credit and Debt Relations among Natchez Planters in the 1820s

Elbra David

In 1820, Natchez, planter and attorney Jonathan Thompson entered into a partnership with his longtime friend and associate James L. Trask to plant cotton across the Mississippi River in Louisiana's Concordia Parish. The terms of their agreement called for each man to pay half of all expenses associated with the enterprise and for each to collect the proceeds from cotton on alternate years. Thompson put to work in the Louisiana enterprise a bound labor force of thirty-three mortgaged slaves. Meanwhile, back in Natchez, he sold his Mississippi plantation to two other planters, accepting a mortgage against the property as payment, even though, by his own admission, Thompson regarded these two planters as untrustworthy "rascals."

When Thompson died in 1823, he left behind an estate deeply in debt. His land and slaves were heavily mortgaged. Still outstanding was his share of the expenses Trask had advanced during their partnership. Also outstanding was the balance of two other mortgages held against his property by another planter. Thompson's indebtedness, though, had not prevented him from extending approximately $59,000 in loans of cash and credit, many unsecured or uncollateralized, to forty-six individual debtors in the locality.

Contrary to the view that credit, tightly monitored, was extended only to trustworthy friends and family, the $52,049 lent by Thompson as creditor and entered in the column entitled "doubtful" in the probate ledger, testify to both the impersonal nature of credit as well as the inherent risk of such loans. And yet, evidence suggests that, rather than being an anomaly, his extensive use of such personal IOUs, as well as other informal means of obtaining and extending credit, occurred with increased frequency not just in Natchez or the outlying regions, but in markets throughout the new nation as early as the colonial era, and continued into the early national period.[1]

This study explores the role of unsecured loans and the promissory notes that recorded such debts in the Natchez area. How prevalent were these informal exchanges and what relevance do they have for understanding the development of a larger plantation economy? As my research project developed, I realized that the material in the collection suits filed in the Adams County, Mississippi, Court house in 1826 recorded transactions that took place outside the limits set by commerce and banking. Indeed, few if any were based on disputes over land, cotton, or slaves, and none of them included indications of the region's commercial orientation, or the typical barter exchange that was quintessentially part of the "frontier" economy. Yet, this absence has analogous implications for the study of Delta credit relations. To date, descriptions of the credit and debt system, especially with regard to earlier developments in Mississippi's history, tend to characterize exchange either in terms of a primitive "semi-barter" carried over from an earlier period of frontier activity, as described by Daniel Usner Jr., or as a set of "complexities" in the forging of numerous plantation empires produced by the alchemy of the entrepreneurial spirit and a seigniorial vision. Usner's detailed account of frontier relations aptly recognized the need to focus on the "interstices" of exchange—the narrow and forgotten spaces within which people bartered and distributed goods in small quantities "in pursuit of their livelihood." Though his discussion necessarily shifted the view to the "internal relations forged by inhabitants," the domestic, colonial market of the Delta is strongly set among the barter and deerskin trade between Indians, slaves, and settlers.

At the other end of the spectrum, Tom Scarborough's detailed account of the economic strategies used by four generations of the Bisland family of Natchez illustrates their adaptability to a credit system that "rested on a foundation honeycombed by the numerous mortgages and notes . . . given to relatives and other planters." Both descriptions, while accurate, stand on opposite sides. Credit was a mixed bag of both the simple and complex to the degree that creditors and debtors defined those exchanges. Thus, the relegation of credit relationships to either of the two labels—"primitive" or "complex"—obscures our ability to view the "dynamics of pre-modern societies" and the "gradualness" of the phases of development.[2]

In contrast to this "either-or" view of credit, the cases examined here suggest, first, the importance of considering the whole range of activities that lay within the locality, and second, that large economic actors accessed credit resources outside the local market on favorable terms that allowed for far longer repayment options. Third, they suggest that a growing secondary market for credit existed whereby a circulating medium, mostly made up of promissory notes, was used between private individuals, economic actors to be sure, without recourse to, or in need of, the liquidating facilities of the bank and which provided access to credit for those individuals considered perhaps the antithesis of the planter class.

The rise in collection proceedings yielded a vast array of material that together present a sphere of activity that, but for a default or death, would never have been available to historians.

To be sure, economic historians have long known that a private market for credit functioned in the pre-banking period and remained in use long after. According to such historians as Winifred B. Rothenberg, in places such as Middlesex, Massachusetts, between 1642 and 1773 "there was a marked increase in the density and geographic spread of personal credit networks" and a "high incidence of endorsements that enabled personal IOUs to pass among strangers." The informal market intensified after Independence. Creditors were more willing to hold on to "scraps of paper" that were "symbolic capital" because of an increase in overall liquidity and a rate of return that enabled farmers to divert their savings accumulations from physical improvements on their farms to debt instruments and securities.[3]

The "great void" in our understanding of early financial markets remains, however, with an especially large piece missing for the plantation enclaves of the Lower Mississippi River.[4] Part of the reason lies in the emphasis placed on cotton and the wider transnational net of marketing and finance in which the region was involved.[5] Morton Rothstein's "dual economy" conceptualizes the regions' wealthiest staple-producing enclaves as economically divided into two distinct sections—one, an export-led sector dominated by cotton planters and yeomen farmers, the other made up of self-sufficient agricultural units. Rothstein's suggestion applied to the lower South, especially Alabama, Mississippi, and Louisiana, where small groups of influential planters, specifically the Natchez elite, strongly resembled the elite agricultural groups found in Latin America and Asia.[6]

Over time, the persistence of this two-part typology downplayed the "within-group variation" found among market producers by lumping together their economic activities. Studies centered on southern commodity production, and especially the operations of the area's largest planters, emphasized their links to the outside world.[7] The ability to exploit their access to external markets depended on the planter-factor relationship and reflected the use of credit instruments as mechanisms that functioned according to the exigencies set by the financing of the cotton crop.[8] The literature concurrently regarded unsecured advances of cash and credit, and the paper on which they circulated, to be inferior and inflationary.[9]

A break with this interpretation came with the publication of Richard H. Kilbourne's *Debt, Investment, and Slaves*, in 1995. In his examination of East Feliciana Parish, Louisiana, Kilbourne argues that accommodation paper was not simply a "necessarily evil," but a vital part of a functioning debt market.[10] According to this author, the division between "real bills," instruments based on the sale of actual goods or commodities, and "accommodation paper" (i.e., drafts, bills of exchange, and promissory notes), which accessed outright advances of cash or credit, ignores the fact that much of the financing for plantation agriculture was conducted informally, well outside regular banking channels.[11]

The variety of credit instruments functioned on the basis of their "ultimate liquidity," or convertibility into specie or cash.[12] Accommodation paper, in particular, added a layer in the local economy by acting as a currency substitute even after the planter-factor relationship became prevalent. Likewise, Kilbourne argued that the focus on the financing of the cotton crop obscures the role of the factors, since they were actually "one tier in a hierarchy of liquidating agents" and as such lent, not capital, but their endorsement. With this contingent guarantee in place, the promissory note could be sold to a third party on the money market. Hence, the distinction between short- and long-term commercial loans masked the relative levels of liquidity for different kinds of credit instruments, while the market determined the value of such endorsements. Using mortgage records, bank portfolios, and collection suit judgments, Kilbourne found that the credit market in the locality was not only large, but generated a diversified layer of credit. As such, debt levels for middle-tier planters versus the elite were based on "risk-reward ratios."[13] The view of credit generated through banks and factorage firms is subordinate to the market in private lending. According to Kilbourne, "a study of chartered banks and their impact in the parish would not be without interest, but of limited importance in piecing together the credit history of the area."[14]

Yet, even amid an overall increase in impersonal credit networks, the development of Natchez and other agricultural enclaves in the Lower Delta had taken on a different hue. The highly capitalized nature of slavery required a large volume of unsecured credit. In particular, the high savings and wealth accumulations in the region allowed savers to invest in the highly liquid and mobile assets consisting of slaves, debt instruments, bank and steamship stocks, and, later, railroad bonds: "As a basis for credit, land was distinctly inferior, illiquid, and immobile. In this respect, southern plantations constituted a more 'advanced' and financially sophisticated form of agriculture."[15]

This paper proposes a more balanced view, one that incorporates more fully the internal, or secondary, markets as a complement to the wider commodity-driven market for the early history of the Natchez district. While the notion of a dual economy may correct for a once static view of Natchez cotton producers, and by implication the rest of the Lower Mississippi River region, evidence suggests that at least some middling planters had indeed emulated the larger planter-bankers through their access to local markets of formal and informal credit. Studies have shown that southern planters, with their cash reserves in New York and Philadelphia, exhibited "a sharp contrast to the chronic picture of indebtedness usually ascribed to [them]."[16] Yet, evidence drawn from local credit networks illustrates the ways individuals exploited local sources of credit and held large amounts of debt.

In fact, an early secondary capital market made up of personal IOUs, drafts, and an array of other informal credit instruments existed to meet economic demands. As a counterpoint to the wider commodity market, it filled a void relative to banking by providing a flexible currency substitute to meet the demand for small sums on a day-to-day basis.

On another level, regional credit allowed a segment of the population to bypass the liquidating facilities of banks and international factors. The case of middling planter Jonathan Thompson suggests, first, that intra-group lending had a trickle-down effect whereby, in contrast with planters of an earlier generation, people such as Thompson accessed local networks, obtaining credit from those higher up the financial ladder and, in turn, extending loans to those lower down the scale. Second, Thompson's case suggests that despite a large debt load, those who acquired the planter's status in a later period emulated the activities of the old planter elite; but by lending on the basis of unsecured promissory notes to regional and local debtors with a small portion of secured mortgages, they also contracted to local debtors. Finally, Thompson's financial assets and debts as a share of his total assets are compared with the portfolio of a first-generation planter, Benjamin Farar. In particular, this case study can help us avoid the tendency to restrict investigation to a few planters falling within the typology identified by the older interpretation.

The increasing volume and spread of personal IOUs and other informal financial instruments in the Natchez district indicates that slavery and cotton could support increasingly complex local financial arrangements. The Natchez market experienced a rise in liquidity, a feature it shared with other markets of the time, channeling savings through credit networks that became increasingly spread-out: in other words, "multilateral and impersonal."[17]

The cases examined signify a strong preference among private lenders and borrowers for quick access to funds in the course of ordinary, day-to-day needs. A few aspects of these types of debt are worth noting: the negotiability and flexibility of this kind of lending, the notion that almost anything could become a debt, and the fact that the local market maintained standards apart from national or international standards for verifications of claims.

In the context of daily business that did not require the resources (or delays) inherent in formal arrangements, accommodation paper in the form of promissory notes, drafts, and bills ensured quick access to relatively smaller credit sources. This informality translated into maneuverability; individuals could either liquidate the note at a bank with a factor's or planter's endorsement, for an upfront cost known as a discount, or transfer the note as payment to someone else for the full value. Debtors, as well as creditors, had much to gain. By substituting their own payment to a creditor with the debts they held against others they could generally avoid paying hard currency. Transferred from one creditor to the next, often several times, a note, which was a liability, became an asset and a form of currency. For example, in the 1826 case of *James C. Williams v. Mary P. Brooks,* the original creditor, or payee of the note, was David Lattimore. The pleading filed with the court outlines the ease and informality with which a note traveled:

> The Defendant made her certain Note in writing, commonly called a PROMISSORY NOTE, her own proper hand-writing being thereto subscribed . . . and then and there delivered the said Note to David Lattimore and thereby promised to pay . . . David Lattimore to whom, or whose order, the payment of the said sum of money in said Note specified . . . and before the payment of the said sum of money . . . endorsed the said Note, his own proper hand-writing being thereto subscribed, by which said endorsement the said David there and then appointed the said sum of money in said Note specified to be paid to one Samuel Ivey. After the making of the said promissory note and before the payment of the said sum of money . . . to be paid to the said Plaintiff, and then and there delivered the said promissory note so endorsed to the said Plaintiff.[18]

Individual IOUs, transferred in this way, without remittances of cash, and found here among the cases, stand in contrast to the literature on negotiability that views credit instruments as a way to gain access to funds. Cotton provided profits in the long run, but the locality displayed features consistent with a cash-poor economy. Smaller exchanges, then, were denominated in money, but little currency actually changed hands.

The Natchez private credit market was a distinct but interconnected arena. The cases make clear that personal accommodations of credit were abundant and suggest the importance of viewing the wide range of activities that lay within the locality, the growing market for a circulating medium mostly made up of promissory notes, without recourse to, or in need of, the liquidating facilities of the bank.

Informal lending lacked official documentation; there was no provision for recording this kind of debt with the court. In its absence, the court relied on a physical act to solidify the agreement that existed between creditor and debtor.[19] Complaints based on a promissory note had to establish "physical" proof by declaring that the "Defendant made his certain note and *delivered* it to Plaintiff." The physical act of delivery established an acceptance, or assumption, of a debt, regardless of whether the creditor transferred the note later. Time and again, this phrase appears as a standard, boilerplate item in cases based on promissory notes.

There were, however, numerous circumstances that resulted in a debt being owed. Writing from Philadelphia in 1821 to his Natchez business partner, local planter Jonathan Thompson dispensed some legal advice should their debtor, a Mr. Gerley, dispute the unsecured debt owed. In full knowledge of the law concerning informal debts, he stated plainly the precautions that should be taken:

> If Gerley makes any difficulty about accepting the bill as it now stands, under pretence that it is for a quarter sum than is due, let him accept it for less or for as much as he admits is due, stating it so in writing on the bill, thereon 'accepted for____' and put his name to it. I am more particular about this, because I want to have him disposed to pay the money as I may want it, and if I do not you may.[20]

Thompson's need to cover all his legal bases should he be forced to file suit is representative of what was legally known as a "due bill." Knowing that Gerley's signature would prove acceptance of the bill, Thompson also knew it would substantiate the debt as it existed and force or "make due" the payment whenever Thompson or his partner requested. It was therefore a legal technicality used to link the debtor to his debt. Such informal evidence of a debt carried weight in the courts. In *Charles Little v. Martin L. Thomas*, the complaint declared the debt had been for "goods, labor and money lent," but in lieu of supporting documents, the suit rested on a "due bill" and declared that the "Defendant acknowledged to be due and owing by him."[21]

Clearly, not all cases of debt were verifiable with the original debt instrument. When the firm of Wilson & Byrne wrote to Natchez planter William N. Mercer, in 1827, that the order drawn on him by a James C. McClelan was "mislaid" by a Mister Buckholts, Byrne reassured Mercer that he had handed the receipt to Mister Buckholts and that the original order had been signed by McClelan, which "I can at anytime affirm."[22] Byrne offered further reassurances: "McClelan lives now at Port Gibson and was in this city since the time I last seen you. I mentioned to him, from what you told me, it was all settled."[23] In a subsequent letter, Mister Buckholts himself wrote to Mercer: "me thinke you have sufficient evidence . . . and we pledge ourselves to stand between you and any difficulties with McClelan as well as Wilson & Byrne."[24] These examples illustrate the informal, yet highly responsive, workings of local credit markets where trust played a critical role in their operation. The informality of the arrangement that led to the misplaced note, the idea that one had no way of verifying the debt, because it was not recorded, outside the circle of friends and business acquaintances that knew of one's transaction and had knowledge of one's whereabouts and movements, all required a degree of trust among agents as they conducted business.

The hundreds of collection suits filed in the Adams County Court in Natchez document the character of a slave-based, river-port economy from its quasi-frontier status to a mature cotton-exporting economy of astounding wealth.[25] Unopened until the 1990s, they reveal the economic activity hidden behind the more conspicuous trade in cotton and slaves.[26] Summarized in terms of monetary value, the 355 cases filed in 1826 reflect three categories: 78 percent represent debts valued between $1 and $500; 17 percent comprised the mid-tier group of debts ranging from $501 to $2,000; and 4.3 percent of all cases were brought to recover debts of $2,000.00 or more. Moreover, of the 355 cases filed, 209 were transactions based on a promissory note. Thus, the two salient features discovered were the overwhelming use of personal IOUs and the relatively small sums involved. Payment terms ranged anywhere from one day to two years. For example, 16 cases brought on behalf of the estate of Jonathan Thompson were for short-term uncollateralized, unsecured promissory notes payable twelve-months after they had been contracted. Of those, twelve were based on sums of cash or credit valued between $1 and $500.

Promissory notes—those thin "scraps of paper" that Blackstone's *Commentaries* in 1768 called simply a "note of hand, not under seal"—lacked the legal formalities of other instruments, rarely, if ever, stated the intended use for the cash or credit obtained, and contained a terse explanation allowing the option to "order" the payment to someone else.[27] Each promissory note begins with "I promise" and ends with a signature. The absence of a notary or other formality facilitated their use as a form of secondary exchange but also risked challenge as binding instruments.

While the collection suits show a growing rate of default, they also illustrate a steady and increasing reliance on promissory notes. Table 1 presents the volume or quantity of debt cases for 1809, 1820, and 1826 as they

Table 1. Types of Claims Filed in 1809, 1820, and 1826

Year	Promissory Note	Bill of Exchange	Order Draft, Due Bill	Money Lent, Advanced	Open Account	Bond	Rent	Wages Services Professional	Theft Fraud Violation	Barter
1809	59	4	3	5	14	0	1	9	14	3
1820	202	14	7	11	32	1	3	5	22	0
1826	209	7	3	11	40	2	6	28	18	2

SOURCE: Adams County Court Records, Historic Natchez Foundation, Natchez, MS

changed over time.[28] Promissory notes accounted for 59 of the total 115 cases put to suit in 1809. In 1820, that number rose to 202 cases out of 299, with a slight increase in 1826 to 209 cases. All three years reflect a shifting debt market, one that had to do with the way debt was perceived—from a liability payable in the near future with actual cash to one that treated obligations as part of a deferrable asset. The number of cases brought on the basis of instruments that functioned on the immediate availability of funds, namely, the bill of exchange, draft, and order, were on the decline. In commercial parlance, they were "sight" instruments—payable at the time they were presented. One example is the bill of exchange. The increase of bills put to suit in 1820—a change of 250 percent over the base year of 1809—is followed by a sharp drop by 1826. Meanwhile, the preference for other types of accommodationist instruments, namely, promissory notes and open accounts, indicates a need for mechanisms that would delay payment and defray costs, so that while interest was an implicit part of doing business, charges were increasingly deferred until the death of one party forced settlement.

Open accounts contained entries for drafts accepted and funds placed to the credit of clients as well as purchases of supplies charged to accounts and payments made on behalf of clients. This provided one source of long-term borrowing, and payment to individuals who extended such services, be they neighbors or merchants, was made through promissory notes then sold on the market, discounted, or used by the creditors as payment for an unrelated debt to a third party.

Bills of exchange were used less frequently, but also functioned as a form of "accommodation paper" that could substitute for promissory notes. The borrower would get the accommodating party to endorse the note and then negotiate the paper to a lender. Other instruments were also adapted to local needs. Drafts, by definition, operated on an existing credit balance. Regardless of who received the remittance, it was used to request that funds be "laid out and expended" on behalf of the borrower and charged for settlement at a future time. It was then "accepted" by the individual or firm that had agreed to extend either a line of credit or direct funds. The case of *R.L. Smith & Company v. Richard H. May* presents a slightly different situation. On August 25, 1825, a local journeyman, William McCauley, of the Natchez newspaper, the *Ariel*, used a draft to access funds to pay the firm of R.L. Smith & Company. He asked the paper's editor, Richard Langdon, to pay the firm $53.12 and charge the amount for settlement at a later date. On the face of the draft Langdon wrote his acceptance: "accepted, on account of Office." But instead of paying the draft immediately, Langdon opted to debit this charge to his already existing open account with the firm and assumed the debt that once belonged to McCauley. There it stayed until 1826, when a suit was instigated by R.L. Smith & Company on the heels of their recent loss of a partner, one William P. Foster. His death required the surviving partners to settle various debts. That even drafts could be negotiated in much the same way as other credit instruments—to delay payment of a bill indefinitely—and charged to an open account is made clear by the case.[29]

For scholars, the hallmark of the antebellum credit system was its ability to carry a debt from one year to the next. Financially, that capability stemmed from what historian Harold Woodman aptly describes as the "security of cotton grown, growing and to be grown."[30] In its day-to-day setting, the practice of carrying over one year's balance to another was based on accommodationist lending. Examination of the default cases for 1826 Natchez seems to suggest that the pace of development may have been more aggressive than scholars have supposed. For example, over time, two older forms of exchange seem to have been less integral to the economy than in earlier years: the cases show the *decline* of both barter exchange and the practice more commonly referred to as "reckoning"—both having to do with a shortage of cash available.[31] In the first situation, payment for goods and/or services was made in cotton or merchandise, while the latter method, "reckoning," meant that creditor and debtor came together to compare their respective debts, "cross out equivalent debts and then only settle on the difference in cash" or with a note. According to historian Craig Muldrew, because credit was so common, most people accumulated a variety of mutual debts over time. These obligations were either remembered or recorded in an account book and mutually cancelled at a convenient time in the future.[32] Among the collection suits, cases based upon "reckoning" were indicated in the complaint by the words "accounted together" as evidence that the defendant accounted with the plaintiff concerning amounts of money before that time owing and, based upon "such accounting, defendant was found in arrears." For example, in the 1809 case of *Peter Little v. John B. Stout*, the plaintiff claimed a $200 debt. The plaintiff alleged that lumber had been sold and delivered to the defendant and that the plaintiff and defendant "accounted together . . . concerning divers sums of money," resulting in the determination that the "defendant was in arrears." In 1820 a debt case entitled *James H. Caldwell v. Samuel Emberton* was brought to court. Emberton became indebted to Caldwell on March 5, 1820, when the "defendant on the day and year aforesaid accounted with the said plaintiff of and concerning divers amounts of money . . . and upon such accounting the said defendant was then and there found to be in arrears."[33]

The need to "account together," and thus induce payment of outstanding balances, gradually decreased in this transitional era. Only two cases—one in 1809 and another in 1820—cited reckoning as the basis of the suit, and none identified this practice among the cases filed in 1826. But the practice did not entirely disappear. Indeed, it continued to be a part of the legal landscape in those suits in which contested debts were adjudicated at the time of probate. It facilitated older transactions, as seen among the probate records of planter Jonathan Thompson. For example, listed among the probate claims against Thompson's estate were the mutual debts that had accumulated between Thompson and another Natchez individual, James Brown, since 1818. By 1826, the death of both men meant that it was up to their administrators to settle the account.

The accounting depicted in figure 1 shows that the transactions between both men had been on a cash basis. While Thompson had made random payments toward the balance owed, as seen in the form of slaves and cash, it was left up to the probate court to reconcile, or "reckon," the account. Working from the balances that remained since the time of Thompson's death in 1823, the administrators cancelled out the equivalent amounts owed, after having deducted Thompson's payments, leaving a difference of $379.00 due to Brown's estate.

As this document shows, the relationship that existed between these men had never been one of creditor versus debtor. Rather, both men had made mutual indebtedness the key to their operations, until their deaths required administrators to "reckon" the account. In 1826, their longstanding affairs had been reconciled in the Report of the Commissioners labeled simply "Claim Number 44." The main difference has to do with the fact that those in earlier periods who "accounted together" did so periodically as a mechanism of control over finances and in order to bolster their cash flow, in contrast to those creditors and debtors who, at least by 1826, preferred to retain past debts for far longer periods without the aid of reconciliation.

Available clues concerning barter and reckoning provide a window into changing patterns of credit and debt relationships. Although barter never entirely disappeared as a means of settling debts, its use became increasingly rare. In 1809, three cases based on barter came to court, but none in 1820. In 1826 two barter cases appear. *Peter M. Lapice v. Charles C. River* offers an example of what is called a lateral exchange, or triangular barter. The debtor, River, was also the creditor for an amount owed him by John Forsyth. As payment for the debt owed Peter Lapice, River instructed Forsyth to "please deliver to Mr. Lapice my two bales of cotton [owed to Rivers by Forsyth] and this will be your receipt." In this way, Forsyth would satisfy the debt he had incurred with River, and River would have satisfied his debt to Lapice while avoiding the expenses he might have incurred should he have received the cotton, handled it, sold it, or delivered it. Slightly modified, the case provides an example of triangular barter: debtor B owes a debt to creditor A while being the creditor to C. B does not have either the cash or the goods on hand to settle this debt to A, but B is also a creditor of C, who owes money to him/her. The payment owed by C to B is made to A. It means that B has paid A, and C has paid B, though the actual payment, in the form of goods, "in fact move(s) only across the base of the triangle."[34]

In 1826, the case of *Elizabeth Greenfield v. William Dunbar, Margaret Dunbar, administrator and administratrix of James Dunbar, deceased* amounted to the highest dollar value of debt that year, totaling $65,000. Contracted in December 1810, it was to be paid in "cash or merchantable cotton." According to the complaint, James Dunbar

> promised to pay the said Elizabeth Greenfield with legal interest on the above sum in each of the three succeeding years, to wit, in the year 1815, 1816, and 1817 the said James Dunlop promised to pay a sum not less than nine nor more than eleven thousand dollars in cash or merchantable cotton at thirteen dollars per hundred weight English to be delivered at the City of New Orleans on or before the first day of May in each of the last named years, or cash or merchantable cotton at eighteen dollars per hundred weight English to be delivered in the City of Philadelphia on or before the first day of July in each of the three last named years—on or before the first day of August in the year 1818 James Dunlop promised to pay the legal interest there due on or before the first day of May in each of five succeeding years to wit, 1819, 1821, 1822, 1823 the said James Dunlop promised to pay an equal portion of the remaining principal and interest.[35]

That the single largest case of debt was payable with cotton indicates both the difficulties faced by most planters, even those who produced cotton on a grand scale, to come up with significant quantities of cash and the shortage of hard currency in general. The debt from 1810 remained unpaid until it became a claim sixteen years later against Dunbar's estate in 1826.

Martha Jane Brazy begins her account of the life of Natchez planter-banker Stephen Duncan with a letter he wrote to United States senator Josiah S. Johnston of Louisiana in the 1830s suggesting that the region prepare for gradual emancipation and the eradication of slavery. This, he explained, would be in the best interest of all involved; especially in the wake of a recent slave uprising. Duncan, a northerner by birth, became by the Civil War the nation's wealthiest man. He was the embodiment of what Rothstein regarded as the Natchez elite who combined finance and large-scale agriculture with precision and rose through the planter elite to become the president of the Bank of the State of Mississippi, a monopoly bank chartered in 1809. Duncan's connections enabled him to diversify on a wider playing field than other plantations, to have the choice of changing positions on the slavery issue, and, more important, to diversify his portfolio by investing in whatever venture, in the North or the South, he saw fit. Such a secure financial position allowed him not only to withstand the panic in 1819 and the economic downturn in the mid-1820s, but to profit from them.[36]

As president of the Bank of the State of Mississippi he restricted credit in the 1820s when prices for cotton dipped. For "insiders" like Duncan, however, the bank continued to do well, producing "prosperity for those who controlled it," paying its shareholders generous dividends of ten and eighteen dollars per share. By 1829, the bank's board of directors was still in the hands of original settlers and men of the second generation like Duncan.[37] For other planters of Duncan's generation, a different story of diversification occurred.

Jonathan Thompson, a middling Natchez planter, conducted his cotton-growing operations at the same time that Duncan was president of the state bank. His economic decisions reflect a concern identical to that of Duncan's: the need to diversify his portfolio in the face of sinking cotton prices and slave unrest. At times, his access to credit was prevented by the very credit-tightening policies that Duncan had helped put into effect. When Trask's brother Israel required the aid of the two men in obtaining a large loan, he first met with Thompson in Natchez. After attempting to obtain funds from the Natchez bank for Israel, he reported back to James Trask:

> I returned here to indorse with your brother's name and my own, but it would not answer . . . owing as I understand to the extraordinary course now pursued by the banks at New Orleans which makes them careful here how they put any of their means in the power of the banks there.[38]

When James Trask finally obtained funding for his brother, he called upon Thompson to advance the funds from his serve as a conduit:

> Finding an opportunity here of raising the money wanted by my brother I.E. Trask at the Mississippi Bank on the 23rd. I have this day drawn on you at 60 days for the amount, say $15,000 in favor of William Kenner and Company which please accept, and I shall place timely funds in your hands to withdraw the same at maturity.[39]

As a middling planter, Thompson turned to the local market time and again to access credit and was himself a source of funds and resources for others in his circle. His network was much more modest than Duncan's and he did not qualify as a banking "insider" in the region's institutions. By drawing a distinction between planters of the early nineteenth century on the basis of financial status, this study highlights the access that middling planters had to a local capital market and shows that important differences existed between rural wealthholders and patterns of lending that took place within these agricultural areas. The probate records of Jonathan Thompson, a middling planter, and those of the wealthy Benjamin Farar illustrate the ways in which the components of the planter class were linked by debtor-creditor obligations. Both men were second-generation planters; but Farar, as the son-in-law to early settler Richard Ellis and the only son of Dr. Benjamin Farar, also an early setter, acquired a sizable portion of his assets through intergenerational transfers of prime alluvial lands along the Mississippi River originally secured by land-grantees of the Spanish and British Governments.[40] Acquisition of these rich alluvial lands by settlers like the Ellis family enabled them to become sources of local lending and required subsequent emigrants to use private mortgage contracts in the accumulation of assets. Mortgages on slaves and land to access capital as well as the use of private credit instruments suggest that over time these mechanisms intensified, increasing the liquidity in the market, which facilitated credit. Second-generation planters thus accessed latent capital by becoming net debtors to elite, net creditors, such as Farar.

Intra-group lending also suggests that despite huge increases in debt (in absolute terms and as a ratio of total wealth), second-period planters lent money as well as held mortgages against other individuals. Thus, credit "trickled down" to those at the lower end of the financial ladder. Thompson also held financial assets at a ratio to his total wealth that was proportionate to Farar's, suggesting that despite rising debt levels among middling planters, financial assets were an important component in the composition of rural portfolios. This evidence also illustrates the different patterns of lending between first- and second-generation planters, highlighting aspects of financial markets previously hidden by the dual-economy model.

In general, Farar made fewer loans and held fewer mortgages at the time of his death, though the amounts were far larger than those contracted by Thompson. In contrast, Thompson lent short-term petty sums and held mortgages against individuals deemed a credit risk.

Historians generally rank planters according to the number of their labor force: Farar's records indicate that he held four plantations and 241 slaves, all free and clear. In contrast, Thompson's assets included a bound labor force of 97 slaves, of which 33 had been mortgaged to him. In addition, he obtained two mortgaged-plantations in Natchez. Farar's records, by contrast, are an example of an elite decedent's portfolio. His record is important, since it is the Ellis family that Rothstein cites as one of the key figures of his "modernized sector" model.[41] Farar inherited a sizable portion of his property upon marrying into the Ellis family and dealt directly with at least three firms: William Kenner & Company and Hall, Nelson & Company, both in New Orleans; and Wilkins & Linton, headed by prominent Natchez merchant James C. Wilkins. They effectively provided Farar with all his financing needs. In a transaction of December 1818, Farar had advanced the first full payment of $10,000 for a "house and lot" in Natchez sold to him by James C. Wilkins for Farar's sister-in-law. The payment, made "by the hands of Henry Nelson," was arranged as an advance by Henry Nelson, part owner of Hall, Nelson & Company, and was then placed to Farar's account to be paid at a later time. Conversely, as a net creditor, Farar's probate records show Hall & Nelson indebted to Farar for $6,100 at 8 percent.[42]

In contrast, Thompson's records demonstrate that while he also sold his cotton through factors in New Orleans, he conducted his operations mainly through his local connections with other planters. Thompson had arrived in Natchez from Brimfield, Massachusetts, sometime prior to 1814, perhaps as early as 1809. His major enterprise stemmed from owning two plantations in Natchez, acquired between 1816 and 1819, and the operation of a third plantation in Concordia Parish, Louisiana, in partnership with another planter, James L. Trask. Thompson accessed credit from Trask and other wealthier individuals such as Samuel Postlethwaite, future president of the Bank of Mississippi, and Winthrop Sargent, former governor of the Mississippi Territory, even as he advanced petty sums of cash and credit to those who stood at the lower end of the financial spectrum.

A substantial portion of Thompson's financial dealings stemmed from his partnership with James L. Trask, another "outsider" from Massachusetts. The Trask-Thompson enterprise reflects their mutual financial accommodations, and their partnership facilitated a range of activities, from the operation of small cotton plantations with enslaved labor and speculation in bank and steamboat stocks, to endorsing notes and loans for one another for a number of mutual investments. Thompson acted as Trask's agent in assisting him in the management of one of his plantation properties. On other occasions, they pooled the funds and resources necessary for larger transactions and kept each other abreast of the financial climate from Philadelphia to New Orleans. Trask enabled Thompson to access credit sources regionally. Trask acted as a buffer in all financial matters, a qualitatively different scenario than Farar's.

A combination of risk aversion and high transaction costs can hinder development. When measuring economic efficiency, economists usually look for evidence of a convergence of rates of return on risk-standardized investments across an array of enterprises; in other words, a reduction in risk aversion and high transaction costs. Analysis of probate records, however, requires finding evidence that individual credit networks thickened (that a middling planter networked as many if not more credit partners than an elite planter) and widened (the decedent networked to more distant and financially dissimilar credit partners).[43]

The records of Jonathan Thompson and Benjamin Farar indicate increasing capital mobility. Thompson left forty-two debtors in 1823, while Farar left sixteen in 1824. Thompson's creditors totaled sixty-four, while Farar's probate listed eighteen creditors. Farar's smaller numbers could be attributed to his existing ties in metropolitan centers, but evidence from the claims submitted to the Natchez commissioners as standard procedure shows that these were promissory notes given by individuals contracting credit, mortgages, and open accounts for services within the region.

The comparison suggests that Natchez credit networks expanded and grew more efficient as information about borrowers' creditworthiness became more freely available to lenders.[44] The increased use and availability of credit sources in the regional market also illustrates not only that elite planters were able to clear their debts more easily, but also that they did not rely on local credit facilities to the same extent as middling planters did.

While the findings do not represent the universe of creditor-debtor transactions the decedent dealt with over the course of a lifetime, they provide a good estimate of all those debts pending at the time of death. Moreover, because administration accounts at probate contain only those credits and debts outstanding at death—only those unpaid balances left over after a lifetime of borrowing, lending, and litigation—the information available on the size of the networks may be considered as vastly understating the credit networks of the living.[45]

Table 2 presents the decedents' total wealth, financial assets, and debts. The two decedents are ranked and sorted by total wealth, that is, by the value of real estate plus portable physical wealth (PPW) plus financial

Table 2. Total Wealth, Financial Assets, and Debts (in Nominal Dollars) of the Estates of Two Natchez Planters

	Real Estate (including PPW/FPC)	Financial Assets	Debt
Farar	141,203.62	397,337.34	7,654.36
Thompson	36,352.00	66,130.49	166,007.00

SOURCE: Second Recapitulation in account current with William N. Mercer, administrator of the Estate of Benjamin Farar; Summary of Debts Due in account with Mrs. Jane Raplje, *William N. Mercer, administrator of Benjamin Farar, deceased, v. Thomas Butler, executor of Jane Raplje, deceased,* 1826, Adams County Court Records, Historic Natchez Foundation, Natchez, MS; Report of Commissioners, Claims Allowed against the Estate of Jonathan Thompson; Inventory and Appraisement of the Estate of Jonathan Thompson.

Table 3. Distribution of Assets of the Estates of Two Natchez Planters (in Percentages)

	Real Estate as a Share of Total Wealth (including PPW and FPC)	Financial Assets as a Share of Total Wealth
Farar	26	74
Thompson	34	64

SOURCE: Second Recapitulation in account current with William N. Mercer, administrator of the Estate of Benjamin Farar; Summary of Debts Due in account with Mrs. Jane Raplje, *William N. Mercer, administrator of Benjamin Farar, deceased, v. Thomas Butler, executor of Jane Raplje, deceased,* 1826, Adams County Court Records, Historic Natchez Foundation, Natchez, MS; Report of Commissioners, Claims Allowed against the Estate of Jonathan Thompson; Inventory and Appraisement of the Estate of Jonathan Thompson.

Table 4. Value of Financial Assets of the Estates of Two Natchez Planters (in Nominal Dollars)

	Cash	Securities	Loans
Farar	1,912.89	9700.00	367,537.45
Thompson	31.50	800.00	66,098.99

SOURCE: Second Recapitulation in account current with William N. Mercer, administrator of the Estate of Benjamin Farar; Summary of Debts Due in account with Mrs. Jane Raplje, William N. Mercer, administrator of Benjamin Farar, deceased, v. Thomas Butler, executor of Jane Raplje, deceased, 1826, Adams County Court Records, Historic Natchez Foundation, Natchez, MS; Report of Commissioners, Claims Allowed against the Estate of Jonathan Thompson; Inventory and Appraisement of the Estate of Jonathan Thompson.

assets. Financial assets are defined as loans and mortgages, securities, and cash. In the financial assets column of table 2, there is a striking difference in borrowing and lending as a share of wealth. Physical capital (PC), which includes farm physical capital (FPC) as a share of total wealth, either decreased or stabilized at a certain point in both portfolios, while holdings of financial assets as a share of wealth rose. Debts, meanwhile, increased in a way that suggests that debt was a "strategic and logistically-shaped function of wealth" (see tables 3 and 4).

Broadly speaking, an increase in the correlation between financial asset holdings and total wealth might suggest that a rise in wealth increased the demand for credit instruments at the mid-tier level.[46] What the probate accounts show is that both Farar and Thompson actively participated in the local and regional market but that Thompson's participation was qualitatively different than Farar's. Intergenerational transfers of land and slaves initiated by first-generation settlers like Richard Ellis (Farar's father-in-law) went a long way toward providing an economic base. With assets largely free and clear, Farar appears as a specialized lender, a net creditor, whose holdings of financial assets far exceeded his debts (net assets are financial assets minus debts). In contrast, debt increased for Thompson in a way that suggests his use of debt as a strategic function of wealth (in contrast to the simple lending between farmers in all locations). Thus, while the share of funds lent by Farar and Thompson relative to total wealth is proportionally within the same range, 74 and 64 percent, respectively, their financial paths diverge with the pattern of lending and borrowing.

Farar lent far larger sums, though he made fewer loans than Thompson. His records show that he financed John Cook's mortgage for $6,000 in slaves and held notes against Volante Labarri worth over $20,000. Both these figures are included in the total amount of notes and open accounts owed to Farar, totaling $162,159.26. Meanwhile, Thompson made more numerous and comparatively smaller incremental loans. Of the total forty-two people listed as owing sums to him, only two claims had been for overdue mortgages, totaling $6,500. Of the total debt of $66,130.49, the balance of $59,598.99 in loans of cash and credit was based on outstanding and unsecured notes, book accounts, drafts, and bonds. Both decedents had made loans to individuals who stood on an equal or lower social and financial footing.

The evidence suggests two other important aspects of lending. For Farar, financial assets show a 181 percent increase over his real estate holdings. For Thompson, a middle-tier decedent, whose debts exceeded his asset holdings by more than 150 percent, financial assets constituted an 82 percent increase over his real estate holdings (table 2). Farar's loans were larger, fewer, and far exceeded his value in real estate. Thompson's lending activities also exceeded his real estate holdings, but only slightly. Each, however, had devoted a sizable portion of his resources to lending and commercial interests that included bank securities. In other words, a rapid increase in borrowing and lending may have required that an investment be made in financial assets at an ever-increasing rate.

Meanwhile, Farar's financial assets were growing despite a stable or declining share in real estate. However, it is significant to note that the lending activities of both Farar and Thompson were weighted heavily against the other assets in their portfolios, despite, as we shall see, Thompson's mortgaged assets. These considerations suggest that, at least in the early national period, planters may have been increasingly able to diversify into financial investments in the region.

Much of the credit Thompson contracted as both a debtor and creditor was unsecured and had little connection to the larger network of international credit for the production and sale of cotton. Likewise, the credit he obtained by mortgaging his real and personal property was facilitated by his ties to local and regional connections rather than to international sources.

In 1823, his personal property was worth an estimated $13,207. His investment in ninety-seven slaves was worth $30,720.[47] He also owned Pine Grove and Bradley plantations, along with a town home in Natchez.[48] At the time of his death, sixty creditors listed sixty-four claims against his estate, amounting to an uncollateralized debt against him of $84,007.81.[49] Thompson had contracted some of these debts on the basis of secured transactions, including the mortgaging of both plantations to Samuel Postlethwaite. On the credit side, with approximately $66,000 owed to him, some $52,049 was categorized as "doubtful," whether from a lack of security for the debts, the inability to collect on them, or simply a lack of evidence on the part of the administrator to prove the debt was owed.[50]

James Trask, Thompson's partner, also filed his claim to the administrators of Thompson's estate for outstanding debts arising from their partnership in the planting and cultivating of cotton in 1821. Trask forwarded various sums on behalf of Thompson on several occasions, but the largest amount came from advancing all of the expenses arising from the business, a claim that left Thompson indebted to him for over $10,335.83. The claim also included earlier balances such as a loan from Trask to Thompson in 1814, another to Thompson for $1,000, as well as mutual investments in bank stock, which paid dividends in 1819 and 1821. Trask enjoyed the flexibility of credit sources in the eastern parts of the South as well as in New Orleans, and Thompson's arrival in Natchez may have been a function of this regional network.[51]

In the list of debts, Trask claimed the amount of $6,236.75 for his endorsement of Thompson's note at the bank. See table 5. Both Thompson and Trask had an ongoing financial affiliation with Winthrop Sargent, a

Table 5. The Estate of Jonathan Thompson, Deceased: Account with Major James L. Trask and Israel E. Trask, June Term, 1824

Debit			
1814	May 23	(a) To your draft paid by Israel E. Trask	$ 1,000.00
1819	July 3	(b) Dividend on Bank Stock	1,500.00
1821	Jan. 29	(c) Dividend on Bank Stock	463.18
	May 20	(d) Chamber's Note –	742.00
	May 01	(e) Net Proceeds Cotton Received of William Kenner & Company	1,275.88
	Jan. 1	(f) One half expenses of Plantation Concordia in 1821 & 1823	3,259.16
1822	June	(g) Net proceeds 110 Bales Cotton received by you	5,680.27
		(h) One-half hire negro to W. Vancompen	150.00
1823	Jan. 23	(i) Account with Winter	97.39
		(j) My expenses to New Orleans on your business with Nichols in January 1821	150.00
		(k) Cash paid in Bank at Natchez for amount of my endorsement	6,236.75
		(l) To amount of Interest	3,578.51
		Balance Brought Down	10,355.83

NOTE: (debts b-l were charged 8 percent, and debt (a) was charged 6 percent)
SOURCE: Claim Number 34, Account Allowed by Commissioners of the Orphans Court, Adams County, June 1824, Probate Records, Adams County, Office of Records, Natchez, MS.

prominent Natchez politico and planter.[52] Though the extent of this three-way relationship remains unclear, evidence indicates that significant sums were advanced to Thompson as unsecured loans. At one point Thompson urged Trask to pay Sargent his $1,100. This "last sum," he advised, "you *should* arrange *now*."[53] When this payment was not made quickly, Thompson pressed Trask to put the funds in the hands of a New Orleans factor. It is likely that the firm, William Kenner & Co., represented Sargent as his agent in the sale of his crops, meaning that paying Kenner would translate into a credit to Sargent's account.[54]

By the time of Thompson's death in 1823, he personally owed Sargent $13,021 and had contracted another $10,000 debt from Trask in order to clear that debt.[55] The records do not make clear the full character of Thompson's indebtedness to Sargent. The earliest transaction was a note contracted in February of 1819, through which Thompson received a $3,000 loan that included interest and the option to negotiate the note at the Bank of the State of Mississippi. In the month of July, 1819, Thompson contracted a further debt.[56] In addition to this loan there was an "old account" that carried a balance of $2,002.62 and "cash" borrowed in the amount of $6,000.[57] In August of 1821, Sargent's death forced Thompson to settle these debts, and he turned to Trask to facilitate the movement of funds. He asked Trask to accept his promissory note for $10,000, reminding him that his position as bank director should have enabled him to accommodate his request.[58] From Philadelphia he wrote to Trask and explained the situation:

> And as money matters stand (of Mrs. S.) precisely as I told you I supposed they did, let me know if I may draw a bill on you there (Oct. 1) say payable 1. Jan. for the amount of the debt due W.S.'s estate, or some part of it say $10,000, or say what I may do in this respect, and for how much. If [I] do draw on you on my own account as I have your leave to do, you will have nothing to do but accept it. I shall be on the spot ready and able I hope to provide for it.[59]

Trask obtained these funds from a bank loan, by using a promissory note from Thompson to himself, which the bank discounted. Dated July 18, 1823, the note to Trask was due sixty days after it was made.[60] Trask endorsed the note, and it was presented to Gabriel Tichenor, the bank's cashier. Thompson's death, however, sometime in the summer of 1823, prevented the loan from being repaid. Interest charges from September 9, 1823 (the date the note was due), to January 1, 1824, totaled $195, to which was added the notary's fee ($2.50) associated with the protested note.[61] In all, the debt totaled $10,197.50. Another 8 percent per annum was added in interest for the period leading up to the claim in 1824, which totaled $1,141.87. Although "paid by Trask" was written on the face of the note, in the final calculation Trask, as endorser, assumed only partial liability (most likely because Sargent had lent funds to Thompson over the years with Trask as endorser, or security for the debts, and split the debt in half as part of their planting operations). Thompson's estate therefore stood liable for $6,236.75 instead of the full $10,000, with the balance paid by Trask.[62] "Cash paid in Bank at Natchez for amount of my endorsement" enumerated this item in the account rendered by Trask against Thompson's estate and was presented to the probate commissioners accompanied by an additional 5 months and 12 days of interest.

The debts owed to Sargent and Trask, respectively, comprised the two largest claims received by the probate commissioners and encapsulate the depth and duration of informal credit, or unsecured credit, as it operated on a yearly, even daily, basis. They demonstrate how local, agrarian entrepreneurs used the legal instruments of credit, such as promissory notes and bills of exchange and discounting mechanisms with local banks, to engage in planting and to accumulate the resources necessary to facilitate business. These informal debts and credits clearly enabled medium-sized and small-scale planters and agrarian operators like Thompson to function at least on the local scene in ways that vitiated to some degree the shallowness of their resources for credit.

But what role, if any, did mortgage-secured credit have in a planter's operations? Thompson borrowed heavily against his plantations almost from the moment he acquired them. This was the case with the mortgage between Thompson and David Williams in 1816, for Thompson's two plantations, Pine Grove and Bradley, and for the ones involving Josiah Morris and Chauncey Pettibone, respectively dated 1820 and 1821, which saw Thompson as creditor.[63]

By 1820, one year before Trask and Thompson began their partnership, Thompson once again mortgaged his plantations to David Williams. The $47,200 loan was secured once again by Pine Grove and Bradley, along with the slaves on the property.[64] In June 1823, Thompson refinanced the remaining balances on these mortgages with merchant-banker Samuel Postlethwaite for a loan of $11,500 at 10 percent.[65]

The debts owed to Williams and Postlethwaite give added clarity to Thompson's financial position in the 1820s and, by implication, reveal the character of his partnership with Trask: he used noncollateralized debt as seen in the Sargent loans (promissory notes) as well as secured debt (mortgages) to operate his three plantations, pledging his profits from the cotton and the value of his land but not his slaves as the security for his notes.

Thompson also functioned as a creditor. He sold twelve acres of farmland near Natchez on May 11, 1820, to Josiah Morris for $13,500, as well as plantation lands and slaves in Concordia Parish, across the river.[66] Thompson accepted a lien on the farmland in Natchez rather than cash payment from Morris. This mortgage, which included slaves as well as the land, amounted to $8,000, payable March 1, 1822, suggesting that Morris had paid part of the sale in cash. Regarding the Concordia property, Thompson had agreed to the sale reluctantly and for reasons that are unclear:

> I did never offer or wish [*sic*] to sell the property to those fellows. I was about to sell it to [*sic*] who was ready to buy it and had or would I believe acceded to my terms. P&M applied to me while the negotiation with [*sic*] was [*sic*] and stated that they supposed I was friendly to them,

> that they thought the terms of payment, that the purchase was desire-able [*sic*] and that they would consider it an indication of my friendship to them and disposition to aid them if I would break off that negotiation with [*sic*] and let them have the property.
>
> To this I objected that they had no means to [sic] carry on the plantation; that by waiting [sic] while I thought they might find a chance to do better—that as I had paid a high price for the negroes I was determined not to sell at a loss, that I must have an [higher price] for them—and though from their want of means it might be a hard purchase for them to make . . . But they insisted—and I consented much to my sorrow. They were to have the property at precisely what it cost me neither more nor less.[67]

Thompson eventually blamed the problems arising from this transaction on the debtors' character: "I do not wish to enter into any detail in this letter to show you how much I have been injured by these two most indescribable scoundrels, villains, and rascals."[68] And Thompson's initial hunch was proven correct when, in 1821, it was clear that the buyers were unable to make the payment for the plantation in Concordia. He then rescinded the original contract for one that rented them the slaves and land.

A look into the early nineteenth-century economic life of a southern town entrenched in plantation agriculture from the perspective of the collection suits filed in the community's circuit court presents a picture of how credit worked at a local level, within the interstices of the community's larger economic system. From a very early stage of its development, the Natchez district developed local financial markets that efficiently allocated the investment capital that was necessary for the operation and expansion of the slave plantation system. While the financial instruments and arrangements that allocated debt and credit were informal and relied upon trust among agents, it is clear that credit flowed freely between regional borrowers and lenders. Issues such as liquidity and capital accumulation are common elements found in every market. The absence of studies centered on regional and local developments make even a basic understanding of shared mechanisms impossible to identify and any discussion of commodity markets a one-sided affair, since the internal and informal networks of private lenders and borrowers comprise a heretofore unexamined means by which plantation systems operated and flourished in the American South. Yet, this study demonstrates that a secondary credit-tier provided maneuverability and opportunity, even within the realm of an economy tied to agriculture, commerce, and slavery.

NOTES

1. I would like to thank Ronald L. F. Davis for his continued support and insights, Steven Topik, Michele Gillespie, and Susanna Delfino for their help and work on earlier drafts of this article, as well as Louis Kyriakoudes and the several anonymous readers for their helpful suggestions.

2. Daniel H. Usner Jr., *Indians, Settlers, and Slaves in a Frontier Exchange Economy: The Lower Mississippi Valley before 1793* (Chapel Hill: University of North Carolina Press, 1992); Scarborough, "The Bislands of Natchez: Sugar, Succession, and Strategies for Survival," *Journal of Mississippi History* 58 (1996): 23.

3. Winifred Barr Rothenberg, "The Emergence of a Capital Market in Rural Massachusetts, 1730-1838," *Journal of Economic History* 45, no. 4 (1985): 781-808. The literature on informal loans remains largely centered on the Northeast and other eastern seaboard states. The debates in the 1990s, concerned with the origins and timing of capitalism, fueled the need for detailed studies of rural economic exchange patterns.

4. Richard Sylla, "Forgotten Men of Money: Private Bankers in Early U.S. History," *Journal of Economic History* 36 (1976): 173. Sylla originally commented on the absence of studies regarding private lending. In 2000, Howard Bodenhorn reminded readers once again that private lending remained "one of the great voids in our understanding of antebellum financial markets . . . important, if not large." For a discussion of the national integration of banks for the period, see Howard Bodenhorn, *A History of Banking in Antebellum America: Financial Markets and Economic Development in an Era of Nation Building* (Cambridge, UK: Cambridge University Press, 2000), 182. A concise depiction of the lending activities of private banking firms in Virginia has been offered by Howard Bodenhorn in "Private Banking in Antebellum Virginia: Thomas Branch & Sons of Petersburg," *Business History Review* 71, no. 4 (1997): 513-42.

5. Joseph J. Klein, "The Development of Mercantile Instruments of Credit in the United States," *Journal of Accountancy* 12 (1911): 342. As early as 1911, Klein's study examined credit instruments as primarily a function of the trade in agricultural commodities.

6. Morton Rothstein, "The Antebellum South as a Dual Economy: A Tentative Hypothesis," *Agricultural History* 41, no. 4 (1967): 373-82. The "modernized sector" consisted of three categories, (1) the nonslaveholding yeoman farmers who produced surpluses, (2) the planters on the make, who owned from twenty to fifty slaves on one or two plantations, and (3) the true elite of the economic system. The small, cohesive elite at the top of the social order are described as "exploiting their access to external markets and credit." See also Rothstein, "The Cotton Frontier of the Antebellum United States: A Methodological Background," *Agricultural History* 44 (1970): 149-65, and "The Changing Social Networks and Investment Behavior of a Slaveholding Elite of the Slaveholding Elite in the Ante Bellum South: Some Natchez 'Nabobs,' 1800-1860," in *Entrepreneurs in Cultural Context,* ed. Sidney M. Greenfield, Arnold Stickon, and Robert T. Aubey (Albuquerque: University of New Mexico Press, 1979): 65-88.

7. For a monograph that details the function of the Natchez capitalists and their diverse international orientations see Martha Jane Brazy, *An American Planter: Stephen Duncan of Antebellum Natchez and New York* (Baton Rouge: Louisiana State University Press, 2006).

8. While Rothstein conceded that a focus on the planter elite raised issues of representativeness, inviting further testing to confirm whether any or all three of the categories of market-producers "functioned in the manner of a 'modernized sector,'" the goal at that time—to correct for a static view of Natchez cotton producers that saw them as pre-capitalist and "insular"—focused on establishing the diverse capitalist proclivities of the region's largest planters who were not, as the narrative goes, "rooted in the

region of their main economic interest" but who instead were necessarily a part of metropolitan capital markets. By the 1990s, a type of consensus among historians had been reached that acknowledged planters to be rational, profit-maximizing businessmen, and that smaller to middling growers were engaged in production for international markets. Others, such as Douglas Egerton, argued that to confuse "a commercial invasion with a capitalist revolution" is to make market orientation the primary definition of capitalism, which it is not. He cites numerous instances of key Northern elements, especially wage labor, as the fulcrum for full-blown capitalism missing from Southern markets. See Douglas R. Egerton, "Markets without a Market Revolution: Southern Planters and Capitalism," *Journal of the Early Republic*16, no. 2 (1996): 207-21.

9 Harold D. Woodman, *King Cotton and His Retainers: Financing and Marketing the Cotton Crop of the South, 1800-1925* (Lexington: University of Kentucky Press, 1968). This author illustrates the way endorsements made by cotton factors on bills and notes allowed their clientele to access bank funds. Collateralized by staple crops, and endorsed by factors, credit instruments were sustained through the "security of cotton grown, growing, and to be grown." Historian George D. Green in his analysis of Louisiana banking concluded that development in the region from "primitive to commercial" was marked by a "rapid" shift. Coinciding with the period of bank development, this change occurred between the late 1820s and 1830s and had to do with the development and influence of banks, and the "desire for sound money and easy credit," which induced bankers to "devise" credit arrangements. While banks were in no way inconsequential, Green's depiction advances the notion of expansion spurred on by the evolving regional banks, namely, that the demand for flexible credit instruments was supplied solely by banks. Woodman, however, views changes in the South as having occurred before the establishment of state-chartered banks and reflected the ability of cotton factors to access various outside sources of credit and evolved, by the 1820s, into firms that allowed farmers the option to store their cotton and thereby receive the best price on the market.

10 Richard Holcombe Kilbourne Jr., *Debt, Investment, Slaves: Credit Relations in East Feliciana Parish, 1825-1885* (Tuscaloosa: University of Alabama Press, 1995), 16-23.

11. One reason that banks have figured so prominently in the literature is that they provided a set of financial services different than that of private lenders—that of modern, "arms-length" transactions that helped monetize the economy. Armed with the ability to liquidate the book debts held between farmers, planters, and merchants, they handed over banknotes that were then introduced as currency.

12. Ibid., 17. In particular, the ratio of ultimate liquidity to aggregate income is seen as the basis for distinguishing between the debt market and the money market.

13. Ibid., 11. Kilbourne's distinction between planters is consistent with the findings in this study, namely, that it was middle-tier planters who mortgaged their slaves and plantations.

14. Ibid., 17-27. The largest market in paper currency was the one in New Orleans, but Kilbourne estimates that, even here, the banks' collateralized loans during the 1850s amounted to less than 5 percent.

15. Ibid., xi.

16. Rothstein, "The Antebellum South as a Dual Economy: A Tentative Hypothesis," 380.

17. Winifred Barr Rothenberg, "The Emergence of a Capital Market in Rural Massachusetts, 1730-1838," *Journal of Economic History* 45, no.4 (1985): 782.

18. *James C. Williams v. Mary P. Brooks*, 1826, Adams County Court Records, Historic Natchez Foundation, Natchez, MS.

19. The courts recognized debts contracted on an informal basis by what was termed

indebitatus assumpsit. By definition, this means that the debtor assumed a liability that was "not under seal" but contracted verbally or by informal writing. Seeking the intervention of the court meant that the plaintiff was required to prove his/her claim. If successful, the debt would gain the full force of the law. Under the *assumpsit* heading, the law recognized two types of debt evident among the legal cases. The first was a debt for a specific sum. Examples include rent, a bond, a bill, or promissory note. Hence, the cause of action was identified as an "action of debt," reflecting a previously negotiated sum of money. The second type of debt was an "action on the case" in which the parties had not settled on a price, and the debtor assumed a liability based on the nature of the financial arrangement. Typical of an "action on the case" were claims to recover the balance of an open account. For a concise look at the legal history and function of debts, see R. H. Helmholz, "Debt Claims and Probate Jurisdiction in Historical Perspective," *American Journal of Legal History* 23, no. 1 (1979): 68-82, and R. H. Helmholz, "Assumpsit and Fidei Laesio," *Law Quarterly Review* 91 (1975).

20. Jonathan Thompson to Major James Trask, August 4, 1821, Trask-Ventress Family Papers, Mississippi Department of Archives and History, Jackson, MS.

21. *Charles Little v. Martin L. Thomas,* 1826, Adams County Court Records, Historic Natchez Foundation.

22. D. M. Byrne to William N. Mercer, April 30, 1827, Benjamin Farar Probate Records, Adams County Office of Records, Natchez, MS.

23. Buckholts & Richards to Dr. William N. Mercer, May 8, 1827, Benjamin Farar Probate Records, Adams County Office of Records, Natchez, MS.

24. Klein, "Development of Mercantile Instruments of Credit in the United States," 342. Klein cites the example of such an informality at work in pre-industrial America in "a letter to Mr. William Leigh of New Kent, enclosing a probably worthless bill, which the sender believes the addressee might try to collect with greater hope of success, because living near the drawee."

25. In his examination of Natchez planters, Morton Rothstein uses estimates of wealth distribution for the South as a whole, drawn from James H. Soltow's study of the 1850 Census, to assert that the Natchez area had emerged by that date as a "major pocket of affluence." Studies of wealth in Adams County for the 1850s indicate that planters had held a higher proportion of "adult white males whose estates exceeded $100,000 in value than Newport County, Rhode Island or the Eighteenth-Ward in New York City, two comparable enclaves of wealth." In Rothstein's own estimation, these studies do not reflect "the extent of holdings among the wealthiest 5 percent of the population of the Natchez District," which was much larger than the comparison indicates. See Rothstein, " Changing Social Networks," 65-88.

26. The information compiled from the 1809, 1820, and 1826 collection suits that form the basis for this study was gathered during an internship for the Courthouse Records Project. Historian Ronald L. F. Davis recovered and organized the vast arrays of legal manuscripts that make up the Courthouse Records Project, involving 90,000 court cases and more than 1,200 separate volumes, which are now housed at the Historic Natchez Foundation. Graduate students from California State University–Northridge have worked each summer since the early 1990s. To date, approximately 25,000 cases have been preserved and entered into a computer bank for indexing and analysis.

27. John H. Langbein, ed., *Commentaries on the Laws of England: William Blackstone, a Facsimile of the First Edition of 1765-1769* (Chicago: University of Chicago Press, 1979), 153.

28. The choice of these three arbitrary years had to do both with the availability of the sources at the time and also with obtaining a representative sample of transactions to account for the pre- and post-statehood periods.

29. *R.L. Smith & Company v. Richard H. May,* 1826, Adams County Court Records, His-

toric Natchez Foundation. The writ of execution makes clear the combination of instruments and open accounts: "This action is brought to recover the sum of $282.68 of the Defendant . . . being the amount of goods, wares, merchandise and medicines delivered to the journeymen employed at the "Ariel" office, an account and on the faith of an order or letter from the said Defendant to the said R.L. Smith & Co., directing them to deliver said goods as aforesaid, said order or letter bearing the date the 26th of August 1825."

30. Woodman, *King Cotton and His Retainers,* 34.

31. "The extent of such barter probably varied over time in accordance with the amount of paper money in circulation and was a function of the quantity of paper money emitted by colonial governments and of whether the money held its value." Naomi Lamoreaux, "Rethinking the Transition to Capitalism in the Early American Northeast," *Journal of American History* 90, no. 2 (2003): 441.

32. Craig Muldrew, *The Economy of Obligation: The Culture of Credit and Social Relations in Early Modern England* (New York: St. Martin's Press, 1988), 125.

33. *Peter Little v. John B. Stout,* 1809, *James H. Caldwell v. Samuel Emberton,* 1820, Adams County Court Records, Historic Natchez Foundation.

34. *Peter M. Lapice v. Charles C. River,* 1826, ibid. The quote is from Lamoreaux, "Rethinking the Transition to Capitalism," 441.

35. *Elizabeth Greenfield v. William Dunbar, Margaret Dunbar, administrator and administratrix of James Dunbar, deceased,* 1826, ibid.

36. Brazy, *An American Planter,* 1-25. For a discussion of the Bank of the State of Mississippi, see "The State Bank of Mississippi: Monopoly Bank on the Frontier, 1809-1830," *Journal of Mississippi History* 40, no. 4 (1978): 297-318, and Robert C. Weems Jr., "The Bank of the State of Mississippi: A Pioneer Bank of the Old Southwest, 1809-1844" (PhD diss., Columbia University, 1951), as well as "The Makers of the Bank of the Mississippi," *Journal of Mississippi History* 15 (1953): 137-54.

37. Brazy, *An American Planter,* 1-25.

38. Jonathan Thompson to James L. Trask, September 5, 1818, Natchez, MS, Trask-Ventress Family Papers, Mississippi Department of Archives and History, Jackson, MS.

39. Thompson to Trask, December 1, 1818, New Orleans, LA, Trask-Ventress Family Papers.

40. Spanish Grant between Governor Manuel Gayoso De Lamos and the Estate of Richard Ellis, January 1, 1795, and March 24, 1804; Spanish Grant to Richard Ellis, 1788; British Grant, between Peter Chester, British Governor of West Florida, and Richard Ellis, Auditor's Office, Pensacola, June, 1779, Ellis-Farar Papers, HML-LSU-BR.

41. British Grant, between Peter Chester, British Governor of West Florida, and Richard Ellis, Auditor's Office, Pensacola, June, 1779, Ellis-Farar Papers, HML-LSU-BR. While there existed a need for small sums of cash, or its many substitutes, the formality of secure transactions stood as a necessary building block to wealth. "Title is critical," and in those instances when a mortgage was transacted it unlocked the latent capital embedded in land and slaves, the importance of which lay not just in their ability to stand as security for debts and to satisfy the demands of creditors, but in its ability to finance the expansion of settlement. Hence, the preservation of such title as a formal record was crucial to maintaining and transferring wealth to heirs. For distinctions between "productive" and "nonproductive" loans based on mortgages, the belief among some historians is that contemporary people did not distinguish between capital and consumption in their daily business and the legal components of colonial mortgages, see Winifred B. Rothenberg, "Mortgage Credit and Rural Capital Formation in Colonial Massachusetts, 1642-1773" (unpublished manuscript).

Of particular importance for Mississippi and Louisiana are the indications of long-term debt levels afforded by these publicly registered instruments. As security for a debt, the mortgage "effects a conditional conveyance of the property to the creditor" and the contract takes a back seat to the principal obligation, which is the repayment of the loan. Moreover, a recorded mortgage was effective for ten years and then could be reinstated for another ten years. For historians, they represent measurements of "long term debt levels in the locality." For the relationship between mortgage credit, informal debt, and the credit system, see Kilbourne, *Debt, Investment, Slaves.*

42. Second Recapitulation in Account Current with William N. Mercer, administrator of the Estate of Benjamin Farar, deceased, 1825, State of Mississippi, Probate Records, Adams County Office of Records, Natchez, MS.

43. Rothenberg, "Emergence."

44. Jean-Laurent Rosenthal, "Credit Markets and Economic Change in Southeastern France, 1630-1788," *Explorations in Economic History* 30 (1993): 129-57.

45. Rothenberg, "Emergence," 793.

46. Ibid., 804.

47. Inventory and Appraisement of the Personal Estate of Jonathan Thompson, deceased, late of the City of Natchez, State of Mississippi, Probate Records, Folder 2, Adams County Office of Records, Natchez, MS.

48. Thompson had extensive dealings in Natchez real estate that included land on the outskirts of town and plots within the city. The earliest entry is dated 1808 to one John S. Miller. Although the value of Thompson's property, bought and sold, over his lifetime remains to be calculated, in 1824, both his real and personal property were auctioned over a six-day period for a total of $39,436.92. Profits from the sale of real estate totaled $38,275.92, with the terms of sale being a bond with security payable in twelve months. First through Six Days Sale of the Real and Personal Property of the Estate of Jonathan Thompson, December 15-22, 1824, Probate Records, folders 1, 2, and 4, Adams County Office of Records, Natchez, MS.

49. Report of Commissioners: Claims Allowed against the Estate of Jonathan Thompson, deceased, June 1825, Probate Records, folder 2, Adams County Office of Records, Natchez, MS. The total amount of claims, stated here, represent only those allowed by the Commissioners as of June 1, 1825. All of the sixty-four claims are unsecured, *assumpsit* debts for promissory notes, drafts, bills of exchange. The majority, however, had been based on locally contracted open accounts. The one secured claim listed at a later date had been the mortgage contracted with Samuel Poslethwaite. Out of the seven mortgages entered into the land deed records, only the mortgage to Samuel Postlethwaite appears among the probate records (as claim number 80). The other mortgages, dated between January 1, 1816, and June 1, 1822, do not appear in the Report as Commissioners, and other probate documents, possibly due to the fact that Thompson used Postlethwaite's mortgage to refinance any previous mortgages or simply paid them off.

50. Memorandum of Debts Due the Estate of Jonathan Thompson, deceased, March 2, 1824, Probate Records, folder 2, Adams County Office of Records, Natchez, MS. Sixty-one individuals were listed on the basis of a debt owed to the late Jonathan Thompson. Of these, there were listed 39 notes, 5 bonds, 6 open accounts, and 1 draft. Of the 39 notes, 3 were identified as being based on mortgages held by Thompson; John D. Cochran mortgaged "ground in the city," to Thompson for $2,000, another property located within the city was mortgaged to Thompson by Samuel Brewer and John Glover for $4,500, and last, a note given by John Creighton had been for a mortgage on furniture amounting to $281.50. Only these three mortgages appeared as due, owing, and "doubtful." The mortgage for Benjamin Osmun in the amount of $4,592.00, as well as the mortgage for Josiah Morris in the amount of $8,000.00, were not listed among the debts due. The Osmun debt may have been paid off, since it was contracted in 1815, but the Morris mortgage was still on the books at the time of Thompson's debt. The alterna-

tive view—that the "Memorandum of Debts Due the Estate" is not an accurate reflection of the debts outstanding—is plausible. However, nothing in the probate files indicates that this would be the case, and further examination of these transactions is necessary.

51. Jonathan Thompson to Colonel Israel E. Trask, March 19, 1814; William Thompson, Receipt of funds from Israel E. Trask, Brimfield, Massachusetts, May 23, 1814, Probate Claim Number 34, folder 4, Adams County Office of Records, Natchez, MS.

52. Winthrop Sargent arrived in Natchez in August of 1798 as the first governor of the Mississippi Territory, appointed to the post by President John Adams. He was a New England Federalist and had extensive military and administrative experience. A combination of inadequate judges, frontier conditions, and his own alienation of powerful and influential planters made him an unpopular leader. He did, however, establish some authority with a collection of territorial laws, known informally as "Sargent's Codes," or the Laws of the Mississippi Territory (1799), which enacted a criminal code and a county court system and created a probate code and regulations for the militia. For a more detailed assessment of Sargent's career and financial enterprises, see Mary Joan Elliott, "Winthrop Sargent and the Administration of the Mississippi Territory" (PhD diss., University of Southern California, 1971), and George B. Toulmin, "The Political Ideals of Winthrop Sargent, a New England Federalist on the Frontier," *Journal of Mississippi History* 15 (1953): 207-9.

53. Jonathan Thompson to James L. Trask, Natchez, April 7, 1820, Trask-Ventress Family Papers.

54. Jonathan Thompson to James L. Trask, Natchez, April 23, 1820, ibid.

55. There were obstacles to clearing the debt to Sargent. Thompson alludes to some of the problems with regard to Sargent's widow in Philadelphia in July 1823. Thompson's probate shows that the Sargent debt had not been paid with the ten thousand dollars arranged through trask. Jonathan Thompson to James L. Trask, April 11, 1823; Thompson to Trask, Natchez, July 11, 1823, Trask-Ventress Papers.

56. Promissory Note, Jonathan Thompson to Winthrop Sargent, July 18, 1819, Adams County Office of Records, Natchez, MS.

57. Untitled document, May 1, 1821, Jonathan Thompson, Probate Records, folder 4, Adams County Office of Records, Natchez, MS. The interest rate on the $3,000 loan, as well as on the open account for $2,002.62, had been 8 percent. Interest on the $6,000 loan had been 15 percent. Interest had accrued from 1820 to 1825. The debts owed to Sargent also included the amounts of $5,962.59 and $5,206.26. These are listed among the "Claims Allowed" in the Report of Commissioners as Claims 3 and 5. See Report of Commissioners, Claims Allowed against the Estate of Jonathan Thompson, deceased, Probate Records, Adams County Office of Records, Natchez, MS.

58. Jonathan Thompson to James L. Trask, March 17, 1821, Trask-Ventress Family Papers. The bank for which Trask was director is not named in any of the documents researched here.

59. Jonathan Thompson to James L. Trask, August 4, 1821, ibid.

60. Promissory note, July 18, 1823, Jonathan Thompson to James L. Trask, Jonathan Thompson Probate Records, folder 5, Adams County Office of Records, Natchez, MS.

61. Public Instrument of Protest, September 19, 1823, ibid., folder 4.

62. James L. Trask to the Bank of the State of Mississippi, 1824, ibid.

63. Pine Grove and Bradley were situated five miles outside of Natchez, bordered by property owned by members of Mississippi's early planter elite. In 1816, Thompson mortgaged both plantations to David Williams for $20,000. Consisting of 1,000 acres each, the plantations provided the security needed for the mortgage, while sales from cotton would go toward clearing the loan: Thompson pledged to "put to work on the said plantation, called Grove and Bradley all field negro slaves of him, in number 32

from and after December 1816, until the debt is discharged and shall and will appropriate the net proceeds of the crop so made each and every year . . . until sum is paid." These were the terms of the mortgage along with 3 percent interest charged annually beginning on January 1, 1815, and ending January 1, 1817. Another 6 percent accrued annually from January 1, 1817, until the debt was paid. Mortgage, April 23, 1816, Jonathan Thompson and Wife to David Williams, Deed Book I, Adams County Office of Records, Natchez, MS.

64. Payments would be made in the following increments: $5,003.00 to be paid on May 1, 1821, followed by $11,200.00 on May 1, 1822, another $11,800.00 on May 1, 1823, with another payment of $12,400.00 on May 1, 1824, and $6,500.00 on May 1, 1825. Mortgage, February 23, 1820, Jonathan Thompson and Wife to David Williams, Deed Book L, ibid.

65. Mortgage, June 1, 1823, Jonathan Thompson and Wife to Samuel Posthethwaite, Deed Book N,ibid. He gave Postlethwaite "several promissory notes" with the first payment of $500.00 due on January 1, 1823, the second payment of $500.00 on July 1, 1824, and the final $10,500.00 due on January 1, 1825.

66. Deed, May 11, 1820, Josiah Morris to Jonathan Thompson, Adams County Deed Book L, ibid.

67. Jonathan Thompson to James L. Trask, 1821, Trask-Ventress Family Papers.

68. Ibid.

Contributors

Jeff Bremer earned his PhD from the University of Kansas in 2006, completing a dissertation on the antebellum market revolution in Missouri. He is assistant professor of history at Stephen F. Austin State University in Nacogdoches, Texas, where he teaches nineteenth-century American history. Bremer has published articles in the *Southern California Quarterly*, *Kansas History*, and the *Missouri Historical Review* and is revising his dissertation, "Frontier Capitalism: The Antebellum Market Revolution in the Lower Missouri River Valley, 1803-1861," for publication.

Elbra David is in the PhD program at the University of California, Irvine. She earned her master's at California State University, Northridge, and is writing a dissertation exploring the antebellum credit relations and the Atlantic economy.

Susanna Delfino is associate professor of American history at the University of Genoa, Italy. A founder of the Southern Industrialization Project (1996), she has been its first vice president since its formal structuring as an organization, affiliated with the Southern Historical Association (2003). A student of the U.S. South's economic and social history in the slave era, she has published many works on the subject in Italy and in the United States. She has edited with Michele Gillespie *Neither Lady Nor Slave: Working Women of the Old South* (2002) and the first two volumes of the present series, *Global Perspectives on Industrial Transformation in the American South* (2005) and *Technology, Innovation, and Southern Industrialization* (2008).

Gary T. Edwards is assistant professor of history at Arkansas State University, where he teaches courses on the American South, the early republic, and the Civil War. He received his PhD from the University of Memphis (2004), where he was a Woodbury Fellow. Edwards was a Senior Fulbright Fellow (2009-10) at the Free University of Berlin and served as guest professor of history at the John F. Kennedy Institute for North American Studies.

He has published articles in *Agriculture History* and the *Tennessee Historical Quarterly*. He is currently working on his first book-length manuscript on the yeomen families of antebellum western Tennessee.

Michele Gillespie is Kahle Associate Professor of History at Wake Forest College. She is the author of numerous books and articles, including *Free Labor in an Unfree World: White Artisans in Slaveholding Georgia* (2000), winner of the Malcolm and Muriel Bell Award for the Most Distinguished Book in Georgia History. She is working on a book about tobacco magnate R. J. Reynolds and his wife, Katharine Smith Reynolds.

Jennifer R. Green is professor of history at Central Michigan University. In addition to articles, she authored *Military Education and the Emerging Middle Class in the Old South* (2008) and edited with Jonathan Wells *The Southern Middle Class in the Nineteenth Century* (2011). Her work on middle-class formation and culture continues in a current project on nineteenth-century professionals.

Max L. Grivno is an assistant professor of history at the University of Southern Mississippi, where he teaches courses in southern and labor history. He has been awarded the C. Vann Woodward Dissertation Award and the Reed Fink Award in Southern Labor History. He is the author of *"There Slavery Cannot Dwell": Agriculture and Labor along the Mason-Dixon Line, 1790-1860* (2010). He is currently researching the efforts to unionize southern timber and pulpwood workers during the era of the Civil Rights Movement.

J. William Harris is professor of history at the University of New Hampshire. He is the author most recently of *The Hanging of Thomas Jeremiah: A Free Black Man's Encounter with Liberty* (2009) and *Deep Souths: Delta, Piedmont, and Sea Island Society in the Age of Segregation* (2003).

Louis M. Kyriakoudes is director of the Center for Oral History and Cultural Heritage and associate professor of history at the University of Southern Mississippi. A specialist in the social and economic history of the nineteenth- and twentieth-century United States, Kyriakoudes is the author of *The Social Origins of the Urban South: Race, Gender and Migration in Nashville and Middle Tennessee, 1890-1930* (2003). He is working on two projects: a history of cigarette use in the twentieth century and a study of the demography of rural poverty in the American South in the nineteenth and twentieth centuries.

Keri Leigh Merritt is a PhD candidate at the University of Georgia. Her dissertation, "A Second Degree of Slavery: How Black Emancipation Freed the South's Poor Whites," explores how slavery shaped the lives of poor whites.

Michael J. Pfeifer is associate professor of history at John Jay College of Criminal Justice, City University of New York. His major publications include *The Roots of Rough Justice: Origins of American Lynching* (2011), *Rough Justice: Lynching and American Society, 1874-1947* (2004), and "The Northern U.S. and the Genesis of Racial Lynching: The Lynching of African-Americans in the Era of the Civil War," *Journal of American History* (December 2010). U.S. Senator Mary Landrieu (D, LA) drew upon Pfeifer's work in 2005 when she introduced Senate Resolution 39, which apologized to lynching victims and their descendants for the U.S. Senate's historical failure to pass anti-lynching legislation.

Jonathan Daniel Wells is associate professor of history at Temple University. He received his PhD from the University of Michigan and in 2004 published *The Origins of the Southern Middle Class, 1800-1861* (2003). He has recently completed a book on black and white women journalists and editors in the nineteenth-century South and is writing a book on the Fugitive Slave Law of 1850 and the coming of the Civil War.

Robert E. Wright holds the Nef Chair in Political Economy at Augusta College in Sioux Falls, South Dakota. A specialist in financial history, Wright has previously held positions at the Stern School of Business, New York University, and the University of Virginia. His most recent publications are *The First Wall Street: Chestnut Street, Philadelphia, and the Birth of American Finance* (2005) and, with David Jack Cowen, *Financial Founding Fathers: The Men Who Made America Rich* (2006).

Index